The Jews of Eastern Eu

The Jews of Eastern Europe, 1772–1881

ISRAEL BARTAL

Translated by Chaya Naor

PENN

University of Pennsylvania Press

Philadelphia

Originally published as *Me-umah le-le'om, yehudey mizrakh eyropa 1772–1881* by Ministry of
Defence Publishing House, Tel Aviv, Israel

10   9   8   7   6   5   4   3   2

Published by
University of Pennsylvania Press
Philadelphia, Pennsylvania 19104-4112

Library of Congress Cataloging-in-Publication Data

Bartal, Yisra'el.
    [Me-"umah" li-"le'om". English]
    The Jews of Eastern Europe, 1772–1881 / Israel Bartal ; translated by Chaya Naor.
        p.   cm. — (Jewish culture and contexts)
    Includes bibliographical references and index.
    ISBN 0-8122-3887-7 (cloth : alk. paper)
        1. Jews—Europe, Eastern—History—18th century.   2. Jews—Europe,
Eastern—History—19th century.   I. Title.   II. Series.

DS135.E8B3713   2005
940'.04924—dc22   2005042208

Contents

Introduction

This book relates the history of Eastern European Jewry from the time of the Polish partitions at the end of the eighteenth century to the pogroms that broke out in the southern regions of the Russian empire in the early 1880s. In the summer of 1772, the three neighbors of the Polish state tore off large chunks of its territory, embarking on a process that, in less than two decades, led to Poland's demise as an independent political entity. The first partition of Poland was also the beginning of the triple encounter of the Jews of the Polish Commonwealth with the Austrian bureaucracy (in Galicia), the Russian officialdom (in White Russia [Belorussia]), and the Prussian administration (in western Prussia). This encounter, between a populous Jewish community (with an age-old cultural tradition) and the apparatus of the centralized state, was for the Polish Jew the commencement of the modern era. Because the Jews residing in the Polish-Lithuanian kingdom formed an absolute majority of European Jewry, the first partition of Poland can actually be viewed as the commencement of the modern era in Jewish history. Thereafter began a mass immigration movement that greatly increased the number of Polish Jews in other parts of Europe.

In 1772, a complex and multifaceted process of integration and acculturation began in the regions severed from the Polish state. The Polish-Lithuanian Jew became a "Russian Jew," a "German Jew," or an "Austrian Jew." This process was not rapid. Most Jews in the areas annexed from Poland to the neighboring states continued to maintain their old way of life for decades after they were no longer subjects of the Polish king. They regarded themselves as "Polish Jews," and that is how they were seen by German, Austrian, and Russian writers and bureaucrats. As far back as the 1860s, the Yiddish writer Isaac Joel Linetzky called his anti-Hasidic satire *Dos poylishe yingl* (The Polish lad), although he depicted the protagonist as a Jew living in the Ukraine, deep inside the territory of the Russian empire. Jewish socialists in London published a Yiddish newspaper intended for the masses of poor immigrants from the Russian empire and called it (in 1884) *Der poylisher yidl* (The Polish yid). According to one of its editors, this name was chosen to voice the immigrants' protest against the disdainful attitude adopted toward them by the English Jews, who were panic-stricken that "the Poles are coming!"[1] In the 1880s, the German historian Heinrich von Treitschke, in a polemic with the Jewish historian Heinrich Graetz, expressed his fear that the German Reich would be inundated by masses of Polish Jewish immigrants. In Treitschke's view, the fact that these immigrants clung to their national identity was antithetical to the equal political rights they had recently been granted. Moreover, it constituted a real threat to the German character of his country.[2] Thus, over a hundred years after the first Polish partition, the Jews of Eastern Europe were still seen by many as a community that had preserved its "Polishness." And deep into the modern era, they maintained what Gershon Hundert recently described as a positive sense of Jewish identity.[3]

What began as the invasions by Poland's enemies in the last decades of the eighteenth century nonetheless changed the political base of the traditional society's life. Although the masses of Jews underwent only partial integration, some segments of the population were considerably influenced by it. While acculturation did not cause the old Jewish culture to disappear, it did augment it with cultural traits previously unknown to the Jews of the Polish-Lithuanian kingdom. The changes that affected Eastern European Jewry in the nineteenth century also gave rise to a new type of antagonism between them and the various ethnic groups in the empires. The old religious conflict, between Catholics and Jews as well as between the Eastern Orthodox and the Jews, took the form of a radical anti-Semitism in which the influence of national Romanticism merged with messianic revolutionism. In March 1881, 111 years after the Russian army entered the towns of White Russia, Czar Alexander II was mortally wounded by assassins belonging to the revolutionary movement. Six weeks after the czar's murder, the southern provinces of the Russian empire were swept by waves of pogroms against the Jews, unparalleled in their duration and geographical spread. In their wake, many Jews, during the pogroms or in the years soon after, began to abandon the option of integration and acculturation in favor of more radical solutions to the problems of their economic, social, and spiritual existence. The Russian Jew, like his brethren on the Austrian side of the border, began to exchange the incomplete imperial identity, which had taken shape after the Polish partitions, for alternative identities, either by emigrating to new lands or by seeking new Jewish identities unprecedented in the history of Eastern European Jewry

The boundaries of historical periods are determined by subjective considerations. On the basis of ideologies, political interests, geographical links, or ethnic identity, people are likely to draw disparate time lines. The sociologist Eviatar Zerubavel states: "There are many alternative ways to cut up the past, none of which are more natural and hence more valid than others. Any system of periodization is thus inevitably social, since our ability to envision the historical watersheds separating one conventional 'period' from another is basically a product of being socialized in specific *traditions* of carving up the past. In other words, we need to be mnemonically *socialized* to regard certain historical events as significant 'turning points.' "[4]

Indeed, why should we decide that the partitions of Poland constitute a historical turning point in the history of Eastern European Jewry? After all, one of the major claims in this book is that many of the social, economic, and cultural traits that were hallmarks of the link between the Polish feudal system and the Jews continued to exist for many years after 1772. Life in the towns of Galicia and White Russia did not change much until the second half of the nineteenth century. In 1850, very few Jews in the Russian Pale of Settlement or in Austrian Galicia felt at home in the cultures of the state. This was the time when the Hasidic movement, a consummate product of the traditional culture, was crossing the borders of empires and winning the hearts of Jews throughout Eastern Europe. Similarly, one can ask whether 1881 marks a turning point in the history of Eastern European Jewry. Zionist historiography, on the one hand, and the historical research written under the influence of Jewish radicalism, on the other, designate the year of the pogroms as the beginning of a new era in Jewish history. In 1969, the national-radical historian Shmuel Ettinger (1919–88) wrote:

There has been no more dramatic period in Jewish history than the years between 1881 and 1948—a relatively short span of time when measured against the annals of a nation. During those years the Jewish people underwent enormous changes and agonizing tribulations. Yet, at the same time, they manifested an extraordinary vitality. . . . In contrast to the lengthy tradition developed during the Middle Ages to divert the resentment of alien rule and the sufferings of the Diaspora into the inner world of the spirit and abstain from political activism . . . mighty forces now awoke in the people. These forces, operating at a social and political level, transformed a scattered, divided, and mortally wounded people from a passive entity into an active and independent political and social force.[5]

Ettinger was a Russian Jewish intellectual who, in his political and cultural life, moved from a Hasidic ultraorthodox home in Ukraine to Marxism-Leninism in Palestine under the British Mandate and then became an ardent Socialist Zionist in the State of Israel. For him, as for many intellectuals from Eastern Europe, the image of the Jewish past became a dynamic product of a changing worldview.[6] In his transition from communism to nationalism, Ettinger altered the role of 1881 in his historical thinking. In an earlier version of his lectures on modern Jewish history (from which his previously cited work was adapted),

1848—the year of the "spring of the nations"—was a watershed in modern Jewish history.[7] Jonathan Frankel also describes what took place in the year of the pogroms as a radical and unprecedented shift. In his monumental work on the roots of modern Jewish politics, describing events in the wake of the pogroms, he states that "a revolution in modern Jewish politics took place in Russia during the years 1881–1882."[8]

In recent years, there has been a tendency in research on the history of Eastern European Jewry to place less emphasis on the influence of the pogroms on the processes of modernization that the Jewish people underwent in the modern era. Unquestionably, the decline of the political movements that in previous generations had shaped the collective memory of the past of United States and Israeli Jewry contributed to a new way of looking at the role of 1881 in Jewish history. That year was linked in the Jewish collective memory with the emergence of the Hibbat Zion movement, as well as with the search for roots of the mass immigration to the United States. Modern nationalism and the mass immigration were two reactions to the pogroms that distanced the Jews from the Old Country. The pogroms blackened the memory of the past and radicalized trends that until then had not been unequivocal in the complex historical reality. Even after the 1881–82 pogroms, some sectors of Jewish society still sought integration into the imperial cultures. Russian Jewish culture, works by Jewish authors in the Polish language, and aspirations for social and political integration continued to exist alongside trends of separatism and abandonment. At times, these conflicting trends were even intermixed, because Jewish nationalism in Eastern Europe was strongly influenced by the cultures into which many Jews aspired to integrate.

In his groundbreaking research, Benjamin Nathans adopted a Tocquevillian reenvisioning that "seeks not to deny the profound upheaval that occurred in Russian Jewry (just as Tocqueville never denied that a revolution occurred in France in 1789) but rather to reveal the subtle forms of change as well as continuities that bridge the moment of crisis."[9]

In this book, I concur with some of these reservations about the view that the events of 1881 caused a revolutionary leap from a premodern phase in the history of Eastern European Jewry to a totally new phase. For example, I stress the fact that some Jewish intellectuals in the Russian empire were becoming disillusioned with the policy of the imperial government toward Jews quite a few years before the pogroms, which suggests that there was not a sudden shift in the attitude of the Haskalah movement toward the Russian government. Moreover, I assert that the disintegration of the feudal system, which preceded the pogroms of the 1880s, was a decisive factor in the profound upheaval that Jewish society underwent. The pogroms in the Pale of Settlement were, in a sense, a by-product of political, economic, and social processes rather than a major cause of these processes.

Nevertheless, the 1881 pogroms can be viewed as a significant milestone in the history of Eastern European Jewry. The Jews' tendency to isolate themselves from the milieu in which they had lived for centuries was then significantly intensified. Anti-Semitism became an official policy in the Russian empire, and Jewish nationalism moved from its cultural phase to the phase of political organization. Although the massive immigration from Eastern Europe to the West began back in the 1870s because of the famine in the northern provinces of the Pale of Settlement, it became associated with the new anti-Semitism. From then on, it was also linked to the emergence of a nationalist movement that sought to direct the huge stream of immigrants into different ideological channels.

The period between 1772 and 1881 constitutes a vastly significant chapter in the history of the largest Jewish collective in the world in modern times. During those years, a society, immense in its demographic dimensions, spread over a large geographical area on the eastern fringes of Europe and underwent changes that uprooted and shattered centuries-old social and cultural structures and practices, exposing the Jews to the transformative power of modernity. In the hundred years described in the following chapters, historical circumstances engendered the development of large Jewish movements, which later determined the nature of contemporary Jewish society, left their imprint on contemporary Jewish collectives, and played a decisive role in shaping Israeli society. From 1772 to 1881, the founders of the Haskalah movement in Lithuania and Ukraine made their appearance; the first buds of secular Hebrew literature emerged; the first modern works in Yiddish, the spoken language of the Jewish masses, were written; Jewish literature in Polish and Russian was created; and the Jewish press in various languages flourished.

During that period, the founders of the Jewish national movement, the early leaders of Eastern European Orthodoxy, and the pioneers of the Jewish labor movement were galvanized into action. All these movements bore the hallmark of Eastern Europe: a blend of an ethnic Jewish identity, deeply rooted in a large, widespread community, with a profound consciousness of modernity. Even the opponents of modernity, including the rabbis of Lithuania at the end of the nineteenth century, were greatly influenced by it. They understood all too well that the *kahal* (traditional communal leadership), with its rabbis and lay leaders, had ceased to exist, and they adjusted to modern politics and to concepts such as public opinion, equal rights, and nationalism.

The radical revolutionaries and the early nationalists, on the other hand, while they cherished the vision of revolution and change, still felt part of that large community of Jews rooted in their culture. They rediscovered this community, felt connected to it, and wanted to preserve parts of its culture. The histories of the two large Jewish centers in the world—Israel and the United States—are linked not only because several million Jews in the Middle East and in North America are the offspring of Eastern European immigrants; it is impossible to understand political and social processes and to delve into cultural phenomena in the State of Israel without a profound knowledge of what took place in Eastern Europe in the decades before the First Aliyah. We usually seek historical explanations for what was created in the Land of Israel in the last 120 years in the Middle Eastern reality, but we still lack a thorough study of the link between the Israeli political culture and its Eastern European roots.

In this book, I relate the historical narrative of a large ethnic minority, unique in its culture and separate in its social institutions, which was confronted by the power of the centralized state. While that state succeeded in changing the social structure that the premodern Jewish society had maintained, it was not able to erase the ethnic otherness of the Jews. This ethnic otherness continued to exist in social and cultural spheres that were not under state control or that the state showed no interest in changing. The premodern autonomous community that was the axis of Jewish society's traditional life in the Polish-Lithuanian kingdom did come to an end in the wake of the reforms. But as the old formal organizations were abolished or integrated into the state's administrative systems, new social forms led to the emergence of a modern national identity.

It is no simple task to describe the major trends and processes that occurred in Eastern European Jewish society in the hundred years between the partitions and the pogroms. There are several reasons for the difficulties that confront the historian.

First, the historian must grapple with the question of whether the large Jewish community in Eastern Europe continued to exist as one entity, when its various parts were within the political boundaries of several states. To what extent, if at all, did the Ashkenazi diaspora continue to maintain its unity after the partitions of Poland? The question of the unity of Eastern European Jewry is linked to and dependent on another question: Whose history is it? Is the history of the Jews in White Russia (Belorussia) part of the chronicles of Poland, or is it a chapter in the history of Russia, a paragraph in the history of Lithuania, or a few lines in the annals of Belorussia? The various stages of Jewish historiography in Eastern Europe suggest that there is more than one answer to these

questions. The historian Simon Dubnow, who held manifestly nationalist views, wrote the modern history of the Jews with an imperial Russian
keynote. A contemporary of his, Majer Balaban, wrote his books and articles in a Polish vein. Geopolitics changes the historical perspective.
These two historians wrote about the past of their nation (the Jewish
nation) as a reaction to the Germanocentric point of view that saw Eastern Europe as a semi-Asiatic periphery,[10] which they often termed
"Halbasien," in the wake of the stories by the Jewish author Karl Emil
Franzos, a native of Galicia. In any case, where is the boundary between
Europe and Eastern Europe? Isn't Eastern Europe no more than an
invention fabricated by Western intellectuals?[11]

Second, I have alluded to the fact that the writing of the history of
Eastern European Jewry emerged directly from ideological and political
movements that evolved in this part of the world in the nineteenth century. The Jews of the Polish-Lithuanian kingdom did not write history
books: they wrote chronicles of pogroms; poems in Yiddish about expulsions, epidemics, and conflagrations; prayers for the dead, in memory
of the victims of the trials of Jews accused of using Christian blood to
bake Passover matzos—these were some of the traditional genres by
means of which segments of memory were passed down from generation
to generation. Memory of the past was a cardinal element in the worldview of the Eastern European Jew, but it was not a memory centered on
"history." One exception was Nathan Hanover's book *Yeven metsula*
(Miry pit),[12] about the Cossack revolt in 1648, when the inhabitants of
several Ukrainian communities were massacred. In this short book, one
can perhaps discern the first sign, the only one of its kind, of Jewish historical writing in the early modern period. History as a scientific discipline and a focus for the consciousness of a collective identity was not
part of the spiritual world of Eastern European Jewry before the Polish
partitions. A methodical study of the past, and certainly the establishment of societies to deal with the past and disseminate knowledge about
it, or the writing of historical works were all part of the modernization
that Jewish society underwent. Even the conservative parts of this society,
in the Russian empire as well as in the Hapsburg empire, began writing
historical works in light of the heightened historical consciousness of
their coreligionists who were inclined to join the Haskalah movement.[13]
It is no wonder, then, that many of those who attempted to redefine
their identity in an era in which the traditional frameworks of life had
been undermined turned to the past to seek answers to the questions of
the present. In doing so, they often turned their backs on the traditional
collective memory, and sometimes challenged it. This memory, as well
developed as it was, seemed to its critics—the Maskilim, the nationalists,
and the socialists—"unhistorical." Thus, for example, the young radical

Maskil Simon Dubnow (1860–1941), who had recently discovered the national link to the past, could describe his people in Eastern Europe as a tribe of nomads lacking in "historical feeling . . . whose lives are entirely in the present and who have neither a future nor a past. And the few, select ones so inclined to know the shape of the past actually recognize merely fragments of things and scattered incidents."[14]

In an open letter published in 1892, Dubnow called upon his readers to search for and collect ancient community registers and to copy inscriptions from old headstones. Steven Zipperstein noted the tension between historical empiricism and the desire to remain relevant to the present, underlying the historiography of Russian Jewry, a tension that has endured from the days of the radical historian living in Odessa at the end of the czsarist period up to contemporary historical writing. Indeed, the ideological zeal of Dubnow and others of his generation was not extinguished even among those who followed in his footsteps in Europe, the United States, and the Land of Israel. Dubnow, however, greatly exaggerated in depicting the Jewish society of his time as lacking in historical feeling. As far back as the mid-nineteenth century, a previously unknown genre in the traditional culture of writing was popular in the towns of Lithuania and Ukraine. This genre focused on the history of the Jewish communities based on community registers, rabbinical literature, archival documents, and headstones. In 1860 (the year of Dubnow's birth), Shmuel Yosef Fuenn published his book *Kiryah ne'emanah*, on the history of Vilna Jewry. In the introduction to the book, he wrote: "In this generation of ours, a generation that awakens the sleeping from their slumber, the wise-hearted lovers of memories of their people have awoken to publish copies of inscriptions on gravestones found in the cemeteries."[15] In 1895, Solomon Buber (Martin Buber's grandfather) published a history of the rabbis and leaders of his city, Lwów (Lemberg) in Galicia. This was a monumental work that summed up an endeavor that lasted over thirty years and included the copying of inscriptions from gravestones, transcribing community registers, and conducting searches in the archives of churches and monasteries. In the introduction to this book, *Anshei shem*, Buber wrote: "It is my hope that this work of mine will be of benefit . . . and will serve as material for a large building by a scholar who will consent to write the history of the Jews in Lwów in general, and that of her rabbis and talmudic authorities in particular, and that this work of mine will enlighten him so he may draw from it those things he needs for his work."[16] Buber, Fuenn, and many others who wrote local histories in the second half of the nineteenth century still did not see in history what Dubnow saw in it—a road map for the life of the present and the vision of the future. They did, however, replace the traditional collective memory with a historical consciousness of a new sort and attempted to reinforce it by studying community registers, copying inscriptions from gravestones, and searching for documents in archives. Even before Dubnow, Jewish history had already been written as part of the political and cultural discourse of the new Jewish intelligentsia that emerged in the lands of Eastern Europe. These people were fascinated by the world of the recent generations of their people, in which they had grown up and which they had left, but they interpreted it with modern tools. And the further they moved away from the world of traditional Jewry, the more innovative they became. Intellectual Jews, such as Simon Dubnow, the writer Sholem Aleichem (Shalom Rabinowitz) (1859–1916), and the composer Julius (Yoel) Engel (1868–1927), were imbued with the ideas of reforming the world and building a new society that were current in contemporary circles of Russian writers and thinkers. For these men, the Jewish past was not a subject for detached, supposedly objective, research but rather a detailed guide for political and cultural activity. For them, the Eastern European Jewish heritage was a source from which they could draw materials for social rejuvenation or a national renaissance. The literary scholar Ruth Wisse wrote to Irving Howe: "Though [Sholem Aleichem] too felt the impending break in the 'golden chain' of Jewish tradition, and felt the cracks in his own life, he makes it his artistic business to *close* the gap."[17] Dubnow found the history of the super-communal councils that he studied "a source for the restoration of the national Jewish spirit, in order to put it to use in the new political milieu of the multi-national East European state."[18]

While Jewish intellectuals were combing the sources of the past to find materials with which to weave the threads of continuity, they also found in the recent past the roots of crisis and severance. Several generations of Jewish historians assigned a key role to the Haskalah movement in the historical narrative. Scholars of Jewish history in Eastern Europe, from the inception of the Wissenschaft des Judentums in the Russian language up to the research in the spirit of Socialist Zionism that flourished in Israeli universities only one generation ago, exaggerated in attributing power and decisive influence to this movement. They regarded it, first and foremost, as a movement whose essence was one of change and displacement. The Haskalah was, in fact, the first modern stream to emerge in Jewish society, and all the new movements in the modern era grew out of the Haskalah or carried on its legacy in one form or another. Jewish nationalism, which rebelled against some of the more fundamental ideas of Eastern European Maskilim, adhered and still adheres to some of the Haskalah's underlying principles. Orthodoxy, a traditionalist stream, also adopted many elements of the legacy of the Maskilim, whom it had fought against.

However, the Haskalah movement was but one of the diverse reactions to the dramatic changes engendered in Jewish society by external forces.[19] The Haskalah movement was accused by its adversaries of having destroyed the heritage and hastening the assimilation of the Jews into the surrounding societies. Nationalistic radicals and revolutionary socialists said similar things, but in praise of the Haskalah. From the perspective of two hundred years, the Haskalah—the movement whose spiritual world was closely bound to the Bible and the Hebrew language—seems to have been a quite conservative stream. Hence, the anachronistic statements that came from the radical wing of Jewish politics in Eastern Europe are no longer accepted in the new scholarship, but their traces are still evident in the images of organizations, institutions, views, and values from the past. Even decisions about periodization are still influenced by the legacy of the Haskalah. Traces of the influence of the Enlightenment are palpable in the definitions that serve the writers of history. Hence, in determining what is "central" in the processes that took place in the society we are dealing with, or what was a "major trend," we have to be particularly cognizant of the ideological baggage and the social background of the researchers of the past.

There is a third reason for the difficulties that confront the historian. In the decade that has passed since the collapse of the Soviet empire and the opening of archives in Eastern European states to researchers, the documentary base has greatly expanded. Today we know far more about nineteenth-century Jewish society than we knew in 1990. Research is being updated, old generalizations are turning out to be wrong, and perspectives are changing. These days, a scholar of Eastern European Jewry has access to the same archival treasures that were studied by several generations of historians from the end of the nineteenth century. However, he can ask questions about those historical sources that never occurred to his predecessors. He is not constrained by the apologetic needs that affected historians who lived under the rule of the czar or the kaiser. He is not compelled to work under ideological and political restrictions of the sort that hampered the historians who visited those archives during the time of Soviet rule. Today historians know far more about what happened in Eastern Europe in recent generations than do the scholars who preceded them. But can the historical reconstruction of what happened influence, even slightly, the way that the grandchildren and great-grandchildren of the Jews of Polish and Lithuanian towns "remember" the old country? Can the historian contend with the collective memory of the offspring of the Eastern European immigrants?

The children and grandchildren of the founding fathers of the State of Israel are no longer directly linked to the experience of the Eastern European shtetl. The hundreds of thousands of immigrants from the former Soviet Union who, in recent decades, have found an old-new homeland in Israel are also light-years away from the way of life that existed in previous generations. Many of the early immigrants from Poland and Russia brought with them to the old-new land memories of fear, violence, and hatred. Their ideology served as a sensitive sieve that did not allow memories of another kind to pass through it. Native Israelis absorbed the spirit of the shtetl from the militant Hebrew literature that their teachers from Eastern Europe crammed into their lessons in the new Zionist schools. Descriptions of the ugliness of Jewish society in the Pale of Settlement, depicted by Mendele Moykher Sforim, as well as by Peretz in his neo-romantic stories, imparted to several generations of Israeli pupils a store of images very far removed from the real life of Eastern Europe. Stereotypical images, which originated in the Maskilim's criticism of the life of Jews in the cities and towns of Lithuania and Ukraine, were planted in the soil of the evolving Israeli culture. Hebrew books that native Israelis read during the time of the British Mandate and in the first decades of the state were a bridge of consciousness between what had existed (or was perpetuated as having existed) in the Old World and what had been born under the Mediterranean skies. From the complex and multicolored reality in which their parents grew up, only black-and-white pictures remained in the collective Israeli memory: pogroms, blood libels, poverty, and want. The Holocaust, which swallowed up everything and changed everything, reinforced the negative image of the Diaspora.

A change did take place, however, in the Israeli attitude toward the Jews of the Diaspora: no longer were they contemptuous of those who had not partaken of the purifying experience of Zionism; rather they had compassion for and identification with the victims of the horrifying massacre, as well as guilt for having failed them when they were in dire distress. The image of the past, however, is still as monochromatic as ever. What remains today in the Israeli collective memory is a blend of anachronistic ideologies, literary discussion, and the last vestiges of a shallow folklore. In the United States, too, the memory of the Old World has been transformed, becoming, as Zipperstein put it, "an American, not a Russian, story."[20] As in Israel, the immigrants from Europe to the United States wanted to connect to a new reality and tended to remember mainly what was bad and violent in the old. Only a few decades after the mass immigration from Eastern Europe began, a change took place in the way the Jews of the United States remembered the places they had come from. The memory of the violence did not vanish, but after World War II, the continent the Jews had wanted to flee in order to build a new life in the land of freedom and equality became a site of yearning for innocence, for family values, and for religious faith. Jewish nationalism in Israel and the alienation in the American capitalist society ended by shaping a memory of the past that had very little to do with history.

In this book, I challenge the collective memory of the Jews on both sides of the ocean. This memory is not a product of the manipulative use of the materials of the past, nor was it imposed by an oppressive establishment that forced it upon the rememberers. Rather, it was shaped by the circumstances of the time and of the place. The historian's act of reconstructing the past is also an outcome of time and place. The Russian empire vanished from the world more than eighty years ago; very few are alive today who can still recall childhood experiences in the Austro-Hungarian empire. Why, then, shouldn't we look at the recent past in a way that will enable us to see it in its totality and stop clinging obstinately to contour lines drawn in times distant and alien to us? The Jews of Eastern Europe were at one and the same time Maskilim and Hasidim, conservatives and radicals, heroes and cowards. They were Jews: Russian Jews, Polish Jews, Polish-Russian Jews. They lived in large cities and in godforsaken towns. They hated their country, they loved their country. Their historical story contains pogroms, but yearnings for the Russian homeland as well. The Jewish history of Eastern Europe is not a one-dimensional collective memory but a congeries of many memories.

Once subjects of the Polish-Lithuanian kingdom, the Jews—the heroes of this book—became "Russians," "Austrians," or "Germans." Indeed, it was the power of the centralized state that dissolved the autonomy that the Jews enjoyed until the modern era. The decline of the feudal economy and the growth of a capitalist economy undermined the foundations of the old socioeconomic order. But here I have chosen to tell the story of Eastern European Jews not as a passive element but rather to describe them as an active element, one with a consciousness of continuity and strong ties to their brethren in the different parts of the split commonwealth. I have not adopted the approach accepted until now in historiography, which is from the standpoint of the empires that affected the life of Eastern European Jewry from the outside. It is not the discourse of one of the imperial cultures, be it Russian, German, or Austrian, that underpins the writing of the story, nor, indeed, one of the versions of the national history that competed with the imperial histories. I have chosen instead a combined view that underscores the continuity and identifies the background and the causes for the preservation of the Eastern European identity shared by the subjects of the centralized kingdoms. This continuity, whose ancient roots lie in the social, cultural, and religious unity of the Ashkenazi diaspora, surely also is the basis for the growth of modern Jewish nationalism, which reunited what the economic and social processes of the modern age dismantled.

I have tried to depict the history of a society with a unique cultural heritage that, in a little over a hundred years, cast off old forms and took on new ones, a society that within a hundred years was transformed from a religious corporation, an integral part of a feudal system, into an ethnic nation in a multinational empire. When the Jewish identity as a premodern corporation was lost, the Jews of Eastern Europe began to see themselves as a modern political nation.

Chapter 1
The Jews of the Kingdom

The Jews living two hundred years ago in the Pale of Settlement in the western part of the Russian empire and in the eastern districts of the Hapsburg monarchy did not arrive there in the eighteenth century; they were already residing in these areas in large numbers hundreds of years before Russia and Austria annexed them. Although numerous hypotheses exist, some totally legendary and others with some basis in archaeological or literary sources, the beginnings of Jewish settlement in Eastern Europe remain an enigma. Ancient coins engraved with names in Hebrew letters, probably coined by wealthy Jews who supplied financial services to the early kings of Poland, provide the best evidence of the presence of Jews on Polish soil. Scholars of Eastern European Jewish history agree on one point: although there are clear signs that an earlier Jewish settlement existed in Eastern Europe, the Jewish community in Poland grew mainly out of the waves of Jewish immigrants from Germany, and it was the German element that left the most salient cultural and social imprint on the character of the Eastern European community. One can only speak of a continual Jewish presence in Poland from the second half of the thirteenth century. The Jewish society in Poland was a society of immigrants that coalesced into a community over several generations—similar, perhaps, to the way the Jewish community living today in the United States developed. Although for several centuries it was a dynamic society, constantly augmented by waves of immigration, it took a long time to coalesce into a single society. Only over a long period did a cultural character take shape, with traits shared by the entire Jewish population.

What attracted Jews to emigrate from Central Europe to Eastern Europe? What was there in Poland that led Jews to immigrate to that country in large numbers during the Middle Ages and the early modern era, until in the mid-seventeenth century, the largest Jewish community in the world lived there? The explanation, as in every historical instance of immigration, is connected to the places from which the Jews emigrated, as well as with the countries to which they moved. At first, Jews emigrated from Central Europe to the East as part of the overall emigration movement, seeking better economic conditions. As their situation in the cities of Germany worsened, in the wake of persecution and attack, particularly during the great plague in the mid-fourteenth century, the cities of Eastern Europe seemed safer. At the end of the fifteenth century, when relations between Jews and their Christian neighbors in Central and Western Europe were at their worst, hardly any Jews remained in most of the European kingdoms.

After 1500, owing to pogroms and expulsions, nearly all the Jews living in the world were concentrated in two large realms on the eastern and southern margins of Europe—the Ottoman Empire and the Polish-Lithuanian kingdom. This marginality had an impact on how the special character of Polish Jewry was shaped. There were many similarities between Polish Jewry and the Jews of the Ottoman Empire, the largest Jewish communities at the time when the world stood at the brink of the modern era. The ethnic composition and cultural character of these societies were largely determined by the waves of immigration from Western and Central Europe. In both cases, new immigrants arrived in cities where Jews with a different cultural tradition had been living for several generations. In both the Ottoman Empire and Poland, the culture imported by the new immigrants "swallowed up" the local tradition. In the cities of Greece and Turkey, the Romaniot Jews became "Sephardim." In Poland and Lithuania, the local Jews, about whose language and culture we have only fragmented information, became "Ashkenazim." Since Jewish settlement in Poland was part of the general immigration movement from Germany to Eastern Europe, it bore a German character. The organization of the communities, the immigrants' legal status, spoken language, and cultural world were linked to their German roots. The live connection with the German heritage was preserved because of the constant movement of population from west to east and because the rabbis who ruled on halakhic matters in Germany continued to maintain their authority many years after the new settlers had left their former homes. In fact, Jewish emigration to the east expanded the geographical boundaries of the community known as the Ashkenazi Jewish diaspora. This diaspora, which made a modest beginning in the communities of southwest Germany, expanded eastward beyond the boundaries of the Holy Roman Empire, and in the fifteenth century extended up to the eastern border of Lithuania.

Historians and scholars of Ashkenazi Jewish culture often address the issue of the similarities and disparities between Eastern European Jewry and German Jewry, these two branches of the Jewish diaspora known as the Ashkenazi. The similarities between the two, while they diminished as the immigrants became increasingly alienated from their country of origin, nonetheless remained a significant element in the social and cultural life of Polish Jewry for several centuries. Israel Halpern (1910–71), a scholar of Eastern European Jewry, noted three elements common to Polish and German Jewry:

1. Language: The spoken language is the most striking similarity. One language—Yiddish—was the language of Ashkenazi Jewry from northeastern France, the Alsace region, up to the eastern border of Polish Jewry, which was later a part of the Russian empire. There were, of course, various dialects of Yiddish, which differed in their syntax, grammar, and vocabulary. But within this broad region in which Jews spoke one of the dialects of Yiddish, they were able to communicate in writing and in speech in a language that was understood (albeit at times only partially) by all.
2. Religious Practice: The religious practice known as *minhag Ashkenaz* (Ashkenazi custom), which originated in the early Jewish communities in the Roman cities in Germany, spread and was also accepted in the Eastern European communities to which Jews immigrated. There were, of course, significant differences between the Ashkenazi custom and the Polish custom, but basically, all the Jews in Eastern Europe followed one religious practice and one form of prayer.
3. Communal Organization: Methods of communal organization provide a social key to an understanding of the life of the Jewish community in Eastern Europe in the Middle Ages and the early modern era. The structure of the Polish Jewish community was similar to that of the German Jewish communities, so that one can find many similarities between the communal organization in the towns of Kraków or Lublin in Poland and in towns like Frankfurt in Germany.[1]

Moreover, texts used in the towns of Germany formed the legal basis for the communities' existence, in the form of the document known as *privilegium*, granted by the Polish kings to the new settlers. Owing to the similarity and affinity of Polish Jewry to German Jewry in language, religious practice, the form of communal organization, and legal status, we can regard communities shaped by the copious numbers of Jewish immigrants to Eastern Europe as an offshoot of German Ashkenazi Jewry. But over the years, what happened to many other immigration movements happened to the immigrants from Germany. As Polish Jewry grew in number and developed, becoming more socially and culturally creative, it took on more and more singular traits of its own. Further on, we will see how, in later periods, these singular traits also came to denote significant differences between the eastern and western parts of the Ashkenazi diaspora.

The difference between socioeconomic life in the Polish kingdom and in Central Europe greatly influenced the way that the special character of the Polish community was shaped. It was this difference that also brought many Jewish settlers to Eastern Europe. The Jews in Poland, whose numbers greatly increased in the towns and the villages, engaged in a totally different type of economic activity from that of the Jews in

Germany. In Central Europe, the economic activity of Jews was linked primarily to moneylending; in Eastern Europe, although at first the Jews did specialize in finances, they became a part of the feudal economy and managed businesses that they leased from the nobility. This was a total departure from what they had experienced in Central Europe. The Jewish town dwellers engaged in a wide variety of commercial and productive areas, running industries that they leased from aristocrats. An alliance of interests was formed with the Polish landowning nobility, who invited the Jews to settle on their lands. The Jews had a colonizing function, taking part in establishing towns in agricultural areas. This process intensified in the sixteenth century and the first half of the seventeenth, when the Jews played a significant role in the Polish large-scale settlement project. The magnates (members of families of the upper nobility) invited them to settle in towns established in the southeastern borderland of the Polish-Lithuanian kingdom on the fertile lands of the Ukraine. Huge estates were founded in these expansive territories, where grains were grown and exported to the cities of Western and Central Europe. The economic activity of the Jews was integrated into the agricultural economy of the estate structure on different levels, beginning with the supply of services and the sale of products to the serfs in the villages; the purchase of agricultural produce, marketed in the vicinity or shipped to far-off destinations; and the processing of agricultural produce or other natural products, such as lumber and other forest products, areas the Jews engaged in to a great extent. One branch that became a hallmark of Jewish economic activity in the early modern era—the production of alcoholic beverages (beer, mead, and vodka)—clearly attested to the large-scale Jewish involvement in the agricultural economy of the estates in Poland. The new settlement in the eastern areas of Poland attracted Jews from the older, more established communities, where the urban Poles tried to keep them down and limit their economic opportunities.

The Jewish community in Poland, which took shape over several centuries as a society of immigrants, grew in size both demographically and geographically, and at a certain point in the sixteenth century, it became spiritually and religiously self-sufficient. This turning point had a significant impact on the ties between the two parts of the Ashkenazi diaspora. Before then, the halakhic religious authority of German Jewry was still valid for the Jews in Poland, but in the sixteenth century, the center of gravity shifted to the east. At the end of that century, there were at least fifteen talmudic academies (yeshivot) in various towns throughout the Polish kingdom. Talmudic scholarship in the large communities became the central axis in the Ashkenazi religious world and maintained its preeminence until the last days of the independent Polish kingdom. One distinct expression of the change in the status of these two religious centers was the shift in the direction taken by young men seeking to study Torah. Until the mid-sixteenth century, students traveled to study Torah in the communities of Germany; in the seventeenth and eighteenth centuries, it was almost an accepted norm that Jews of a certain social class in Germany, Bohemia, and Moravia would send their sons to study in Polish yeshivot. These young men, the wandering students of the Ashkenazi world of culture, in many cases traveled to the new country to settle there, joining the flow of immigration from west to east that continued at least until the Cossack revolt of 1648–49, during which the Jews suffered greatly.[2] This was one more manifestation of the change in status of the immigrant community in Poland, which became stronger and more eminent than the original community from which the new settlers came.

As noted, the Eastern European Jewish community bore a fundamental resemblance to the German Ashkenazi community. It was a religious-ethnic corporation recognized by law and protected by the monarchy. The legal basis for its existence was the royal *privilegium* granted in the second half of the fourteenth century, which assured the Jews of the king's protection and defined their duties to the royal treasury. This document, which underwent various transformations over time, was still valid in the days of the last king of Poland at the end of the eighteenth century. The broad autonomy maintained by the Jews in Eastern Europe for several centuries will be presented in a later chapter of this book as one of the main questions that preoccupied the Jews as well as the authorities when Poland lost its independence: How can a population maintaining a separate, foreign autonomy be integrated into a modern centralized state? The Jewish community was organized along the lines of an oligarchy. A small group of families that held all the political and economic power within the self-ruling autonomy usually occupied the key positions in the community's leadership. Three factors determined membership in the leading elite: property, family lineage, and religious status. Each of these was the subject of examination and evaluation. Property was a major element in the communal taxation system; family connections were meticulously examined in the matchmaking market; and in the traditional society, religious scholarship was translated into titles, such as *chaver* or *morenu*, and could be quantitatively assessed and examined through discussion of a halakhic issue. All three of these factors were combined in the Polish Jewish elite, which, early in the modern era, was but a small percentage of the entire Jewish population in the kingdom. Its members had "Torah and wealth dwelling together," plus family lineage.

The communities were managed by the *kahal*, a small group of people who possessed these three elements. Members of the *kahal* held the positions of control and governance in the community, replacing one another periodically through rotation as well as secret elections conducted in a complicated manner. The *kahal* collected taxes, provided services to members of the community, and supervised their religious, social, and economic activity. The communal leadership enacted and enforced regulations in all walks of life. The communal court deliberated and judged according to Jewish law, and the *kahal* had the means to enforce and penalize.

Recent studies have highlighted a significant historical feature: the marked connection between the oligarchic Jewish self-rule, on the one hand; and the external ruling systems, on the other. Today it is indisputably evident that the Jewish autonomous organization can be regarded as a well-integrated part of the overall system, not something deviant or exceptional.[3] Moreover, a considerable number of the powers enjoyed by the autonomous Jewish community largely rested on the mutuality of interests of the external political forces, namely, the families of the Polish nobility and the families of the Jewish elite who ran the *kahal*. This situation prevailed even after the last king of Poland was deposed. In the first half of the nineteenth century, many years after the partition of Poland, the ties between the Jewish leaseholders and the owners of the Polish estates were still strong as ever. The Polish Jewish society enjoyed political stability that stemmed from the political and economic interests shared by the Polish elite, the nobility that owned the estates and controlled the lands and means of production, and the families of the Jewish elite. The Jews played a decisive role in operating the means of production in the towns and the estates, and in return enjoyed a broad autonomy, anchored in the Polish political-legal system.

The structure of the Jewish autonomous community differed from one place to another. A detailed comparative study of various communities shows, for example, that the organization of Jewish self-rule in Kraków differed in several respects from that in other cities, such as Poznań or Lublin. In general, despite the disparity in one detail or another, a network of Jewish communities extended across the large kingdom, drawing its strength from the local communal authority. When the Jewish population increased demographically and expanded geographically, toward the sixteenth century, organizations developed that were supra-communal or regional (*va'adei hagalil*, provincial diets), as well as nationwide organizations (*va'adei ha'aratzot*, Councils of the Lands). In the historical consciousness of Eastern European Jewry in modern times, these supra-communal organizations became symbols of a national entity. The Russian Jewish historian Simon Dubnow (1860–1941) regarded the supra-communal Jewish autonomy as an all-embracing parliamentary structure, a sort of substitute for a state. He regarded the autonomous system with all its elements, from the individual community to the Councils of the Lands, as an expression par excellence of a national entity: "A broad and well-ordered social organization, with communities and associations of communities, and with a complex network of religious, social, and cultural institutions. The national and cultural value of this autonomy was very great. The autonomy provided strength and unity to the outcast nation and, at the same time, gave it culture and laws and educated it in the spirit of discipline and self-rule. The Jew felt that he was a part of a living national body."[4] The Councils of the Lands were loosely formed federations of community representatives who drew their strength from below, from the individual local communities. These organizations, which operated separately in the two parts of the kingdom—Poland and Lithuania—were the "Council of the Four Lands," which operated from the second half of the sixteenth to the second half of the eighteenth century (dissolved in 1764), and in parallel, the *va'ad*, or Lithuanian Council, which was active during a similar period and was dissolved in 1765.[5] These bodies functioned as federative parliaments, somewhat like the assemblies of the nobility (the *Sejmiki*), the consummate expression of that class's political power. At the councils, which were convened in several of the major cities for a brief period, elected representatives of the main communities in the kingdom met. According to Israel Halpern's estimates, only 1.08 percent of the Jewish population in Poland participated in electing the leadership of the national organization, and fewer (0.7 percent) voted in the elections for the Lithuanian leadership. In other words, only a very small segment of Polish Jewry (which, according to the official count in 1765, numbered about 590,000) took an active part in this supra-communal political system.[6]

Why were these supra-communal organizations founded, and what was their true function, beyond the myths and national images created later? From the standpoint of the Polish state, the councils served the Polish government as bodies that collected Jewish taxes.[7] The legal basis for the existence of Jews in Poland, the *privilegia* previously mentioned, granted by the kings of Poland, defined their status as "slaves of the royal treasury." As such, the Jews of Poland were required to pay a tax to the royal treasury. This tax, imposed according to the number of persons (poll tax), was to be collected from every Jewish adult throughout the kingdom. Since someone had to organize the method by which the burden of collecting taxes would be divided among the various communities, these supra-communal bodies set tax quotas that were imposed on the communities. They did not deal with the actual collection of taxes but only with dividing the taxation amounts into portions (known as *sechumot*), using a complicated key that was the topic of fierce debates and endless quarrels throughout the existence of these councils, quarrels that did not end even after the councils were abolished. The councils were recognized by the Polish government solely as bodies responsible for apportioning the burden of taxation among the communities. As far as the Polish government was concerned, the councils decided how much each individual community would collect from the residents in its town and transfer to the royal treasury; the government showed no interest in whether one Jew paid less and another paid more. The treasury expected to receive a certain total sum, fixed by the Polish parliament, the *Sejm.*

However, the supra-communal councils, which had not received any legal recognition beyond their function of collecting taxes, became, from an internal standpoint, the coordinating body of Jewish communal activity. They arranged various matters that needed to be coordinated between communities, enacting regulations on joint economic affairs, such as the handling of bankrupts who fled their town for another community. They dealt with the copyrights of book publishers, approved the printing of new books, and intervened in religious matters that were outside the purview of the individual community. When religious movements appeared in Poland that threatened the accepted religious order, the councils took a stand against them. This was the case at the time when Jewish communities throughout the world were greatly disillusioned upon learning that the false messiah Shabbetai Tsevi had converted to Islam (1666). On another occasion, the Council of the Four Lands took action when another false messiah, Jacob Frank, arrived in Poland from the Ottoman Empire at the end of 1755. Then, groups of secret followers of Shabbetai Tsevi came out of hiding and contended with the rabbinical leadership in southeastern Poland. The Council of the Four Lands did its utmost to inhibit and interfere with the activity of these movements, imposing excommunication and enlisting the help of people in government through its connections.

The councils were active on an ongoing basis in representing the interests of Polish Jews vis-à-vis the government. In the eighteenth century, Jews were accused in a growing number of incidents of murdering Christian children to use their blood for religious rituals (blood libels). In such cases, and in others that posed a danger to the Jews, including those in the Polish kingdom, the councils took action, exploiting their connections with government officials and utilizing funds that had accumulated in their coffers. In practice, these bodies, which had not received any official recognition beyond their fiscal capacity, became the representatives of the Jewish community in Poland and Lithuania. They were also recognized by Jewish communities in other locales—for example, in Amsterdam and Frankfurt, as the supreme authority to which they appealed on matters of internal controversies.[8]

The broad autonomy that the Jews in Eastern Europe enjoyed, from the individual community up to the supra-communal organizations, engaged the attention of Eastern European governments when reforms relating to the Jews' status were introduced. In the coming chapters, we will note that this broad autonomy—a feature peculiar to Eastern Europe in the nineteenth, and even the twentieth, century—was the major target against which the Russian, Austrian, and German regimes, as well as the autonomous Polish government, which survived after the kingdom lost its independence, directed all their weapons, in order to change what they perceived as abnormal—a Jewish society that enjoyed a separate, distinctive legal status. Polish Jewry, at the dawn of the modern era—namely, the second half of the eighteenth century—was a product of several centuries of shaping and growth, and it created for itself systems of life whose major component was the communal structure we have just spoken about. Merged within that same communal structure were the economic activity peculiar to the Jews, the religious and spiritual activity of Polish Jewry, as well as the nature of the Jews' relations with the society at large. In the mid-eighteenth century, on the eve of the changes that took place in Eastern Europe in the spirit of the modern era, a Polish Jew in towns like Kraków or Lublin could live his entire life within the framework of the autonomous Jewish community, hardly coming into direct contact with the external political and legal system. The contacts between the community and the outside world were in the hands of agents, whom today we would call lobbyists, appointed by the *kahal.* Their role is worded in florid language in a 1730 letter of appointment, issued to "the agent [*shtadlan*] of the Council of the Four Lands":

He shall be the guardian of the sanctuary; wherever he is sent, he will go and whatever he is commanded to do, he will do. He will be a loyal representative of his principals and will serve truly and honestly in the holy place; he lies in wait at every corner to gain benefits and salvation for the general good both in the great councils [meetings of the *Sejm,* the Polish parliament] of Warsaw and Gródno and the like, and on the committees, and to present the apportionment of the tax quotas to His Excellency the Treasurer, may he be exalted, every year.[9]

According to this letter of appointment, the representative of the Jewish community engaged in "lobbying" in the corridors of the parliament and was the one who submitted the lists of Jewish taxes to the royal treasury. Thus, the Jewish autonomy enabled a populace of hundreds of thousands to live within a familiar internal world, which, as a separate, special unit, was part of the general socioeconomic system. The end of the Polish kingdom brought about the disintegration of this self-rule, which until the modern era was the basis for traditional Jewish life in Eastern Europe.

Chapter 2

The Partitions of Poland: The End of the Old Order, 1772–1795

Now that we have learned some of the unique features of Jewish society in "old Poland" prior to its encounter with the modern age, we will discuss how and when the traditional communal order began to unravel in the eighteenth century. This first occurred when the Polish-Lithuanian kingdom began to lose its political independence, and reached its peak with the changes that Polish Jewry experienced during the partitions of the kingdom, which lasted about twenty-three years, at the end of the eighteenth century (1772–95). The historical reality in which the Jewish communities existed in the eastern part of the Ashkenazi diaspora did not end in a single day. The military and political changes that redrew the boundaries in Eastern Europe preceded the social and economic change, which was far more gradual and spread over half of the nineteenth century. The removal of the Polish-Lithuanian kingdom from the geopolitical map was, however, a decisive milestone in Jewish history. When this kingdom was abolished, the firm basis of Jewish self-rule was undermined, and the way was paved for the liquidation of the Jewish corporation in Eastern Europe.

The last decades of the eighteenth century were a stormy period in world history, the age of revolutions. Old regimes fell and new states were born, attended by political change, war, and rebellion. A few years after the first partition of Poland, the colonies of North America fought against British rule and gained their independence. While the armies of Russia, Prussia, and Austria were carrying out the second and third partitions of Poland, France was experiencing the horrors of revolutionary terror. During the revolution and the war that gave rise to the United States and abolished the *ancien régime* in France, the Polish-Lithuanian kingdom ceased to exist as an independent political entity, and its territories were divided among three powers that surrounded it on three sides. The partitions of Poland erased from the geopolitical map of Europe a large kingdom, which in the seventeenth century had extended over broad areas between Prussia and southern Ukraine, and from the mid-eighteenth century gradually dwindled into a powerless autonomous area, until it was finally swallowed up by the neighboring states. The partitions of Poland also led to the dissolution of the largest Jewish collective in the world, which at the beginning of the modern era lived within the boundaries of a single kingdom. They created political and administrative barriers between communities that found themselves on different sides of the new boundaries.

In the last decades of the seventeenth century, the Polish-Lithuanian kingdom greatly weakened, both politically and militarily. One of the main causes for the great kingdom's loss of power was the disparity in the form of government and administration between it and its neighbors who were growing stronger and later swallowed up Poland and deprived it of its independence. To the east lay Muscovite Russia, which gathered in strength on the Lithuanian and Ukrainian border; on the south and southwest was the Austrian kingdom, which expanded its provinces at the expense of the Ottoman Empire; to the west was Prussia, a small kingdom (with territories in northeastern Poland as well) that had a centuries-old military tradition of fighting and settlement on the Polish borderland. Prussia augmented its military strength while casting a covetous eye on the western territories of the kingdom.

In the decades that preceded the partition of Poland, these three states introduced a series of administrative reforms, primarily aimed at increasing the power of the sovereign and fortifying his status vis-à-vis that of the nobility. The king became an absolutist monarch, and the kingdom under his rule became a centralized state. This combination of the monarch's increased power and the centralization of the government apparatus significantly improved the functioning of the various systems in the state. Effective mechanisms of governance were established that supervised economic activity and increased the income of the royal treasury. The centralized government deprived autonomous bodies of their powers and placed them under its authority. And what may have been far more important for the fate of Poland—absolutist rule considerably bolstered the military strength of these three states, enabling them to expand their boundaries at the expense of Poland, their large, militarily powerless neighbor, and to intervene in her internal affairs. In 1683, Poland still took part in an important military campaign against the Ottoman Empire, when the Polish army fought at the gates of Vienna. This was probably, however, the last time that Poland appeared as a significant military and political player in Europe. After that, the Polish state began to lose its prestige as a meaningful military power. While its neighbors organized as centralized states with capital cities, the seats of a sole ruler with nearly limitless powers, a totally different process was taking place in Poland. The political strength of the nobility, rather than weakening, became stronger at the expense of the central government. Poland was and remained after its loss of independence a republic of aristocrats. The members of the noble class enjoyed broad political powers; elected, and were themselves elected, to the national parliament (the *Sejm*) and to regional parliaments (the *Sejmiki*). It was a parliamentary form of government in every respect, with all the attendant weaknesses and shortcomings in the economic and military domains.

This Polish democracy (and that is what it was called: "a democracy of the nobility") carried on a representative pattern of governance that was typical of many European states until the rise of absolutism. The Polish parliamentary system was similar to the British system at the end of the seventeenth century, and there were thinkers and statesmen in Poland who attempted to remedy the flaws of government in their country based on the British political model. The excessive political rights of the nobility, anchored in law, weakened the state at the very time when the threat from the centralized states that wanted to grow at Poland's expense was becoming ominous. A significant weak point in the Polish form of government related to the authority to employ military power. In wartime, the army was mobilized through parliamentary decisions, and military activity had to be financed by taxes that were collected in a cumbersome and inefficient manner.[1] Some of the great nobles, known as magnates, kept private armies they financed themselves, waged wars from time to time with one another, entered into alliances with foreign powers, and ran what amounted to their own states within the kingdom. The strength of the upper nobility and the independent policy that the nobles conducted were detrimental to Poland. They helped the neighboring powers to intervene in its internal affairs and hastened the loss of its independence.

What happened to the Jewish community as Poland declined militarily? How did the kingdom's weakened military strength in the international arena affect the status of the Jews? Poland's political weakness, instead of adversely affecting the Jewish community, had a strong influence on its social stability and economic prosperity. The Jews were allies of the nobility, and the nobles' nearly absolute autonomy constituted a solid foundation for the broad autonomy they enjoyed. Families of the nobility strengthened after the invasion of the Cossacks and the wars of the mid-seventeenth century. Even after 1648, they continued to establish new towns and invited Jews to settle in areas that had been destroyed in battles. The colonization of the kingdom's southeastern borderland went on, not stopping even in the eighteenth century. The decentralized character of the Polish government was of great benefit to the Jews, since the Jewish community existed under the aegis of the nobility. Its representatives exploited this and were adept at maneuvering between the various powers in the complex political system within which they lived. Through their agents, or lobbyists (shtadlanim), Jews were involved at various levels in the activities of bodies of the Polish administration. These Jewish lobbyists, who were appointed by the communities or represented the supra-communal organizations, were frequently active at sessions of the regional parliaments and the national parliament that convened in Warsaw or Vilna, the capital of the Lithuanian duchy that merged with Poland. They were engaged in enlisting the support of these members of parliament, with the aim of influencing the decisions of the *Sejm*. In the 1730 letter of appointment of the *shtadlan* for the Council of the Four Lands, cited in the previous chapter, the representative of the Jews was authorized to act, in the name of those who had appointed him, to represent their interests before the members of the Polish parliament, in order to "gain benefits and salvation for the general good."[2] This subtle wording hinted at the variety of the *shtadlan*'s activities behind the scenes of the *Sejm* sessions, which included making payments, exploiting family connections, and providing financial services.

The aggressive activities of the Jewish lobbyists angered some members of the Polish aristocracy, who claimed that these activities behind the scenes of the Polish parliament were causing financial losses and political damage to the state. In his memoirs, R. Dov Ber of Bolechów, an eighteenth-century wine merchant, described the hostility of the Jews' opponents:

In those days the Polish nobles asserted that the Elders of the Council of Four Lands, the Chiefs of Israel, who had always to meet at Warsaw during the sessions of the Diet in connection with the poll taxes to be paid by the Jews to the Crown, caused the dissolution of the Diets, which had been convoked at great expense. Every Diet was attended by many deputies, Jew-baiters, who denounced the Jews for every kind of wickedness, in order to deprive them of the liberties they had always enjoyed, and proposed to forbid the Jews to carry on profitable businesses in wine, cattle and other goods. Under the constitution of Poland one member of the Diet, i.e., *Szlachticz* (noble), could stop the business of the session by declaring: "I do not agree to this matter." The Polish nobles believed that the leading Jews bribed some of the deputies to bring the sessions of the Diets to an end by this means.[3]

In the eighteenth century, Poland was involved in a series of wars that the armies of the neighboring states fought within its territory as if it were their own. For example, the Russian empire, under the rule of Peter the Great, waged wars in the northeastern part of Poland, causing much damage and destruction. Poland, which was gradually losing its military strength, looked like easy prey to its neighbors, who finally concluded that they could forgo the independent existence of the large kingdom and divide its lands among themselves. The process in which Poland's independence was abolished, known in Polish history as the "partitions of Poland," took a little over twenty years. The first partition occurred in summer 1772, when Russia, Austria, and Prussia each swallowed up areas on the border they shared with the Polish-Lithuanian kingdom. Russia annexed regions in the northeast, Austria took over a considerable part of the southeastern area (which became known as Galicia), and Prussia annexed areas in the northwest. The Jews residing in the annexed areas passed in one day from living under the rule of a feudal state with a parliamentary regime of the nobility to residing in states with a centralized government. The centralized system of the occupying states naturally constituted a threat to the broad self-rule that the Jews enjoyed. From the first days after the annexation, the new rulers began to place obstacles in the path of the Jewish autonomy, in an attempt to subject it to the authority of the central government.

Between the first partition in 1772 and the second (1792) and third (1793), several political changes took place in Poland that greatly affected the legal status of the Jews in the countries of Eastern Europe. Eight years before the first partition, Stanisław August Poniatowski, the last king to rule an independent Polish kingdom, took the throne. Poniatowski, who was profoundly influenced by the ideas of the French Enlightenment and greatly admired England's system of constitutional monarchy, attempted to introduce administrative and legislative reforms in his country. Well aware of the changes occurring in the structure of government in the neighboring states, he understood that to save Poland from the loss of its political independence, a great measure of centralization in running the affairs of state was necessary. In addition, he aspired to promote science and education in his kingdom and to train a new generation of skilled, professional public officials. His intentions to introduce reforms naturally met strong opposition from groups of aristocrats who wanted to maintain their power and the nearly anarchic decentralization of government. The neighboring powers were also involved in the controversies that raged between the various factions and influenced events on the internal political scene. The king himself, who had been one of Empress Catherine II's lovers, was under the strong influence of his Russian neighbor. The internal rifts and outside interference also led to wars between the rival factions. R. Dov of Bolechów described the doleful political situation of the kingdom in the early days of the last king's reign:

The majority of the nobles said to one another: "The Polish people has been free from time immemorial. We have no dealings with Poniatowski, nor any

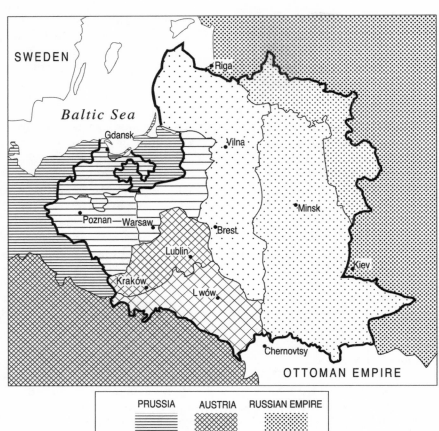

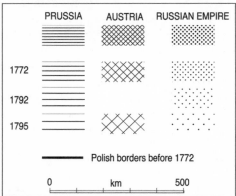

Map 1. The partitions of Poland-Lithuania

counsel with his Senate at Warsaw." So the powerful nobles made a great conspiracy and concluded a strong covenant. They raised large sums of money
among themselves, and as they acted on the advice of France, 200,000 ducats
were sent to them from Paris. I saw this with my own eyes, for the officer who
brought the money stayed with me a whole day. The turmoil lasted for five years
throughout the whole of Poland. During that time there was no law nor justice
in the country, but "might was right."[4]

Despite the opposition, both domestic and external, several reforms
were introduced in the state. One that was announced in the first days
of Poniatowski's reign was the annulment of the Jewish supra-communal
councils in Poland and Lithuania (the Council of the Four Lands and
the Lithuanian Council). This was clearly a step taken to centralize the
administration for the benefit of the state. The *Sejm*'s decision nullifying
the Council of the Four Lands, adopted on June 1, 1764, stated, among
other things:

Since it is known to us that the leaders of the Jews are accustomed to collect,
in accordance with their private regulations and apportionments, by applying
considerable pressure on all the Jews, in particular those residing in the towns
of the kingdom and the nobles, sums far greater than the Jewish poll tax established in the 1717 constitution, a total of 220,000 Polish guldens, and are in the
habit of using them for their benefit and personal expenses, and the state, based
on a correct calculation, can without difficulty extract a far greater income from
the Jewish taxes. Hence, we are rescinding . . . the above-mentioned sum of poll
tax agreed upon in advance, and establishing a general poll tax from all the Jews
and the Karaites.[5]

In other words, the government strove to make the collection of taxes
more efficient and to do without the mediation of a corporative organization, which made the process of collection cumbersome and used the
monies for its own purposes. The legislator's aim was to create a direct
connection between the individual subject and the government administration and to liquidate an autonomous body that acted as a buffer
between the Jewish subjects and the state authorities. By divesting the
Council of the Four Lands (and a year later, the Lithuanian Council)
of their taxation powers, the state deprived these organizations of the
government's recognition, since as far as the kingdom was concerned,
the supra-communal councils had no powers other than those related
to Jewish taxes. Despite the intentions underlying the liquidation of the
councils, it seems that the abolishment of the autonomous supra-
communal organizations did not significantly increase the state's reve-
nues. Historical sources show that although the kingdom conducted a
population census throughout the land, many Jews managed to evade
the census takers. R. Dov Ber of Bolechów relates that several hundred
of the residents of his town were not counted at all. Moreover, according

to him, the number of persons that the representatives of the Jews swore was the accurate count was officially registered as the basis for the new poll tax. In other words, it is not clear that the state enjoyed greater revenue as a result of the reform in the method of taxation, since the Jews managed to influence the outcome of the census that determined the amount of tax. But the abolition of the supra-communal councils was undoubtedly a meaningful stage in the move to make Poland a centralized state, a moment before it lost its independent existence.

Two decades later, the Jews were once again confronted by far-reaching reforms affecting their status. In 1788, the Polish *Sejm* convened in the capital city of Warsaw, and in opposition to the custom that had lasted several centuries, continued its deliberations for nearly four years without a break. "The four-year *Sejm*" or the "long *Sejm*" attempted to hold a thorough discussion on a comprehensive reform of the Polish-Lithuanian kingdom's government and society.[6] The delegates were all too aware of the dangers posed to the nation, weakened and torn by internal strife, by its aggressive neighbors who craved its lands.

An entire series of reforms, proposed during the four-year *Sejm*, concerned the Jews. These proposed changes in the Jews' legal status and economic activity were largely influenced by the ideas of the eighteenth-century Enlightenment and by political and economic theories that were widespread at the time in Western Europe. The reformers' intent was to make the method of government more efficient, to enhance the kingdom's economic strength, and to bolster her military capability. The economic activity of the Jews, a weighty demographic element in the population, was highly important to the owners of the towns and the rural estates. At this point, the long-standing opposition between the Jews and the urban class was starkly revealed. Some reformists understood that it was impossible to maintain a strong and economically prosperous centralized state without granting at least partial rights to other classes in the country. This was an unprecedented idea in Polish history, since until then only the nobility had been regarded as the Polish "nation." In contemporary terms, the idea was to add the town dwellers to the Polish nation, and this raised the question of the place of the Jews in the new political order. The urban class, whose social and political influence were limited (with the exception of several towns that enjoyed special rights), had viewed the Jews for centuries as economic competitors. Now, when there was a possibility that the Jews would also enjoy certain rights, the enduring hostility brimmed over, arousing protests and riots. In certain places, the Jews were a fairly sizable minority, while in townlets and towns, particularly in the eastern regions of the kingdom, they often were an absolute majority in the urban population. The reformers' intent to improve the legal status of the town dwellers, which entailed a bitter public debate about the legal status of the Jews, drew special attention to their economic activity. Memoranda were submitted and essays were composed underscoring the ways in which the Jews were different and proposing ways to minimize the damage they were allegedly causing to agriculture, trade, and small industries.[7] The reformist programs that were proposed clearly reflected the influence of Enlightenment ideas on the Polish statesmen. They ranged from a demand to abolish the communal self-rule through the deportation of the surplus "nonproductive" Jewish population to the areas of new settlement, to the retention of the autonomy under state control.

The public debate conducted in France on the eve of the revolution reverberated up to Warsaw and Vilna. Material of a distinctly emancipatory nature about improving the civil state of French Jews was distributed among political activists. The essays of the Christian clergyman Henri Grégoire and the radical Jewish Maskil Zalkind Hourwitz were translated into Polish and read with interest by members of the Polish *Sejm*.[8] These were the days of a political awakening of a new type, which until then had been unknown to Jews active in public affairs. Jewish representatives did their utmost to influence the decisions of the *Sejm* relating to the Jews, not in the modern political sense but by the familiar method of lobbying, organizing delegations, and writing memoranda. There were Jews who enjoyed the patronage of the Polish aristocracy and who, with their support, wrote essays on the situation of their coreligionists in Poland. The best-known text of this kind is a work written in French published by the Maskil Mendel Lefin, whose patron was the magnate Adam Kazimierz Czartoryski. The aims of the Jewish lobbyists were not similar to those of the Polish reformers, at least not to those of the more radical among them. The Jewish representatives probably wanted, as far as possible, to preserve the existing political and economic system. The ideas of the Enlightenment and the influence of the French physiocratic school threatened their traditional way of life as well as the social and economic infrastructure that sustained it. The Jews and the nobles would seem to have had identical interests, since, as we noted, the Jewish community was the nobility's basic economic prop, and therefore the owners of towns and estates would gain nothing by diminishing the *kahal*'s power or depriving it of its authority. The Jews, however, who were a part (albeit a special, separate one) of the urban class in Poland, were also perceived in it as a different, foreign population. Taking these contradictions and contrasts into account, the *Sejm* sought to redefine the status of the Jews, who did not seem to merit being a part of the "nation." Finally, on May 3, 1791 (to this very day, a national holiday in Poland), a new constitution was proclaimed, which did not grant the Jews political rights.

In revolutionary France, too, which at that point was a constitutional monarchy, a lengthy debate took place on whether the Jews could be integrated into the nation. There was vociferous opposition to the emancipation of the Ashkenazi Jews living in the towns and townlets of Alsace. Much of what was written denigrating the Alsatian Jews is similar to what was written in Poland about the Jews' economic activity, their separatism, and their bizarre customs. In September 1791, a decision was made to grant civil rights to the Ashkenazi Jews and to abolish the self-rule of the communities. In Poland, the autonomy remained in the framework of a class-based state in which the nobility continued to be the only class enjoying full political rights. In France, the self-rule of the Jews was annulled in the framework of a centralized state in which classes were abolished and the "nation" encompassed all sectors of the population. As we shall see, the link between the political power of the aristocratic class in Poland and the existence of the Jewish autonomy continued well into the nineteenth century. Many Jews and Poles understood the meaning of this link and preferred it to the modern alternative in the form of a centralized state.

The neighboring states, which closely followed the course of the four-year *Sejm*'s debates, were opposed to the May 1791 constitution. Several months after it was proclaimed, the armies of Russia, Austria, and Prussia invaded the kingdom and tore more territories away from it.

After the second partition (1792), the area of the independent Polish state was greatly reduced. The third and last partition of Poland (1793) finally destroyed the last vestige of its independence. The remaining parts of the kingdom were annexed to Prussia and the Russian empire. The partition powers froze all the decisions taken by the four-year *Sejm*. They also tried to dismantle the Polish army, but in March 1794, led by Tadeusz Kosciuszko, an engineering corps officer who had fought alongside George Washington in the American Revolution, the army rose up against the Russians. Kosciuszko, who held republican views, led the army to several victories in the vicinity of Kraków.

The atmosphere in Poland was charged with revolutionary fervor, and "Jacobin" slogans in support of human and civil rights, in the spirit of the French Revolution, were widespread. The leader of the revolt promised the town dwellers, as well as the peasants who joined his forces, that their social and political status would be improved. He also turned to the Jews, calling on them to support the revolt and assuring them that they would be granted political rights in the future. The radical ideas of the republican leader were not favorably regarded by the conservative wing of the Polish nobility, whose aim was to preserve a somewhat modified version of the "republic of the nobles." Needless to say, the Polish town dwellers were not enthusiastic about national unification with their historical competitors. Nor was the large Jewish public in Poland-Lithuania, which then numbered close to a million, inclined to favor Kosciuszko's ideas of freedom and equality or the Polish nationalism of the nobles. Nonetheless, some Jews in Warsaw did join the Polish fighters and together with them, drove the Russian garrison force out of the city in April 1794. Kosciuszko had warm words of praise for the Jewish merchants and tradesmen who took part in the war of freedom against the Russian invader: "On April 17 and 18, when Warsaw waged a bloody war against the Muscovite invaders, the Jewish residents of the city took up arms, fought bravely against the enemy, and proved to the world that whenever humanity is likely to gain, they are prepared to risk their lives."[9]

Following the victory over the Russian garrison force in the capital, a Jewish light cavalry unit was formed under the command of a Jew called Berek Joselewicz. Notwithstanding the opposition of the leadership of the Warsaw Jewish community, the commander of the unit (*pułkownik*) received financial aid from the Polish government to purchase weapons and military equipment and began collecting volunteers and forcibly enlisting unemployed Jews. Historians disagree about whether the Jews of Joselewicz's unit actually fought in a real battle. At the time, unsubstantiated rumors spread that the regiment had fought in a battle in the suburb of Praga on November 4, 1794. Other rumors held that the Jewish soldiers never took part in any fighting. In any case, in the autumn of 1794, the Russian army, coming from the east, invaded the Polish areas that were still independent, attacked Warsaw from the northeast, and set upon Praga, then inhabited by many Jews. The Russian soldiers massacred the Jews, killing several hundred of them. More than any other event, Warsaw's fall to the Russian empire symbolized the end of independent Poland. The role of the Jews in the last struggle for Polish independence, which in truth was marginal and insignificant, later was chosen as the symbol of the pro-Polish Jews' trends of integration in the coming 150 years. The commander of the Jewish regiment, who deviated from the political norms of traditional Jewish society, was lavishly praised by the nationalist leaders of the Polish aristocracy: "You were the first to provide an example of the resurrection of your people's heroism and the revival of the valiant men whose death the daughters of Zion wept over in the past."[10]

With these words, Prince Potocki eulogized this Jewish war hero, who fell in a battle near Kock on May 5, 1809. This romantic Polish nationalism was utterly foreign to Joselewicz's fellow Jews, and decades passed before a nationalistic pathos of this kind began to fill the hearts of the first proponents of the Jewish nationalist movement in Eastern Europe.

The years from 1772 to 1795 were a turbulent period in Jewish history.

Owing to the military conquests, events occurred the likes of which Polish Jewry had never experienced. The most striking change caused by the partitions was the opening of the Russian empire. A country that, for age-old religious reasons, had never permitted Jews to reside in it now had annexed regions inhabited by hundreds of thousands of descendants of the "God killers." When the Polish cake was divided up, the Russians took the largest slice for themselves, annexing Lithuania, White Russia, and the Polish part of eastern Ukraine. Instantaneously, the majority of Poland's Jews came under the new, alien, and unfamiliar rule. On the other side of the divided kingdom, Prussia, a state with a centralized government under the rule of King Frederick the Great, annexed other districts in the north and the west. The new areas created a land connection between western and eastern Prussia. In the first years after the suppression of Kosciuszko's revolt, Prussia also ruled Warsaw and its surrounding area. This small and conquest-hungry kingdom was also the land in whose cities the Jewish Enlightenment movement began at the time of the first partition of Poland. Here the Jews came up against the most rigid instance of an absolutist regime. There were not as many Jews in the area occupied by Prussia as there were in the area annexed by Russia, and that number was considerably reduced because of the expulsion of the poor (the *Betteljuden*).

At first, the Prussian *Reglement,* which had been in force in that country from 1750, was applied to the Jews of the annexed regions, and over time, the new government enacted a special system of laws for the Polish Jews. The restrictions on self-rule and economic activities were similar to those in force in other areas of Prussia (the 1797 constitution). Within a few years, the Jewish society underwent social and cultural changes that brought it closer to German Jewry. In the area annexed by the Austrians, the Jews also encountered a centralized regime, but their large numbers (about a quarter of a million) and the religious difference (the influence of Hasidism) apparently enabled them to preserve the special Eastern European character of Galician Jewry.

Over the next hundred years, in the wake of the partitions, two parallel historical processes took place. On the one hand, the link between the Jews and the Polish nobility still remained intact. The fact that independent Polish rule was over did not mean that the aristocratic class had lost any of its special rights and privileges. The centralized states—Austria, Russia, and Prussia—integrated the Polish aristocracy into their own class systems and allowed them to maintain their political and economic rights. A social revolution did not take place, nor did anything change in the order of life on the local level. The Jews of the cities, towns, and villages continued their lives under the old economic relationship; the feudal system was not abolished but remained intact for several decades.

On the other hand, the imperial government, administered from Berlin, Petersburg, or Vienna, was eager to curtail Jewish self-rule and to integrate the Jews into the urban class in those states. These were two contradictory processes, which became part of the life of the Jews living on the lands of partitioned Poland for nearly a century. The Jews' existence was dependent on the feudal economic system owned by the Polish aristocracy, but they had to contend with the imperial officialdom that strove to quash the power of the Jewish autonomy that was linked to this aristocracy.

The Polish nobility continued to maintain its influence on Jewish life not only because it preserved its class privileges but because it retained a considerable measure of autonomous rule. Although the kingdoms that split the Polish state tended to greater centralization than was customary in the annexed areas prior to the partitions, they did not abolish Polish independence at one stroke or in equal measure everywhere. Some parts of Poland still retained some autonomy; for instance, a large part of central Poland that was annexed by the Russian empire enjoyed autonomy, and there the internal administration remained in the hands of the Polish aristocracy, the same political stratum that had ruled the areas previously. Self-rule in the regions of central Poland and Lithuania was reduced as Russian opposition to the Poles' nationalist aspirations grew, until it was totally rescinded after the 1863 Polish uprising failed. The preservation of Polish self-rule, even after the loss of independence, had considerable implications for the Jews. The changes that occurred in Polish Jewish society in the areas annexed to each of the three powers did not depend only on the relations with the new rulers. Contacts with the Polish elites continued and sometimes even influenced Jewish life far more than the activity of the imperial government. In the history of the Jews in every area of divided Poland, and sometimes also in every town, there was a "Polish" story, one that continued under Russian rule or, alternatively, under the Austrian government.

Polish autonomy continued to exist because the aristocracy maintained its special privileges, and the feudal infrastructure, still legally preserved even after the partitions, was retained, although there were differences between what happened in this regard in Russia and in Austria. As we shall see in the coming chapters, one result of this continuity was that traditional Jewish life continued to exist well into the nineteenth century, thus maintaining the economic infrastructure of the Jewish community, preserving the old frameworks, and delaying the introduction of new forms of living. In his memoirs, Yehezkel Kotik, from the town of Kamenets-Litovsk in Belorussia, writes about the Jewish traditional way of life under the protection of the Polish aristocracy until the 1863 Polish uprising (scores of years after the area was conquered by the Russians). Among other things, he notes: "In those days, what was ruinous for the gentry was no less so for a large section of the Jewish population, who derived their livelihood from the lords. And now all this affected them as well."[11]

However, the same forces that destroyed the old way of life in Jewish society also operated against Polish autonomy. When the feudal economy crumbled and the power of the premodern, class-based organizations declined, the Polish nobility weakened. What changed the power of this nobility, from a class that enjoyed broad autonomy to one that had no autonomy at all, were its abortive attempts to rebel against Russian, Austrian, and Prussian rule. These attempts were a tale of repeated failures, in which the 1794 uprising was but the first chapter. In 1830–31, a second revolt against the Russian invader also failed and ended in a further curtailment of Polish autonomy; in 1846, a revolt in the Austrian area suffered defeat; during the 1848 revolutions, similar attempts were made in the Prussian area and again in the Austrian. The 1863 revolt against Russian rule brought to a close the series of Polish uprisings, after which the Russians eradicated every last shred of Polish autonomy within the empire.

In all these rebellions, the Jews were caught between the central imperial government and the families of the Polish nobility, under whose protection they had lived for generations. Many actually tended to support the Poles, which shows that even decades after Poland's loss of independence, the old ties of loyalty between the Jews and the Polish nobility had not been severed. In the Austrian area, the situation was different. Here, in 1867, the Poles actually gained what they had been deprived of in the Russian area. This difference had particular significance, as we shall see later, in the history of Galician Jewry.

The partitions of Poland ended one chapter in the history of Polish Jewry and opened several parallel historical paths. From the political standpoint, one story of Polish Jewry ended here and at least three separate stories began to unfold: the story of the Jews of the Russian empire, the story of the Jews of Austrian Galicia, and the story of the Jews of the districts annexed to Prussia. But as we have seen, the geopolitical factor was not the only one that shaped the historical story. Although the Jews of Poland were divided among several separate political units, the elements common to them continued to exist and to influence their lives many years after the split created by the partitions. A political boundary was established between one district and another, but many of the characteristics of the old Jewish life in Eastern Europe—ranging from the economic reality to the relations between Jews and Polish nobles—

remained unchanged. This may explain the gap between the pace of the political changes that took place in Eastern Europe and the pace of the social and cultural development of the Jews in this region. In the following chapters, we will trace the historical avenues along which the history of the Jews of the Polish-Lithuanian kingdom moved in the states that put an end to the political independence of the Polish nation.

Chapter 3

Towns and Cities: Society and Economy, 1795–1863

What happened to Eastern European Jewish society after the huge kingdom that stretched from Germany to Russia fell apart and was swallowed up by three powers? What changed in the social and economic life of the Eastern European Jew after these partitions? The social and economic history of the Jews of Poland-Lithuania can be sharply divided into two distinct periods: the first, from the partitions to the mid-nineteenth century; the second, from the 1850s to the beginning of the mass immigration in the 1880s. This periodization of the social and economic history of Eastern European Jewry is based on the fact that the 1850s mark the beginning of a totally different period in Eastern Europe. This was the time of the massive penetration of the capitalist system that, within a few years, upended Jewish life.

In the first period the processes of capitalism were in their infancy, so that a significant gap was created between the economic development in Western and Central Europe and that of Eastern Europe, which also affected the role of the Jews in the various parts of Europe. Although during these years, processes of industrialization, as well as of urbanization, did begin in several areas of the Russian empire, the corporative legal structure and the old economic ways of a feudal economy still continued to exist, with all their social implications for the Jewish community.

The economic activity of Eastern European Jews was underpinned by social, religious, and cultural processes that took place in the nineteenth century, which were particularly influenced by the enormous demographic change that occurred in the first half of the century. This was an immensely large community that grew rapidly and spread throughout the area where it resided, particularly within Eastern Europe or on its fringes (mainly in southeastern Europe). This population expansion did not include the massive emigration to North and South America (which only began in the last decades of the century). The reason for the huge demographic growth of Eastern European Jewry is still a matter of controversy among scholars,[1] but one thing is clear. Throughout the nineteenth century, the Jewish population in the areas annexed to the Russian empire increased more than tenfold (about 400,000 in the 1764 Polish census, compared with more than five million in the 1897 Russian census). In the previously mentioned census, conducted by the Polish authorities when they abolished the Council of the Four Lands and the Lithuanian Council, nearly 600,000 Jews were counted in Poland and Lithuania, but that was the official figure based on the total counts in the various towns and cities. Unofficially, about 750,000 Jews were then living in Eastern Europe. The discrepancy between the official figure and the "true" number stemmed from the problems involved in conducting a census in Eastern Europe at the time. Jews, like other groups in the large kingdom, were not eager to report the true number of their community. Taxes, and later conscription into the armies of the various states, were based on the lists of inhabitants. Whenever we speak about the number of Jews in Eastern Europe, we have to bear in mind that tens of thousands, and perhaps even more, were never registered and were in a sense "unknown."

From three-quarters of a million, then, the number rose to more than five million Jews in the Russian empire only. If we add the more than a million Jews in the Austrian part of Poland, count the Prussian Jews (who emigrated in masses to Germany), and include the emigrants who left the area in the last decades of the century, the picture is one of enormous growth unprecedented in Jewish history. The demography of Eastern Europe had several features that did not exist in other Jewish diasporas (with the exception, perhaps, of the Ottoman Jews in large cities like Izmir or Salonika). First, the Jews formed the majority in certain types of settlement: small cities and towns (shtetls), sometimes constituting more than 80 percent of the population. These cities and towns were in a rural vicinity with an absolute majority of a non-Jewish population. Second, in certain areas of partitioned Poland, the Jews were between 10 and 14 percent of the overall population (in towns and villages). Not only the relative size of the Jewish population, but its absolute size as well, were exceptional compared with any other diaspora. Third, there was a large internal immigration, a constant movement of hundreds of thousands that resulted in the spread of the Jewish population living within the boundaries of the Polish-Lithuanian kingdom to other regions of Eastern Europe that opened for settlement only after the partitions.

A case striking in its geographical scope and demographic dimensions is the massive Jewish emigration to districts in southern Ukraine, particularly to the three southernmost districts, known in the Russian empire as the "new Russia." The areas of new settlement in the southern part of the empire, where no European Jews had lived until the end of the eighteenth century, attracted thousands of immigrants from the older, established communities. For example, in 1789, in Odessa, a developing port city and bustling commercial center on the shores of the Black Sea, there were six Jews (at the time, there was nothing there but a fortress called Khadzhi-bei). In 1855, there were 17,000 Jews residing in the city, and in 1897 when the imperial census was taken, there were 138,915.[2] Within a century, widespread immigration from other regions of Eastern Europe turned the city into the largest Jewish urban center in the Russian Pale of Settlement.

This is what Ben-Zion Dinur (Dinaburg), the eminent historian of Eastern European Jewry, wrote about the connection between the special demographic nature of Russian Jewry and its particular social and cultural character:

Four basic features in the existence of this Jewish collective gave it its special place in the life of our people in recent generations. One, it was the largest in size; two, it was the most concentrated in the settlements it inhabited; three, it led the most elaborate lifestyle; and four, it was the most deeply rooted in traditional Jewish culture. These were the four features that shaped the historical image of Russian Jewry and endowed it with its three main traits: a) It was a strong Jewish entity with a remarkable, distinctive mode of life; b) it was plagued by constant internal tension that affected its fate and the course of its history; and c) it steadily gathered strength as it defended itself and struggled against outside forces.[3]

Dinur noted the dimensions and the concentration of this population as its most salient features. Indeed, the enormous growth in the number of Jews led to such crowded living conditions that internal emigration alone could not lessen its social and cultural implications. It was a population that was "urban" in nature, and even if it did not reside in a city or town, it remained in close touch with urban life. Because Eastern European Jews were crowded into large blocs of settlement, they always had a clear sense of being an ethnic group with a separate, unique identity. Integration into the non-Jewish milieu was a very slow process that hardly existed in the period in question. Not only did a considerable part of the Jewish population continue to maintain autonomous systems of rule, which were not yet abolished by the government, but in many cases a Jew lived within an environment in which Jews were the majority, hardly coming into contact with other populations. Even if he were influenced by one non-Jewish population or another, this happened through Jewish mediators (for example, the Maskilim) or through a few, limited instances of encounter. For example, from 1772, the Jews of White Russia lived for nearly ninety years under Russian rule and still understood no Russian, the language of the state.

The Jews of Eastern Europe were a mobile population, constantly on the move, and in the modern era, they maintained patterns of internal immigration that had existed from the early days of the formation of Jewish society in the Polish-Lithuanian kingdom. In the period under discussion, internal immigration was still motivated by economic considerations, but the directions changed, owing to political changes and revisions in the economic structure and the way it functioned. The Jews moved from the areas where economic opportunities had dwindled to places where better ones were available to them. I previously mentioned the massive immigration to regions of southern Russia, which began when the Russians conquered the area from the Ottoman Empire. The Russian government encouraged Jewish immigration to the new territories in the south, and large numbers of Jews were attracted there by the wake of the accelerated economic development and the growth of new urban centers.

After the Napoleonic wars, Congress Poland—formerly the Grand Duchy of Warsaw—became another destination for immigration. (The name "Congress Poland" reflects the creation of this political region by the 1815 Vienna Congress, at which the powers that defeated Napoleon redrew the political boundaries of the European continent.) Jews began to emigrate from the northeastern districts of the Pale of Settlement (Lithuania and White Russia) to southwestern parts of partitioned Poland, where modern industry was in the early stages of development. Three cities attracted Lithuanian immigrants (Litvaks)—Białystok, Lodz, and Warsaw—and in all three, the Jewish population grew rapidly, thanks to the development of new industry, trade, and financial activity.

Jews from Galicia, which under Austrian rule had experienced an economic decline and remained on the fringes of the new capitalist economy, embarked on a third direction of emigration, seeking to move to the heart of the Austrian kingdom. But because of the harsh restrictions that were in effect until the 1848 revolutions, many emigrated to the south of Russia. A part of the new Jewish community in Odessa was made up of Galician immigrants. The Haskalah of Galicia made its way to the new city together with the immigrants, who came from communities that had lost their economic vitality (Brody, Tarnopol). According to the image that still prevails today, the Jews led harsh lives in Russia, but the emigration from Galicia to "new Russia" indicates that Jews preferred to move to Russia and settle in districts where economic opportunities were better than those in Galicia. During those years, the process of urbanization, which later became a hallmark of modern Jewish history, was moving ahead at a rapid pace. Jews began to concentrate in cities. Odessa in the south of the Pale of Settlement, Warsaw in Congress Poland, Lwów in eastern Galicia, and Kraków in western Galicia attracted Jewish immigrants from the nearby towns and new settlers who came from afar.

The feudal economy continued to exist. A considerable number of Eastern European Jews, "townsmen," according to the legal definitions, lived in villages. At the end of the eighteenth century, nearly 30 percent of the Jews were linked to the estate lease economy, and managed means of production owned by the nobility: distilleries, breweries, flour mills, lumber mills, and the like. Some of them leased forests, felling the trees and moving the logs over the rivers. Although many continued to live in villages, a significant emigration from the villages and towns to the cities was beginning, caused by the immense growth in the number of Jews and the expulsions from the villages (in Congress Poland in the twenties and thirties), as well as changes in the status of the Polish estate owners. The Polish nobility, on whose estates the Jewish leaseholders had been active for generations, had lost its political power in the wake of the Polish revolts against Russian rule. After each failed Polish revolt, land assets were confiscated, Polish property was expropriated, and estate owners emigrated to the west. As a result, the Jews were also cast out of the old feudal economic cycle and forced to seek other sources of livelihood in the newly developing cities.

What did Eastern European Jews engage in during the first half of the nineteenth century? We have mentioned their role in the leasehold economy, and the traditional economic stratification was still maintained in other areas of activity as well. In the more developed areas, a new brand of capitalistic entrepreneurs, bankers, industrialists, and merchants was making its appearance. A considerable proportion of the Jews were tradesmen, specializing in particular trades and providing a large share of the demand of the non-Jewish village and town population. These trades included tanning, fur making, and watchmaking (a typical Jewish occupation in Eastern Europe). Certain occupations were specific to Jews, because they were unable to use products and services of non-Jewish tradesmen for religious reasons. Tailoring, for example, was a singular Jewish trade, because of the laws of *shatnez* (which forbid the use of cloth mixing linen and wool). Tailoring was apparently the most widespread Jewish occupation, and there were a great many tailors in Eastern Europe. Hebrew printing also flourished. At the beginning of the century, several printing houses were in operation in the Russian empire, which also disseminated the teachings of the new movement of Hasidism. Later, in 1836, publishing activity in the Pale of Settlement was restricted to two printing houses that were granted a monopoly by the government. The great demand for holy books, such as prayer books, was supplied by a large number of printers in Galicia and in the autonomous areas of Poland.[4] Although tailoring was the most widespread occupation, Jewish tradesmen engaged in a large variety of other vocations. In the town of Biała (near Brisk [Brest-Litovsk]), there were, in the middle of the century, 127 artisans engaged in twenty-five different occupations, fifty-one of them Christians and seventy-six Jews. The Christians engaged in fourteen different occupations and the Jews in twenty-one, including tinsmiths, carpenters, tanners, builders, harness makers, shoemakers, jewelers, and, of course, tailors.[5]

Peddling and retail commerce were popular occupations among Eastern European Jews, many of whom traded with the rural population around the towns. In many cases, the Jews living in the villages owned general stores that stocked products brought from outside the region. They would often engage in more than one type of work; for example, they might run a tavern where the peasant would come to drink his vodka and a store where he could purchase "urban" products, such as tools and nails. The Jew also lent money and acted as a pawnbroker. In addition, the tavern (*shenk* in Yiddish) also functioned as a road inn, offering food, lodging, and stables for horses. The leaseholder of the *shenk*, which was owned by a Polish noble, ran this entire economic setup together with his wife, sons, and daughters. The Jewish tavern keeper played a very important role in the rural economy of Eastern Europe. Linking city and village, his tavern was an island of capitalistic activity in a feudal environment, perceived as both foreign and local.

The economic activity of the Jews in the villages was a major topic in reform programs in Poland, Russia, and Austria. They were blamed for the drunkenness of the peasants and for the poor conditions of the members of the low social classes. The image of the Jewish tavern keeper was deeply imprinted on the collective memory of the peoples of Eastern Europe.[6]

Jews also dealt in wholesale trade, both interregional and international. They continued to fill, as they had in the previous centuries, an important role as importers and exporters, and some served as supply contractors for the armies of the Eastern European states (the Peretz and Notkin families from Shklov in White Russia; the Bergson and Kronenberg families in the Duchy of Warsaw). They specialized in several typical Eastern European branches of export, including lumber export, river trade, and the import and export of alcoholic beverages (importation of wine and exportation of vodka). The shackles of feudalism constituted heavy obstacles for Jewish commercial initiatives, since many economic rights were still the province of the nobility. Hence, Jewish entrepreneurs entered primarily into totally new branches or found special niches in the economic system through which they could embark on unusual enterprises. For example, Jewish bankers were involved in establishing the first railroads in Congress Poland. Jews played almost no role in the first textile plants established in Lodz, since the Polish government deliberately restricted their involvement, but Jewish importers brought raw materials from the industrial centers of Britain and the United States, gaining control over the supplies to the factories. Jewish entrepreneurs in the autonomous part of Poland were also adept at exploiting the fact that the Russian empire favored the industrial products of Congress Poland. The same explanation holds true for Jewish initiatives in the sugar-processing plants in Congress Poland and Ukraine. This was a totally new product (the use of beets to extract this sweetener only began in Europe in the Napoleonic period). Here, too, the Jewish entrepreneurs were forced to circumvent the restriction that limited the beet growing to lands owned by the nobility. They continued to use the long-standing method of leasing lands from their owners. Until the second half of the nineteenth century, Jewish capitalistic initiatives to establish modern factories were limited only to those areas where the industrial revolution had already begun. When such plants were first established at the government's initiative (in Białystok, Warsaw, Lodz, or Kiev), Jewish ventures were connected primarily to the textile, food, and tobacco industries.[7]

After the partitions, the autonomous social organization of Eastern European Jewry changed at a varying pace in the different parts of the Polish-Lithuanian kingdom. Jewish autonomy was legally rescinded in Russia only in 1844, while in Austria it had been abolished in the 1780s. This was an extremely significant difference. A gap was created between the social processes that occurred on the Austrian side and those on the Russian. Where Jewish autonomy was preserved, the social character of the Jewish community in Poland that had existed prior to the partitions was also preserved, continuing to exist until the mid-nineteenth century. The old oligarchy, when the society was ruled by a number of elite families, remained in place from the time of the partitions until the middle of the century, resulting in stability but also slowing down social mobility. At the same time, a social process began in which various types of voluntary organizations that had existed before Jewish self-rule was abolished were supplanting the *kahal*. The Hasidic court, a social organization that took shape on the basis of religious faith centering on a charismatic leader, took over social and economic functions that for generations had been in the hands of the community. Another voluntary organization, the society (*hevrah*; pl., *hevrot*), which had existed in Poland many years before the partitions, filled a social function similar to that of the Hasidic community. The *hevrot* were corporative bodies that had existed within the community in previous centuries as suborganizations. Some were associations of artisans (like the guilds in Christian society); others were societies for charity and mutual aid (such as financial aid for weddings, the burial society, and visits to the ill); others engaged in the study of the Talmud, the recitation of Psalms, or the nighttime study of Torah, or specialized in the study of a particular book (such as *Ein Ya'akov* or *Hayei Adam*). Across the vast area of Eastern Europe, these societies spread a dense network of organizations that, to some extent, were under the supervision of the Jewish community. But when that community's power declined until it was abolished, these organizations did not disappear but grew in strength; in the first half of the nineteenth century, they became an organizational focus that served as an alternative to the community leadership. They preserved the traditional way of life by providing it with a social basis. Moreover, they served as focal points for socialization at a time when the Jewish communities were being affected by external forces that threatened to vitiate them. When the Russian government officially abolished the *kahal,* and some members of the Vilna community wanted to carry on all types of social functions that the authorities were no longer permitting, they transferred the community's activities to one society (*hevrat hatsedakah hagedolah*). Similar changes took place throughout Eastern Europe, so that Jewish social organization underwent a form of decentralization. In some cases, this decentralization was connected to new religious phenomena, such as the Hasidic courts of *tzaddikim,* which took over certain social functions; in other cases, it was connected to organizations that had existed before autonomous rule was abolished (the *hevrot*) but that now augmented their social power as the strength of the formal organizations diminished.

During this period, a new social class emerged in Eastern Europe, one that had never existed before the partitions: a Jewish bourgeoisie that was integrated into the country's culture. These were the Jewish entrepreneurs in the Russian Pale of Settlement and in Congress Poland I referred to earlier, such as the Peretz, Notkin, Bergson, and Kronenberg families, who had become affluent and gradually were severing their corporative social ties and linking their cultural life and social identity with the non-Jewish society. This phenomenon was not connected to the Haskalah movement, but was a more general one, known as acculturation. Some of the Jewish elites, particularly in the big cities, but not only there, came into contact with circles of the Polish and Russian aristocracy; or, influenced by German culture—then considered the ideal European culture by a certain segment of Eastern European Jewry—they adopted new lifestyles and abandoned traditional Jewish customs. In the first half of the nineteenth century, this social trend was becoming increasingly evident, although it remained marginal from the demographic standpoint, with only a few thousand such Jews in all of Eastern Europe.

The members of these circles went far beyond the ideas or aims of the Haskalah movement, and many of them did not share these aims but wanted to become Russians, Poles, or Germans of the "Mosaic faith." They regarded cultural change as an expression of genuine integration into the Russian, Austrian, or Prussian state and used their money and political connections to persuade their coreligionists to undergo similar cultural changes. For them, political identification was bound up with financial betterment and cultural transformation, expressed, first and foremost, in a language shift—from the spoken language (Yiddish) to German, Russian, or Polish. The sons and daughters of these new bourgeois Jews no longer needed to remain within the traditional educational settings. For the first time in the history of Eastern European Jewry, Jews studied in the *gymnasium* and even attended universities, such as those in Vilna and Kraków, which in those years first opened their doors to admit Jews. From this group came writers, scientists, and political activists who contributed to the receiving culture. Although these circles were still small in number in the first half of the century, they made a salient impact on the political and social character of Eastern European Jewry in the years to come.

Chapter 4

Hasidim, Mitnagdim, and Maskilim

During the waning years of the Polish kingdom's political existence, a religious and cultural transformation took place in Eastern Europe that altered the face of traditional Jewish society. It was not a direct result of the political changes but rather drew upon the inner world of Ashkenazi Jewry. "Hasidism is the creation of part of the Ashkenazi world, which rejected Sabbatianism and Frankism, on one hand, and the Enlightenment, on the other." This is how the kabbalah scholar Moshe Idel defined the role of Hasidism as a mystical phenomenon peculiar to Eastern Europe.[1] While unquestionably an internal development, it joined together with the external upheavals caused by Poland's partitions to reshape the Jewish community. Rapid changes in customs, the way of life, and modes of thought engendered by new religious streams were absorbed by communities that passed from the rule of the Polish kingdom to the rule of centralized states. The spiritual world operated within a given political reality, influencing social life and modes of economic activity, and in turn was influenced by them.

In the decades prior to the Polish partitions, Eastern European Jewish society was in the process of a spiritual awakening. The most pronounced religious phenomenon, although not the only one, was the meteoric rise of the Hasidic movement in the second half of the eighteenth century. It originated in Podolia, Ukraine, on the southeastern boundary of Poland, in the first half of the century, beginning with a small circle of students of Jewish esoterica that centered on R. Israel ben Eliezer (c. 1700–1760). Better known as the Ba'al Shem Tov (the "Besht"), he engaged in magic and the study of kabbalah and, with his charismatic religious power, attracted disciples including rabbis, talmudic scholars, and students of kabbalah, many of whom resembled him in their personality and behavior. The Besht offered them a new way of worshiping God and developed a means of achieving communion between man and God, a matter of extreme importance to the group of mystics that had gathered around him.[2] In addition, he supposedly cured the sick and helped those seeking his advice on matters of livelihood and business. In his personality, authority, and influence, R. Israel embodied a new model of leadership, one that achieved an unprecedented success in Jewish history.[3] After his death, Hasidism spread from Podolia to other regions of Eastern Europe, until, from a small circle of scholars studying esoteric doctrine, a mass movement emerged that, in the mid-nineteenth century, encompassed hundreds of thousands of Hasidim.[4]

The Hasidic movement was based on the leadership of men possessed of spiritual power and strong religious influence who gathered around them a community of believers. The leader of the Hasidic community, the *tzaddik*, presided over a "court" in the town where he lived. His close associates lived there, along with providers of various services to the believers who came to seek a cure, spiritual support, or commercial advice. The Hasidic *tzaddik*, or the rebbe, was the spiritual and social core of Hasidism. The rapid spread of the movement after the Besht's death began when men of religious charisma dispersed throughout Eastern Europe. Within only a few decades, *tzaddikim* were in many communities in White Russia and in Lithuania in the north (there were even Hasidim in Vilna, the largest and most important community in Lithuania), areas that were annexed to the Russian empire from 1772 to 1795. Communities of Hasidim also formed around *tzaddikim* in the west and northwest, areas that had recently been annexed (in 1772) to the Austrian empire and became known as Galicia. Later, courts of *tzaddikim* were established in central Poland, which, early in the nineteenth century, was under Russian rule but enjoyed a large measure of autonomy. The spread of Hasidism stopped only when it reached the invisible border that separated German Jewry from Eastern European Jewry—the boundary between the western central part of the Ashkenazi diaspora and its eastern part. With the exception of one quasi-Hasidic community established in Frankfurt, the Hasidic *tzaddikim* did not succeed in gaining a foothold in Germany as the movement spread. Was this because of the great linguistic difference between eastern Yiddish and western Yiddish that set up a barrier to the movement, most of whose propaganda was transmitted orally, through preaching, conversations, and the sermons of the *tzaddik*? Or was it because of the change that took place in the autonomous Jewish community under Prussian rule? In any event, Hasidism, unlike the Sabbatian movement that preceded it by only a few years, did not become an international movement, remaining instead a phenomenon peculiar to Eastern Europe, except for those Hasidim who emigrated overseas in the last decades of the nineteenth century and the emergence of small Hasidic communities in Palestine from 1777 on.

Scholars of Jewish history have suggested many reasons for the amazing success of Hasidism. Some studies have focused on the movement's ideological aspects and its innovative thought. Some scholars regarded the new movement as a response to the spiritual, social, and economic travails that Jewish society suffered in the eighteenth century, and linked the spread of Hasidism to the religious crisis engendered by the Sabbatian movement and the role of the messianic idea among the early leaders of the movement. Others tended to see in the new movement ideas of social reform and expressions of social protest by the disadvantaged class against the wealthy and more powerful classes.

I will deal with the social significance of the new movement's expansion and the influence of its religious messages on the pace with which it spread throughout Eastern Europe. Among its other religious innovations, Hasidism strengthened the influence of esoteric learning on the religious behavior of its followers. New practices that originated in kabbalistic thought, as well as kabbalistic explanations for the observance of the commandments and customs, were adopted by broad sectors of Eastern European communities. A list of religious practices that differed from the Ashkenazi practice accepted until then (the "practice of Ashkenaz-Poland") aroused the opposition of scholars, rabbis, and communal leaders. These practices were derived from kabbalistic literature, nearly all of which was written by mystics who came from the Sephardic Jewish culture. Members of the scholarly Jewish elite did not reject the kabbalah or kabbalistic practices. On the contrary, they viewed kabbalah as an esoteric doctrine intended only for the select few, and its practices as restrictions that only men of a special religious status were permitted or fit to observe. What was intended for a select religious group, like those studying in the exclusive group in the Brody community (the *kloiz* of Brody) was not permissible for others.[5] They found it outrageous to widely disseminate kabbalistic practices among Jews of all classes and to turn them into a religious norm. At times, in addition to this objection, which often reflected social-class consciousness, there was opposition for economic reasons.

For example, the early Hasidim were very strict with regard to the technique of sharpening slaughtering knives (polished knives, called *geshlifene* in Yiddish). This strict adherence to the technique, for the purpose of producing a smooth, sharp knife, free of any defects, stemmed from the kabbalistic belief in reincarnation. The sharp blade was intended to help amend the soul that had been reincarnated in the body of the cow or chicken that was being slaughtered. The Hasidic ritual slaughterers were in the habit of passing the already very smooth knife over a leather strap, in addition to sharpening it as usual on a grindstone. This small, seemingly insignificant technical detail aroused bitter controversies in Eastern Europe and was perceived as the introduction of a practice that, while halakhically legitimate, was not binding on the society as a whole. A far more mundane reason for opposition to

Hasidic slaughter was the fact that the supply of kosher meat was one of the most important sources of income of the Jewish autonomous rule at the time when Hasidism was on the rise. The fact that certain Jews refrained from eating meat slaughtered under the supervision of the *kahal*, but ate only what was slaughtered by a ritual slaughterer approved by a certain Hasidic *tzaddik*, caused the community serious economic damage. It also amounted to a challenge to the authority of the *kahal* by an extra-communal body, which was intervening in matters that until then had been solely in the hands of the local leadership. The dispute over the appointment of ritual slaughterers continued for several decades, until Hasidic slaughter was recognized and permitted in communities, as a result of the social reality created by the spread of Hasidism. Chone Shmeruk, a scholar of Ashkenazi-Jewish culture and Hasidism, of the Hebrew University in Jerusalem (1921–97), cited this case as an example of the influence of a kabbalistic religious practice that originated in the desire to avoid tormenting a soul that had been reincarnated in an animal, on the social and economic reality of Eastern European communities.[6] The uniform method of slaughtering under the supervision of the *kahal* was replaced by alternative methods. Moreover, the disciple of a specific *tzaddik* was not prepared to eat the meat of an animal slaughtered by a ritual slaughterer approved by another *tzaddik* in the same community. This was the beginning of the religious-organizational heterogeneity that typified Eastern European Jewish society until the beginning of the twenty-first century.

Another example of the influence of spreading Hasidism on the institutions of Jewish autonomy is linked to the intervention of *tzaddikim* in the supervision of activity in the leasehold economy. Many scholars have been intrigued by the social implications of the spread of a religious movement, most of whose power stemmed from a new type of leadership that became accessible to members of the traditional Jewish society in Eastern Europe. This new leadership no longer drew its authority from the accepted social values spoken of in earlier chapters—namely, family lineage, religious knowledge, and financial standing. The rebbe's authority stemmed from his believers' subjective faith in his supernatural powers and in his link to the upper worlds. The *tzaddik* had charisma that seemingly could not be transferred to a system of normative values and redefined in formal terms.

Nonetheless, as Hasidism's influence grew and it took on greater momentum, this charismatic leadership began to take the place of the formal leadership, or at least to act alongside it in similar roles. The new social phenomenon did not abolish the older, existing systems but became an integral part of the functions of the autonomous rule. Chone Shmeruk also studied the authority of the *tzaddik* and the leasehold economy,[7] which was central to the economic activity of the Jews within the feudal estate structure. From the internal Jewish legal standpoint, the *kahal* regulated the participation of leaseholders in the lease market, using the method of *hazakah*, or holding. If a Jew leased a certain asset or means of production from a Polish noble, the laws of *hazakah* protected him from the competition of other leasers. According to the law, which was supervised by the communal leadership in each locale, it was impossible to deprive him of the lease by offering a higher payment to the leasing noble. This method ensured social stability and prevented the nobles from demanding exorbitant prices for leases. In the eighteenth century, there were many cases in which Jewish entrepreneurs ignored the regulations and offered a higher price to the Polish noble for leasing an asset or means of production that were already held by another Jew. The leadership of the Jewish community was generally unsuccessful in enforcing the law on those who violated it. From the second half of the eighteenth century, the Hasidic *tzaddikim* became a new authority and played a decisive role in supervising the *hazakot*. Their followers' fear of the *tzaddikim*'s supernatural powers and strict compliance with their moral code replaced the regulations of the *kahal* or the supracommunal councils, enabling the *tzaddikim* to enforce the law of *hazakot*. A story is told, for example, about R. Yehiel Mikhel of Zloczów, who angered a Polish noble because he intervened in a financial competition between leaseholders and caused the noble a loss of profit: "He decreed that no one should encroach on the affairs of his Jewish brethren, nor should he cast his eyes upon that which is not his, even if it be given him at half the cost. And if any man should disobey him, he will punish him with his magic and his witchcraft."[8]

In this case, a clearly economic function, devoid of any direct religious significance, passed to the charismatic authority of the *tzaddik*, and as a result the laws of *hazakah* were enforced. The role of Hasidic ritual slaughtering in the communities, as well as the intervention of *tzaddikim* in economic activity in the Polish feudal economy, shows how much social power was wielded by this new type of leadership that took Eastern Europe by storm.

Within a few decades, the spread of Hasidism changed the sociological map of Jewish society in the partitioned Polish kingdom. In the previous chapter, we related to the change that occurred in the functions of the autonomous community in Eastern Europe in the wake of the partitions. At the time when the authorities were interfering in the internal affairs of the Jewish community, Hasidism made its appearance as a factor that tended to preserve the existing order. Alongside the traditional leadership of the *kahal*, which continued to maintain its frameworks for a long time, it emerged as a new, alternative focus of power, driven by the leader of the Hasidic community.[9] It did not openly challenge the power of the community leadership but rather offered to serve as a supplementary authority. In many cases, as we can see from the case of the *tzaddik* R. Israel of Ruzhin, not only did the influential *tzaddik* refrain from challenging the existence of the community institutions or trying to change anything in the structure of the *kahal* or the functions it filled, but he placed his followers in key positions in the community.[10] In other words, the Hasidim of a specific rebbe took over existing points of power. What actually happened was that the outer shell of autonomy was preserved while the inner contents were greatly altered. Those in positions of authority no longer drew their power from the formal local communal system but from the religious charisma of a leader living far outside the boundaries of the city. This change, which at first was an internal one within the traditional world, soon became a decisive factor in the ability of this world to survive and contend with the threats of modernism.

We have noted that Hasidism paid no heed to the political boundaries that separated the parts of the fragmented Polish state. The Besht died in 1760, four years before the last king of Poland took the throne. In 1764, the Council of the Four Lands, which, in a sense, was a unifying extra-communal factor, was abolished. In 1772, the year in which R. Dov Ber of Mezhirech died, the first partition of Poland took place. Then the movement began to spread into the territories of two empires: Russia and Austria. The new political borders did not stop the *magids* (preachers) who moved from town to town disseminating the movement's message. The first books of Hasidism were published early in the 1780s in Volhynia (then still within the boundaries of the Polish-Lithuanian kingdom) and also were distributed beyond its borders. Why didn't Hasidism halt at the border between Podolia and Galicia? Why, within a few years, did the young movement spread into the central area of independent Poland (by the 1790s) and acquire supporters in Vilna as well, where the Poles ruled until the 1794 Kościuszko revolt?

The spread of Hasidism across political borders was apparently linked to the informal character of the movement. Government officials in Russia and Austria did not regard the Hasidic community as an organization that required a permit. The administrative apparatuses in the new areas focused their attention on the *kahal*, the recognized corporative organization in the Polish kingdom. An informal organization that was not anchored in the laws of the states and needed no political approval could function independently alongside the formal organizations. Added to that was the fact that the Hasidic communities emerged in Russia and Austria just at the time of the partitions, when there was no known legal or administrative precedent of the Polish state that could be applied to them. When the centralized states began to curtail the power of the formal organizations, and then to abolish them, Hasidism survived and continued to fill their functions well into the nineteenth century. The spread of Hasidism also shows that despite the creation of political boundaries between the different regions of the Polish-Lithuanian kingdom, a large measure of unity and uniformity was preserved in Polish Jewish society, even many years after the partitions. In many cases, Hasidim lived on one side of the border while their rebbe was on the other. Borders never stopped the Hasidim, nor did they inhibit the distribution of their books and doctrines.

It is no wonder that the young Haskalah movement, whose founders observed the success of Hasidism with anxiety and aching hearts, also saw it as a political enemy that endangered the modern concept of the state. In the eyes of the Maskilim, Hasidism not only embodied the evil of irrationality but also inhibited progress. They did all they could to convince the authorities in Russia, Austria, and the autonomous regions of Poland that the spread of Hasidism should be halted, because it posed a political danger and even the threat of rebellion against the kingdom.

The Maskilim were not the first opponents of the new religious movement. In certain parts of Eastern Europe, the amazing success of Hasidism aroused principled religious opposition to the dissemination (or popularization) of practices based on the Lurianic kabbalah. These practices were not new; Hasidism had not introduced them but rather had only expanded the circle of those who adopted them. It took modes of religious conduct that had been the sole province of elitist circles and made them accessible to all. Every Jew could observe them, if he so wished—the tailor and the shoemaker, as well as the rabbi and the scholar. The Hasidim replaced the Ashkenazi version of prayer, which had been accepted in Poland for many generations, with a prayer book based on the Lurianic doctrine.

This does not mean that Hasidism represented the low social classes or that it aspired to make their status equal to that of the elite. Recent research on Hasidism no longer sees in it what scholars in previous generations did: a movement with a popular social message in the spirit of twentieth-century movements of social radicalism. This image of Hasidism was particularly prevalent among Jewish historians in the interwar period and was influenced by political movements, many of whose members came from the Jewish intelligentsia of Eastern Europe and the countries to which they had emigrated. Even if Hasidism did not bear a radical social message, the movement's expansion engendered a significant change in the religious world of broad sectors of the population, as well as in their religious conduct. The religious elite was disturbed not only by the popularization of the esoteric doctrine but also by the order of priorities that the Hasidim assigned to study and worship. They suspected that they were downgrading the place of Torah study in favor of kabbalistic and Hasidic texts. They also accused the early Hasidim of disregarding the times for prayer and indulging in improper behavior, as a result of their ecstatic form of worship.

At the end of the eighteenth century, several writings harshly critical of the Hasidim, their practices, and doctrines, were distributed among Eastern European communities. One of their greatest opponents, the scholar David of Makow, a disciple of R. Elijah, the Gaon of Vilna, wrote about the prayer of the Hasidim: "In their prayer, their voice is as the roaring of the lion, the whimpering of his cubs, a barren tree and willows of the brook. Like a swarm of locusts, the spreading vine, a braying donkey, and a galloping horse. From the sound of their clamor, their throats are parched. They have changed the prayers to leave the bounds of the world, but their voice cleaves the earth. The din of their voices makes the deep boil like a cauldron. They have changed their clothing and tongue, but forgotten their maker and savior."[11]

Some religious leaders, foremost among them the eminent eighteenth-century scholar R. Elijah ben Solomon, the Gaon of Vilna (1720–97), perceived the new religious movement as a sect of heretics.[12] In 1772, the year in which R. Dov of Mezhirech died and the first partition of Poland took place, the Hasidim were banned in two Eastern European communities: Vilna in Lithuania and Brody in Galicia. The attempt to halt Hasidism by excommunications failed. In different cities, a variety of attempts were made to persecute the Hasidim and to prevent them from praying in separate minyans, but to no avail. Hasidism just stepped up the pace of its expansion and penetrated deep into Lithuania, the stronghold of Torah scholarship. In the early nineteenth century, the Hasidim in Vilna even succeeded in gaining control of the *kahal*, holding positions of leadership in the community for some time, several years after the death of the Gaon.

One intriguing way of coping with the challenge posed by Hasidism to the scholarly elite was to internalize several of its messages. The man who created a theological basis for this approach and also established a social organization that imparted the new method to the contemporary scholarly elite was the great Lithuanian scholar R. Hayyim ben Isaac of Volozhin, in White Russia (1749–1821). At the time, Hasidism was well established in the traditional society, and it was hard to imagine that any attempt to suppress it was likely to succeed. Unlike his mentor, the Vilna Gaon, R. Hayyim did not regard Hasidism as a deviant sect but as "a dangerous and failed attempt to achieve aims that are sublime in themselves." In his view, these lofty aims could also be achieved through traditional Torah study, through a revised understanding of the value of study, its role and relationship to the worship of God and to faith. He proposed innovations to the non-Hasidic scholarly society that were both a reaction to and an internalization of the religious messages of Hasidism. For example, he assigned preeminence to the study of Torah on the basis of kabbalah. He also presented Torah study as a way of achieving communion with God.[13]

R. Hayyim of Volozhin introduced an important educational innovation that greatly influenced spiritual life in Eastern Europe when he created a new type of higher religious study in the yeshivot. Until the end of the eighteenth century, yeshivot in Poland were communal institutions supported by the community or by local donors. R. Hayyim established a voluntary supra-communal organization of support for the yeshiva, which extended far beyond the boundaries of a single city. He chose, in 1802, to establish his yeshiva in the town of Volozhin in Lithuania (today in Belarus). Its unique feature was the fact that it was a supra-communal institution that existed within a certain community but was totally autonomous. Later, this type of organization became an important focus of social and political power in Eastern European Jewish society.[14] Although the supra-communal yeshiva differed greatly from the Hasidic community, there was a salient parallel between the two on the social level. Both the Hasidic community and the new yeshiva were voluntary organizations based on a particular religious principle. While the "formal" autonomy was subject to government control, the new voluntary organizations played an important role in intercommunal relations and hence exerted an influence beyond the local religious context in which they were originally founded.

While Hasidism was rapidly spreading over the large geographical space of the Polish-Lithuanian kingdom, the first buds of the Haskalah movement, to which we will devote a detailed discussion in coming chapters, were emerging in Eastern Europe, and in the last decades of the eighteenth century, the initial manifestations of its opposition to Hasidism were apparent. Concomitantly, the first signs of Hasidism's counterreaction appeared.

One of the most fascinating Hasidic *tzaddikim*—R. Nachman of Bratslav (1772–1811, who was born in the same year that Poland was first partitioned)—embodied the almost inevitable conflict between a rational worldview and openness to Western culture, on the one hand, and the figure of the *tzaddik* and the all-encompassing influence of mysticism in everyday life, on the other. R. Nachman, who, from his home in Ukraine observed the political changes of Napoleonic times, predicted that "a wave of heresy is coming into the world." He was outspoken in warning against the dangerous influence of the "German" Haskalah on traditional Jewish life in Eastern Europe. This *tzaddik*, aware that the intactness of Jewish tradition would be endangered if any of his believers came into contact with a speck of anything connected with the Haskalah movement, which was hateful to him, called upon his followers to abstain from engaging in any form of science and philosophy. R. Nachman was also opposed to the reforms that the Russian government proposed to make in the status of the Jews, and he employed acts of magic (mystical dances) to prevent what he called the *punkten* decree (the 1804 constitution of Czar Alexander I).[15] R. Nathan Sternharz (1780–1845), R. Nachman's pupil who also compiled his teachings and stories, carried on this acrimonious anti-Maskilic trend for decades after R. Nachman's death.[16]

The Maskilic response to the positions taken by the Bratslav Hasidim was not long in coming. It was more pronounced on the Austrian side of partitioned Poland than on the Russian side. The Galician Maskil Joseph Perl (1773–1839), from Tarnopol, made R. Nachman, his writings, and his flock of disciples the targets of his counterattack against the Hasidic movement in general. R. Nathan did not emerge unscathed, either. Among his other anti-Hasidic writings, Perl wrote a "sequel" and a new version to one of the Ukrainian *tzaddik's* folk tales, in which he jeered at the spiritual world of the Bratslav Hasidim.[17] Perl devoted a large part of his literary work in the second half of the nineteenth century to a fierce attack on the Hasidic movement, which he regarded as a dangerous distortion of traditional Jewish life. The early Maskilim did not appeal to the traditional society in the name of ideas of change, nor did they place an emphasis on the European influence. Rather, they argued for ideological, cultural, and social change in the name of the values of traditional Jewish society. In their writings, the Maskilim invented an ideal "imagined community," which had existed in the past and had been destroyed in recent generations. They assailed Hasidism as a perversion of the Jewish religion. Perl and like-minded friends called upon Jewish society to return to the scholarly, rational values, that had (supposedly) existed before the spread of kabbalism in the Jewish diasporas. The Maskilim wrote a series of blatant anti-Hasidic texts portraying the Hasidim as ignorant fools who waste their time on trivial matters, and the *tzaddikim* as charlatans who steal the money of naive believers.[18] In his satirical book *Megaleh temirin*, published in Vienna in 1819, Perl lashed out against the influence of Hasidism on the spiritual and material life of the Jews.[19] It centered on a Hasidic book published only four years earlier, in 1815, entitled *Shivhei haba'al shem tov* (usually known as *Shivhei habesht*).[20] Perl regarded this book as a kind of manifesto that helped the Hasidim to disseminate their movement. This Galician Maskil, blessed with literary talent and well versed in the Hasidic book, made very clever use of it. He mocked its language, scoffed at its readers, and invented stories based on the legends it contained. Perl's virulent witty satire was in the form of a dialogue between two types of discourse, that were diametrically opposed to each other but used the same language taken from the Jewish sources.

The conflict between the Haskalah and Hasidism, which began in the early nineteenth century, intensified over the years. Throughout the nineteenth century, the two rival movements were locked in an uncompromising struggle, in which neither side was loath to engage in persecutions, informing to the authorities, and even physical violence. To a great extent, the struggle was conducted on the pages of books: the Maskilim printed witty satires, and the Hasidim retorted with polemic broadsides. It was an extremely blatant struggle—a *Kulturkampf* between two spiritual streams, each claiming a monopoly over the definition of the "true Judaism."

At the same time, the turbulent dialogues between the Hasidim and the Mitnagdim and between the Hasidim and the Maskilim were, viewed from another time and place, part of one cultural system that connected Eastern European Jewish society on both sides of the border between Russia and Austria throughout the first half of the nineteenth century. Everyone argued with everyone, everyone quoted everyone, everyone read everyone. Even if they openly denied doing so, they did so in secret. Everyone replied to everyone. It was a dynamic cultural life, and scholars must look at it as a whole, rather than focusing on the one-sided nature of each of the movements in itself. Only then can they understand how Hasidism, Lithuanian scholarship, and the Haskalah all exerted an influence on the new cultural streams that emerged in the coming years in Eastern Europe.

Chapter 5

Russia and the Jews

In the fall of 1772, Jews, arriving at the synagogue of Polotzk in White Russia for the High Holiday service, found a proclamation (*plakat*) attached to the door. Like many others affixed to the doors of synagogues in all the towns and townlets by Russian soldiers, who had occupied the northeastern regions of the Lithuanian duchy, this proclamation addressed the Jewish residents in a new language, one almost unknown in these parts of the country. It announced, in a solemn tone, that the Russian empress, Catherine II, was assuring the Jews of White Russia that they would enjoy the freedom to observe the commandments of their religion and to retain their property and assets, as they had until then in the Polish-Lithuanian kingdom. "It is understood . . . that the Jewish communities dwelling in the towns and on the lands joined to the Russian empire retain and preserve those freedoms that they now enjoy by law regarding the control of their property, because the humaneness of Her Imperial Majesty will not permit anyone to be excluded from Her all-encompassing generosity and from the welfare to come under Her benevolent protection, as long as they, for their part, with the appropriate compliance of loyal subjects, live and pursue their present trades and business according to their callings."[1]

With this solemn affirmation, a new page opened in the history of Eastern European Jewish society, a period marked by the encounter between Jewish communities and the systems of the centralized state. How did the partitions of Poland affect Jewish society in the three kingdoms that swallowed up the large state? What was the fate of the Jews in the different countries? The Russian empire took the largest portion of Poland's territories, and a considerable part of the lands of the Polish kingdom became provinces in the western Russian empire. Until 1772, no Jew could legally reside in the lands of the empire, and now with one stroke of a pen that drew a revised map, a vast Jewish population was annexed to it. After 1795, hundreds of thousands of Jews lived in the western provinces under Russian rule. As the proclamation mentioned above shows, the imperial government began to deal with the question of the Jews' status in the annexed areas as soon as the Russian army entered White Russia. Two problems engaged the attention of the authorities: how to integrate the Jewish population into the administrative systems; and how to direct their economic activity so that it would be of benefit to the state and at the same time not harm the economic interests of other groups in the population.

The issue of the Jews' integration was connected with the self-rule that continued to exist even after Poland lost its independence. In the economic sphere, the problem was linked to the feudal economy, in which the Jews played a significant role as leaseholders of assets and means of production that belonged to the Polish nobility. The various czars—beginning with Catherine II, who ruled at the time of the partitions, and ending with Nicholas I, who ruled until the second half of the nineteenth century—dealt with these two issues through legislation intended to transfer the large Jewish minority from the frameworks of the Polish republic of nobles to those of the Russian absolutist state.

Two basic trends underpinned the Russian government's attitude toward the Jews. On the one hand, it acted in the spirit of enlightened absolutism, according to the Central European model. On the other hand, it maintained the Christian-Orthodox attitude toward the Jews, a legacy of a centuries-long religious hostility.[2] In the first years after the partitions, the trends of enlightened absolutism were dominant. Based on the absolutist model, any population, regardless of its religion or the attitude of other population groups toward it, was judged primarily by utilitarian criteria. Hence, the Jews in Russia were not necessarily perceived according to the traditional Christian image but as a population of great economic value. The new Russian attitude toward the Jews, one unprecedented in that country, was already revealed in the imperial proclamation of 1772. Based on its content, the Jews would enjoy the grace and protection of the sovereign and were called upon to continue engaging in activity that contributed to the wealth and prosperity of the state. Moreover, the Jews were explicitly included in the group of subjects deserving of "humaneness," which also reflects the influence of Catherine's enlightened ideas.

There was, however, something more in the imperial *plakat*: the Russian government recognized the previous political status of the Jews, namely as set forth in the *privilegia*, the documents that had regulated their status during the time of Polish rule, while at the same time, the czarist regime strove to politically integrate them into the state. Within a few years after northeastern Poland was annexed to Russia, the Jews were granted the status of townspeople and were able to elect and be elected to the institutions of urban government. The Jewish residents of White Russia were not required to give up their institutions of self-rule as a prerequisite for receiving rights from the state.[3] However, this integration was only partially implemented, because of the opposition of the Polish town dwellers, the long-standing enemies of the Jewish residents of towns and cities in Eastern Europe.[4] Nonetheless, Russia was the first state in Europe to grant Jews a certain type of "emancipation" (equal rights to members of the urban estates) before the French Revolution. We need to bear in mind, of course, that the Russian empire was an estate-structured state whose subjects did not enjoy equal rights, so that one cannot speak about full emancipation, since each estate had a different legal status. As the result of a series of administrative reforms (1775, 1785) that determined the structure of government in the districts and redefined the legal status of the townspeople in the empire, the Jews also were integrated (1786) into the Russian urban class. They were given urban political rights (namely, they could elect and be elected to the local city government). Moreover, not only were they integrated into the urban administration as holders of active rights, but these rights did not cancel out the old *privilegia*. Hence, the Jews of Russia gained something that the Jews of France did not enjoy during the French Revolution, a few years later: they were not required to forgo their previous legal status as a condition for receiving new political rights.

Catherine's policy, reflected in these reforms, was a clear manifestation of enlightened absolutism. Its aim was to integrate the Jews into the centralized state and exploit their economic usefulness without taking into account their different nature and their special religion, which until then had been banned in all parts of the empire. However, the old Christian-Byzantine tradition, which regarded Jews as a hostile religious group, endured in Russia. Until the Polish partitions, it had been the cause of the prohibition against Jews entering Russia or remaining there except temporarily, as merchants or in transit. The clergy of the Russian church retained this tradition, and since the czars were also the heads of the church, there was an obvious contradiction between Catherine's enlightened absolutist political position and the religious role of the ruler.

Some elements in the population were opposed to the granting of urban rights to the Jews, particularly because the stiff economic competition of the Polish Jews, recently integrated into the Russian empire, posed a serious threat to the Russian merchants. The opposition between the absolutist legislator's intentions to make the Jews part of the urban estates and the local interests of the residents of the Russian cities was also a source of the dualism that typified the Russian government's policy toward the Jews from 1772 until the 1917 revolutions. Several examples show how the government vacillated between trends of integration and the opposition of the urban population. In 1791, merchants in the "inner" cities of Russia (namely, within the borders of the empire prior to the first partition of Poland) were complaining that merchants from the new eastern areas were exploiting the urban rights granted them by the 1785 reform, and settling in Russian cities far beyond the boundaries of the area annexed from Poland. These complaints were clearly motivated by economic considerations: the merchants of White Russia were competing with Russian merchants in Smolensk and Moscow. As a result of these complaints, the Russian senate approved a ukase, stating that from then on, while the Jews would retain the urban rights granted them under the reforms, they could do so only in areas where they had lived prior to the partition of Poland: "We find," Empress Catherine proclaimed (in the plural, as was customary in imperial ukases): "that the Jews do not have any right of registration in the merchantry in inner Russia's towns and ports; only by Our ukase are they permitted to exercise the rights of citizenship and the privileges of townspeople in Belorussia."[5]

This ukase meant that in other areas to which Jews might come, they would be unable to legally register as permanent residents enjoying urban political rights. However, since during those years, the Russians captured extensive parts of the Ottoman Empire, reaching the shores of the Black Sea, the Jews gained a benefit along with the restriction: they were permitted to immigrate to the new areas conquered from the Ottoman Empire from the Black Sea to southern Ukraine. There they were allowed to enjoy urban rights. This was the wording of the imperial ukase: "While approving the strict observance of the regulations enacted in this regard [prohibition against registration in the inner cities of Russia] we have deemed it right to extend the said privilege beyond the White Russian government, to the vice-royalty of Yekaterinoslav and the region of Tavrida, and we hereby order our Senate to issue the proper instructions to the persons concerned."[6]

This ukase, while expanding the Jews' rights to settle in extensive areas in the southeast of the Russian empire and limiting their right to enter the northeastern parts of the kingdom, led to what later became known as the Jewish Pale of Settlement. It created a map on which a line was drawn determining where Jews were permitted to settle permanently and where they were forbidden to reside. This demarcation was based not only on a prohibition against settlement; it also contained an expansion of the Jews' rights, permitting them to settle in districts that the empress wanted to develop. The Pale of Settlement shaped the character of Jewish society in the empire and established demographic patterns whose influence was felt until the days of Soviet rule.

In the coming decades, the trends of enlightened absolutism continued to have an impact on the situation of the Jews in the empire. In

1804, Czar Alexander I, who began his reign with a series of reforms, introduced what was known as the "Jewish Constitution." It was a complete set of laws that, for the first time, systematically defined the status of the Jews in Russia. The "1804 Constitution" was influenced by the Austrian and Prussian legislation regarding the Jews, as well as by the deliberations of the four-year *Sejm* (two of the members of the committee appointed by the czar to formulate the constitution—Adam Czartoryski and Seweryn Potocki—were Polish magnates who now held office in the Russian government). It was intended to promote the integration of the Jews into the imperial administration, to increase the economic benefits they provided, and to improve their character in the spirit of the European Enlightenment.[7] According to this constitution, elementary and secondary schools, as well as universities, were open to the Jews. On the one hand, it encouraged Jewish agricultural settlement in order to change Jewish economic activity in the leasehold economy, which enlightened critics (influenced by the physiocratic school) regarded as harmful and unproductive. On the other hand, the framers of the constitution wanted to remove the thousands of leaseholders from the villages and to abolish the economic symbiosis that had existed for many years between the peasants, the Jews, and the estate owners. They even set a final date for the liquidation of the leasehold activity in the villages: "No Jew, beginning on the 1st of January 1807, in the provinces of Astrakhan and Caucasia, and in those of Little Russia [Ukraine] and New Russia, and from the 1st of January 1808, elsewhere, in any village or in the countryside, is allowed to hold a lease on a tavern, drinking house or inn, either in his own name or in another's, nor to sell liquor, nor even to live where this is done, except when passing through."[8]

This clause ordering the expulsion of the Jews from the villages, which was not implemented on the dates set forth in it, remained hanging over the heads of Jews in the villages for decades. The constitution granted Jewish subjects total freedom of religion and also recognized the right of various religious groups (the Hasidic communities) to worship God in their own prayer groups. But most important, it defined the Jews as an inseparable part of Russian urban estates. The Jewish society in large part received this constitution favorably. Some early Maskilim in Eastern Europe, such as Mendel Lefin and Judah Leib Nevakhovich, were also involved through their aristocratic patrons in the deliberations of the constitution committee. But as we learned in previous chapters, some *tzaddikim* regarded openness and the Enlightenment as a basis for material improvement, which was likely to cause a spiritual decline. It is no wonder that the *tzaddik* R. Nachman of Bratslav (1772–1811), one of the fathers of the militant Orthodox position in relation to the Haskalah and the Enlightenment, protested against the constitution that he called the *punkten* decree, or the decree of clauses. He tried to forestall it with "dances and clapping of hands," namely, acts of magic. The *tzaddik* was astute enough to discern the link between the ideas of the European Enlightenment and the social and cultural reforms that Alexander I wanted to apply to the traditional society.[9]

In the final years of Alexander I's reign, after the Napoleonic wars, Russian policy took an extreme turn in relation to the Jews. The trends of enlightened absolutism were weakened as part of the reaction to the influence of the French Revolution and its Napoleonic reverberations. The Christian orientation reemerged with greater vigor, and Alexander acted resolutely in cooperation with religious organizations that had missionary aims. Now he believed, contrary to his previous view, that the Jews could be integrated into the Russian state if they converted to Christianity. In 1817, he founded the Society of Israelite Christians, which promised converts land for settlement in the areas of New Russia. He also cooperated with the London Society for Promoting Christianity among the Jews and supported the activity of the British missionary Lewis Way. This trend was strengthened during the reign of his successor, Czar Nicholas I, who ruled from 1825 to 1855. During those years, Russian identity began to be perceived as a combination of state, church, and czar, and Jews could only be fully integrated into a state of this kind if they embraced Christianity. At the same time, the government continued its attempt to change the economic activity of the Jews by expelling leaseholders from the villages.

The conscription of Jews into military service was an effective means of "correcting" their character. The rise of the absolutist centralized state led to the establishment of large armies and the mass conscription of members of various social classes, and no exception was made in the case of the Jews.[10] In Galicia, under Austrian rule, they were already required, in 1788, to provide a quota of soldiers for the army. Forty years later, in 1827, the Russian army began conscripting Jews into its ranks. Czar Nicholas I's issuance of the ukase of military conscription was inscribed for generations in the collective memory of the Jews as a traumatic event. It required not only a quota of adult men to serve in the army for twenty-five years, under very harsh conditions, far from the Pale of Settlement and traditional Jewish life, but also included instructions for the abduction of Jewish children, aged six and older, to provide them with pre-military education in what were known as units of *cantonists*:

I. 8.1 The Jewish conscripts presented by the Jewish communities shall be between the ages of 12 and 25.

X. 74. Jewish minors, i.e., below the age of 18, shall be placed in preparatory establishments for military training.

XII. 90. The active service of Jewish minors in relation to their right
to be discharged from service shall be calculated from the
age of 18.[11]

This event, painful as it was, affected only the demographic fringes of
Jewish society, but it further weakened the status of the *kahal*, since the
government assigned it the duty of providing the quota of conscripts.
The traditional society, which was unable to openly resist the new
decree, dealt with it in a rather cruel manner, by enlisting the less useful
members of the community—beggars and indigenous, uncertified
tradesmen. Young Jews of conscription age fled to neighboring countries, and scores of them even got as far as Palestine.

The Constitution of 1835 was another step taken to forcibly integrate
Jews into the Russian state. It redefined their legal status on the basis of
all the regulations enacted since the proclamation of the 1804 constitution and institutionalized the Pale of Settlement, whose boundaries had
been fixed at the end of the eighteenth century. But this time, it
restricted rather than expanded them. Jews were forbidden to reside
permanently in central cities of some of the provinces (Kiev, Nikolayev)
and in the villages of White Russia, and restrictions were placed on their
economic activity. The *kahal* was defined as the body held responsible
by the government to see that the laws were observed and taxes collected. Thus the autonomy that had lasted for so many years officially
became a system of supervision and control in the framework of the
apparatus of the centralized state. Nonetheless, the separate Jewish corporation still acted as a buffer between the imperial bureaucracy and
the largest ethnic group in the west of the state.

From the early 1840s, Czar Nicholas took steps to introduce a comprehensive reform in the status of the Jews and to intervene in their internal
cultural life. Traditional education and its key text, the Talmud, became
the major target. To the czar and his ministers, the Jewish religion was
an extremely influential element that prevented the Jews from becoming integrated into the Russian state. They believed that the religious-
intellectual pursuits of the Jews—in particular, their intensive study of
the Talmud and rabbinical literature—engendered xenophobia, offen-
sive traits, and economic damage. In other words, Jewish scholarship was
officially perceived as a political element hostile to the state. The negative, almost demonic image of the Talmud as hostile to Christianity and
spreading hatred of human society in general (a long-standing motif in
medieval European culture) became, during Nicholas I's reign, a major
issue in the various texts describing the behavior of Jewish society.
Although the Minister of Education in the early 1840s, Sergei Uvarov,
was influenced by the French Romantic trends of the early nineteenth

century, he also held that the best way to correct Jewish society was by reducing the influence of the Talmud. He believed that the texts on which the Jews were educated ought to be fundamentally changed and that this could be done in various ways.[12] For example, there was the claim put forward by the Central European Maskilim that the Bible ought to be restored to its rightful central place, which had been usurped by the Talmud. Various, even contradictory, trends joined together against the Talmud. For example, the Russian government supported the publication of a revised edition of traditional texts to reeducate the Jewish population. Maskilim like Ribal, taken aback by the ferocity of the opposition to the Talmud, wrote books in its defense. For "reeducation," a real revolution in the curriculum studied by Jewish children was necessary, one that would introduce science, languages, and new ideas to the Pale of Settlement and remove the hostile rabbinical literature from the classroom (*heder*). Uvarov invited a "progressive" German rabbi, Max Lilienthal (1815–81), to persuade the Jews of the Pale of Settlement to support the establishment of modern schools. After Lilienthal returned from his campaign of persuasion, Uvarov appointed (June 1842) a commission that included four Jewish representatives and assigned them the task of coming up with a proposal on how "to establish, on the existing general foundations of education, the supervision of the Ministry of Public Instruction over all the Jewish institutions of learning and science, the rabbinical seminaries, the houses of study, and others, whatsoever their names may be, in which Jews engage in scientific interpretation of their religion and the Holy Scriptures, as well over the education of youth."[13] The four members of the commission—two prominent religious leaders from the north of the Pale of Settlement (the leader of the Lubavitcher Hasidim, Rabbi Menahem Mendel Shneerson; and the head of the Volozhin yeshiva, Rabbi Yitzhak ben Haim); a Jewish banker, lobbyist, and supporter of the Hasidim, R. Israel Halperin of Berdichev; and a Maskil and educator from Odessa who arrived as an immigrant from Galicia, Bezalel Stern—could not openly oppose the aims of the Ministry of Education. Jewish society in general was in a thorny situation: it was impossible to unequivocally object to the imperial policy, but it was also hard for anyone supporting it to agree to the style and means adopted by the government. The Maskilim in the cities of the Pale of Settlement to which Lilienthal traveled to request support for the new educational program were divided in their views. Some regarded it as a consummate manifestation of the enlightened nature of the Russian government, while others took exception to the fact that the government had not applied to the local Maskilim but rather had invited a foreign "expert" with extremist intentions.

The religious leadership in the Pale was very apprehensive about the new schools but could not openly interfere with the government's activities. The members of the commission had their own suspicions about the government's true intentions and tried to minimize the damage by giving their partial agreement. The four men on the committee represented, despite their differing views, informal Jewish organizations, not the official communal rule. This suggests that the authorities understood well who possessed the power to influence the large population in the western provinces. Indeed, after a short time, the government abolished the formal apparatus of self-rule (or what was left of it). A month after the law relating to "the Establishment of Special Schools for the Education of Jewish Youth" was issued (November 13, 1844), another law was published (December 19, 1844) abolishing the Jews' autonomous rule.[14] The abolition of the *kahal* in 1844 placed the Jewish subjects under the direct jurisdiction of the general municipal administration. This would have seemed to be the completion of a process that began during the reign of Catherine II—to abolish the duplication of functions that had lasted for years between the special Jewish administration and the municipal administration, into which the Jews had been integrated in 1785. What actually happened was that in the absence of any ability to effectively control the Jewish masses, the Russian government was compelled to go on maintaining special alternative bodies to deal with their affairs ("representatives," "collectors," and the like).[15] Paradoxically, the czar achieved the very opposite of what he had intended: alternate organizations that were not under the direct control of the imperial administration supplanted the *kahal* and its institutions. The government lost its ability to directly influence internal processes in the "native" society. Although the old Jewish corporation did disappear, frameworks of social organization and cohesion continued to operate, preserving the distinctive identity of the Jewish *ethnos*. What the Russian government sought to eradicate through formal integration grew in strength and found other channels of continuity.

The imperial project to enlighten and reeducate the Jews in the spirit of the autocratic Russian state was to be implemented through the establishment of a system of Jewish schools, with instruction in Russian. The actions of the authorities in the days of the affair of "government-sponsored enlightenment" were similar to those taken by colonial regimes that sought to disseminate European culture among the natives in their overseas colonies. The local inhabitants also reacted in a similar fashion. Some of them were captivated by the charms of the high culture and became its agents among their own people; others accepted some things from the imported culture but sought to combine them with their traditional culture; yet others totally rejected the new culture and adopted a hostile, separatist position. This affair, which we will return to later in connection with the Haskalah movement in Russia, greatly exacerbated the alienation between the traditional Jewish population and the Russian Ministry of Education and the government bodies that tried to interfere in the shaping of the culture of the Jews in the Pale of Settlement.

But despite all the efforts of the Russian government, after seventy years of rule over the areas annexed from Poland, the majority of Jewish society maintained traditional lifestyles. The government introduced comprehensive reforms, both in the legal status of the Jews (incorporating them in the urban estate) and in their self-rule (abolishing Jewish autonomy). It attempted to limit traditional communication through the channels that disseminated beliefs and doctrine (control over books, censorship, and limitations on printing [1836]). In fact, the government's intervention did not achieve real results: the number of Hasidim did not decrease, the study of the Talmud was not discontinued, and the knowledge of the state language was limited, until the 1860s, to a very small group of wealthy merchants. Thirty years of Nicholas I's rule did not give rise to a decisive change in the relationship between the Russian government and the Jews annexed from Poland. And the traditional political basis on which Jewish autonomy had rested for centuries—their fundamental loyalty to the government as such—was shaken.

The actions taken by Czar Nicholas I in relation to the Jews, which reached their peak in the 1840s, reverberated even beyond the boundaries of Russia and aroused the interest of Western Jewry in the fate of their coreligionists in Eastern Europe. When Russia first began inducting Jews into the army, Western philanthropists tried to intervene with the government to persuade it to cancel the practice. The new Western philanthropy, however, was not the same as the traditional help that donors and persons close to the government had given their brethren in times of trouble. In many cases, those proffering aid from Germany, France, and England believed that the Jews of Poland and Russia were indeed deficient in their character and in need of reform. In this sense, they—consciously or otherwise—accepted the negative image of Eastern European Jewry that was held by Austrian, German, Russian, or Polish rulers, government officials, and intellectuals. Moreover, the Jewish philanthropists from Western countries were not prepared to help unless there were some change on the part of the society they were supporting. Their help was conditional on the readiness of those in need of help to change and reform. This position, too, was compatible with the views of the imperial official in Eastern Europe: he also made any change in the legal status of the Jews conditional upon their changing their language, religion, and occupations and acknowledging the total authority of the centralized state.

Sometimes the Western philanthropist only partially agreed to cooperate with the absolutist ruler, and sometimes the ruler exploited the solidarity between Western Jews and their brethren in Russia to achieve aims of his own. One example of this kind of cooperation was the 1846 journey taken by the British Jewish philanthropist Sir Moses Montefiore to Saint Petersburg in an attempt to influence the Russian government to curb the reforms and to mitigate their effect on the Jews. On his way to Russia, Montefiore met with representatives of some of the important communities in the empire. This journey is an invaluable historical source of information about the economic and social situation of Russian Jewry in the middle of the nineteenth century. Montefiore collected documents and papers and recorded the content of his talks with the community representatives and government officials. These sources indicate that he intended to moderate the government's intensive activity in its effort to "correct" the Jews and integrate them into the society. But Montefiore unwittingly became a pawn in the hands of the Russian government: the czar and his ministers used the British philanthropist's journey to claim that Western European Jewry identified with the aims of the Russian government and agreed that traditional Eastern European Jewish society was deficient and in need of reform.[16]

The affair of "government-sponsored enlightenment" also led to the invitation of a foreign "expert," the German rabbi Max Lilienthal. While the British philanthropist Moses Montefiore gained the distinction of being remembered as a righteous benefactor, Max Lilienthal was commemorated in the folklore of Eastern European Jewry as a malefactor who wanted to see the Jewish masses convert to Christianity. A contemporary Hasidic legend even invented a lineage for him, linking him to the dynasty of semi-demonic "Maskilim" who for generations fought against the *tzaddikim*, defenders of the faith.[17] But history tells us that the activity of these two men, Montefiore and Lilienthal, was very similar: both intended to act for the good of their coreligionists, both believed that some reform ought to be introduced in the traditional lifestyle; and both were convinced that the government wanted to ameliorate the situation of the Jews in the Pale of Settlement. Similar, too, was the cynical use that the Russian government made of these two public figures from the West, who failed to realize the true aims of the Russian government, neither their aim to forcibly integrate the Jews nor their secret intention to Christianize them.

The play between the aim of integrating the Jews in the spirit of enlightened absolutism, on one hand, and the hostile Christian attitude toward them, on the other, prevailed from the time of the Polish partitions. In their policies, the Russian rulers mixed these two trends and they were in constant play. Sometimes one had the upper hand, sometimes the other. During Catherine's reign, it was enlightened absolutism that determined the principles of her policy toward the Jews in the areas annexed from Poland; in the first years of Czar Alexander I's reign, the enlightened absolutist trend of integration was dominant, but in the later years of his reign the Christian tendency was ascendant. Nicholas I adopted a distinctly Christian position but used models and methods taken from the enlightened absolutist regimes in the neighboring countries. Hence, he introduced military conscription of the Jews, established a special imperial school system for Jewish children, and abolished the *kahal*. All these actions were similar to those taken by Joseph II in Galicia in the 1780s.

The Maskilim in the Russian empire believed that the policy of Nicholas I and that of Joseph II were two similar stages in the era of enlightened rulers. The defenders of traditional society regarded the reforms of Nicholas I as a war of religion that he was waging against the Jews. The former became agents of the imperial culture among the "native" population; the latter, who could not openly come out against the empire, directed their anger against those they identified as agents of the hostile culture. In Immanuel Etkes's view, the affair of "government-sponsored enlightenment" engendered a radical change in the image of the Haskalah movement in the eyes of the traditionalists. This change, he averred, gave rise to Orthodoxy among Russian Jewry: "In effect, we find here what may be properly designated the beginnings of Orthodoxy in Russian Jewry: that is, a traditionalist society confronting processes and phenomena that threaten the authority of its tradition, and whose consciousness of these threats, as well as its attempts to deal with them, leave a deep impression upon its very being."[18] The struggle of a "native" culture to maintain its existence in the face of an imperial culture, disseminated by the government with the help of local agents, elicited a new type of counterreaction: Orthodoxy. In the coming years, other counterreactions, which accepted some aspects of the new influence but wished to bridle it and preserve elements of the old identity, played a decisive role in shaping a new type of Jewish identity.

Chapter 6
Austria and the Jews of Galicia, 1772–1848

So far we have dealt with what happened to the Jews of Poland when its eastern regions were annexed to the Russian empire. What happened in those very same years in the southeastern part of the country, which was annexed by the Austrian kingdom? In 1772, in the first partition, Austria took a very large part of southeastern Poland and created a vast administrative region known as Galicia (Galizien in German), which from then until the end of World War I in 1918 was under Austrian rule. The scholar Abraham Brawer (1881–1975) wrote about Galicia:

Very few countries like Galicia have had such unnatural and unhistorical boundaries fixed on the map by diplomats. Its only link with Austria, to which it was annexed, was a rather narrow strip in the west, which also served as a corridor to the West as a whole. In the south, the Carpathian Mountains separated it and pre-1919 Hungary. In the north and east, it had closed borders, at first with Poland and later with Russia, which became in the nineteenth and twentieth centuries an iron curtain for the Jews, the merchants of Galicia, owing to the decrees of the czars relating to Jews in general and the Jews from other countries in particular, and to the high tariff rates on both sides.[1]

Indeed, the new area captured by the Austrians in the summer of 1772 was patched together by the partition powers from a number of administrative units in two separate parts of the Polish kingdom. Western Galicia included territories from "Little Poland," most of whose inhabitants were Catholic Poles, while eastern Galicia took in territories of "Red Russia," whose population was Ukrainian and Greek Catholic. The border between the Roman Catholic part of Europe and the Greek-Byzantine part of the continent divided the two parts of the area. It is interesting to compare the fate of the Jews under Austrian rule with that of their brethren under Russian rule. In both cases, these were absolutist states with distinctly centralized governments, military powers in the Europe of the second half of the eighteenth century. At one stroke, both states absorbed an extremely large population of Jews with similar social, economic, and cultural characteristics. But despite this great similarity, the Jews in each of the two areas followed a different historical course.

One reason for the disparity in the situation of the Jews in Austria and that of their coreligionists in Russia was the pace of change in their legal status. In Russia, the process of integrating the Jews into the administrative systems, including the abolition of their self-rule (the *kahal*) in 1844, took over seventy years, from the first Polish partition until the mid-nineteenth century. In Austria, this process moved much more rapidly, nearly ending in the first decades after the annexation of Galicia, and, in some cases, the administrative reforms relating to Galician Jewry preceded the Russian reforms by several decades. Moreover, the way that the Austrian authorities dealt with the large Jewish population in the annexed areas served as a model for the Russian state. The Russian legislators in the first half of the nineteenth century were mindful of some of the changes that had affected Jews in Austria at the end of eighteenth century. Moreover, unlike the Russian case, Austria had other Jewish communities before the Jews of Eastern Europe were added to its population. The Austrian legislator, therefore, had at his disposal several precedents dealing with the status of the Jews and their economic activity. From this standpoint, the case of Galician Jewry was more similar to that of the Jews annexed to the Prussian kingdom.

When Galicia was annexed in 1772, Empress Maria Theresa ruled over Austria. A devout Catholic and shrewd when it came to state affairs, she was not known for her fondness for Jews. Her attitude toward them was based on considerations of economic benefit, similar to the absolutist policy of the Prussian government. In the Germanic parts of her kingdom, the empress enforced a rigid policy toward the Jewish communities, restricted their rights of residence, and strictly controlled their economic activity. Occasionally during her reign, Jews were expelled from certain cities. The first eight years of Austrian rule in Galicia, between 1772 and 1780, were the last years of Maria Theresa's reign. In principle, the empress continued to relate to the new Jews added to her kingdom according to the principle applied to them in other parts of the country: she strove to derive the maximum benefit from their economic activity while severely limiting their numbers, their residence in certain areas, and their occupations.

Joseph II, her son who was placed in charge of the new area, added a soupçon of "enlightened absolutism" to his mother's policy. One of his first acts after the occupation was to hold a census, a move typically carried out by a centralized state to strengthen its control over the demographic movements and economic activities of its population. In the winter of 1772, the heads of the Jewish communities were required to submit a detailed report of the property of the *kahal*, its income, and its expenditures and to record the names of the Jewish residents and their families, their ages, and sources of livelihood. In this census, 225,000

Jews were counted, 9.6 percent of the overall population. These figures served the Austrian government in its aim of introducing an economic policy in the spirit of the French physiocratic school, then considered a model economic theory by state officials in France, Prussia, and Russia, according to which a nonproductive surplus population was detrimental to the state economy. The census enabled the government to locate the economically excess population and to transfer it to other areas. The new government, which defined a considerable number of the traditional Jewish occupations in the Polish feudal economy as "unproductive," began to expel the surplus Jewish population, particularly the members of the lower classes—beggars and people with undefined occupations—beyond the borders of the state. The Austrian authorities also adopted another step, intended to curtail the uncontrolled growth in the number of Jews: restrictions on marriage. In 1773, soon after the results of the census were processed, the following order was issued:

Having learned from the submitted documents and other reliable information that the early marriages, numerous marriages, and the resulting tremendous growth of families are one of the reasons for the poor economic state of the Jews, which leads them into poverty and beggary, we hereby strictly forbid them, under penalty of expropriation of property, and, in certain cases, corporal punishment, to enter into the covenant of marriage, in the country or over the border, without a license from the government and without paying the set tax in advance. Moreover, all the Jewish beggars, whatever their names may be, shall be removed immediately. The property of the heads of the synagogues, and, in some cases, their persons, shall serve as surety that this order is executed in all its details.[2]

Many poor Jews left Galicia and emigrated southward to the territories of the Ottoman Empire and to the east, to the areas annexed by the Russian empire in southern Ukraine. In Galicia, they circumvented the order limiting the age of marriage in a variety of ways. One method was to marry off minors. In 1781, the famous *posek* R. Yehezkel Landau wrote about the panic aroused by the government's decrees: "For several years now, there have been rumors that the Jews will not be free to marry, and they have been arranging marriages for very small children, even those six and seven years of age."[3]

It seems that Eastern European Jewish society in all the different parts of partitioned Poland coped with the decrees relating to family life in a similar way. They arranged marriages for very young boys and girls whenever a rumor spread about some new piece of legislation by the absolutist government. That was the practice in Galicia in the early days of Austrian rule, and hasty marriages of children were held in Poland during the reign of the last king, Stanisław August Poniatowski. In the Prussian area of the partition, there was a deluge of marriages of minors in the period prior to the enactment of the 1797 Jewish law, and there were more "marriages of panic" during the rule of Nicholas I in Russia.

One method that the absolutist state employed to increase its control over the Jews was to make their institutions of self-rule subject to the authority of government officials. As the Austrian government had done decades before the partitions of Poland in certain regions of the empire, in Galicia it established a chief rabbinate. The appointed rabbi was supposed to be a supreme official supervising all matters of religion and education and overseeing the community rabbis. This meant that the rabbi was given a role that he had never had in the framework of the traditional community; from being a salaried employee of the *kahal*, he now was endowed with administrative powers. Obviously, the system of the chief rabbinate, which was extended throughout Galicia, stripped the Jewish community of its authority and functioned as a branch of a government ministry. The concept of a chief rabbinate (including the chief rabbinate of the State of Israel) did not exist in premodern Jewish society but was an innovation introduced by the Central European centralized state in the eighteenth century. The first chief rabbi appointed by the state, in 1778, was Judah Leib Bernstein. He supervised the religious administration on behalf of the state and collected payments for "religious services," until this new government post was abolished after a few years. An innovation of this kind was never introduced into the areas of Poland annexed by the Russian empire. The czarist government did establish an apparatus of state rabbis (crown rabbis) in the communities, but they never established a chief rabbinate for the entire empire.

In 1780, eight years after the annexation of Galicia, the empress died. She was succeeded by her son Joseph II, who was imbued with the ideas of enlightened absolutism and had already gained much experience in managing the affairs of the new region. From a political and social standpoint, his reign can be compared with that of Empress Catherine II in Russia. Joseph II aspired, among other things, to curtail the power of the church in the state and to limit the political influence of religion on the monarch. As an enlightened absolutist, he believed that there was a link between the enlightenment of the population and the good of the state. Hence, he wanted to integrate the Jewish population of the Austrian kingdom, including Galician Jewry, into the state's social and economic system not only by means of administrative reforms but also through education and the dissemination of knowledge. In the first ten years of his rule, Joseph introduced a series of reforms for the purpose of changing the "defective" character of the Jews of the region and turning them into "useful" subjects of the state and the society. Among other things, the Jews were required to take German surnames, to replace traditional Jewish dress with German clothing, to change their

occupations, to provide a quota of conscripts to the army, and to relin-
quish the institution of the *kahal.* These reforms culminated in the Tol-
eration Patent for Galician Jewry (1789), which defined the legal status
of the Jews and the relationship between them and the state. This edict
was one of a series of similar orders issued to various groups of Austrian
Jews in the different areas of the country, from the early 1780s. But it
severely limited those types of economic activity regarded as unproductive, in particular striking a blow at leaseholding, from which thousands
of Galician Jews earned their livelihood. The emperor wanted to create
a class of Jewish farmers and to transfer leaseholders and middlemen to
the crafts and free professions, all in the spirit of the physiocratic school.
However, both the Jewish inhabitants and the Polish estate owners strove
to retain the old method of leases. The "Patent" completed the integration of the Jews as urban subjects into the state administration, a move
that closely paralleled what took place during those same years in Russia.
But in the Austrian case, these changes occurred at a rapid pace and in
a far more energetic form.

As a ruler profoundly influenced by the European Enlightenment,
Joseph II displayed special interest in the education of his subjects. He
introduced comprehensive educational reform in all parts of his kingdom, and the Jewish communities in the different districts were called
upon to participate in the grand project. The first members of the
Haskalah movement in Central Europe enthusiastically embraced
Joseph II's initiative. The most well known of all the reactions to this
unprecedented initiative was that of Naphtali Herz Wessely (1725–
1805),[4] a poet and linguist, one of a group of Maskilim in Berlin. In
response to an appeal sent to him by the Trieste community in northeastern Italy, he composed a special work, *Divrei shalom ve'emet* (Words
of peace and truth, 1782), on the new educational program. In this
work, he praised the emperor, whose intention was in keeping with the
ideas of the Haskalah, and called upon the communal leaders to wel-
come the new program:

And here, the few details we spoke of in this regard, and many more about which
we did not remark, the exalted emperor, His Majesty Joseph II in his wisdom has
foreseen, and in a royal decree he has issued has included all the aforesaid in
brief, choice words, and commanded the Jews to establish schools of study in
which the children of Israel will learn the German language fluently. Every wise
man should rejoice upon hearing this commandment and understand the great
good that will come of it to their future offspring, and you, my dear brethren,
ought to hasten to carry out this excellent work, to establish schools and to make
all the necessary reforms required for it.[5]

In Galicia, too, a government network of education was founded,
intended to draw the Jews closer to the preferred imperial culture (in

German). The money to finance the new education for Jewish children was supposed to come from Jewish sources. In 1787, Herz Homberg (1749–1841), a Maskil and native of Bohemia who had been a member of Moses Mendelssohn's group in Berlin and acquired educational experience in the new school founded by the Trieste community, was invited to supervise the new system of education. In this matter of educational reform, Homberg played a Janus-faced role: he represented the intentions of the government to "civilize" the "native" population, the same population of which he was a part, although he had moved into the new Jewish cultural elite. This duality later became a distinct social and cultural trait of members of the Eastern European Haskalah movement. Homberg addressed the leaders of Galician Jewry in a letter written in Hebrew, in which he explained the aims of the new education (1788), but his words apparently made hardly any impression on the addressees.

Herz Homberg's name is inscribed forever in the collective memory of traditional Jewish society in Galicia. The abhorrent image of the imperial superintendent of schools endured for generations not only because the government schools he supervised were regarded by the Jews as the source of dissemination of religious heresy and a threat to the traditional culture; many remembered him for the corrupt method he installed and the fact that he exploited his position to make easy profits. For several years, he inspected the government schools for Jews and also served as an expert official on matters of Jewish culture and as a censor of Hebrew books. In other words, vis-à-vis the government, Homberg represented the culture that it wanted to change, and at the same time vis-à-vis the Jews, he represented the state culture that sought to reform their culture.

The governmental school system for Jews was a network of elementary schools (also called "normal" schools) that were also a contemporary innovation of the centralized state. Joseph II established the Jewish system as a small branch of a system of elementary schools founded throughout the Austrian empire. These schools—intended merely to teach the Jewish children reading and writing in the state language (German) and simple arithmetic and other subjects considered useful for a loyal subject of the state, such as his civic duties toward the ruler and the Jew's obligation not to cheat his non-Jewish customers—were perceived by the Jews as a serious threat to the traditional way of life. Homberg, as the superintendent of the government schools for Jews, devoted much space to these subjects in the textbooks he wrote for Jewish children.[6] For example, he wrote about the "bad traits" of the Jews: "And now there are foolish men who hate those of other religions and think that everything the Torah has cautioned against, not to lie or to take a false oath, not to steal, deceive, or cheat on measures, not to bear a grudge and the like, only applied to relations between one Jew and another, and its commandment to love your neighbor as yourself meant only that a Jew should love his fellow Jew and not a non-Jew. These men are misguided and are angering God, for whom all innocent and pure-hearted humans are equal."[7]

The Jews of Galicia grappled with the cultural danger posed by the government schools in a variety of ways. They preferred to send the children of the poor to acquire their education in the new institutions. A rather amusing example of the attitude of this society toward the government schools and the extent of their influence was cited by one of the great advocates of Austrian rule in Galicia. Joseph Perl (1773–1839), author of the biting anti-Hasidic satire *Megaleh temirin* (1819), writes about the total ignorance of a Galician Hasid who learned the German language in a government school: "I took the *bukh* and showed it to mine son-in-law, he should live, who's from Galicia and studied there in the German schools. Even though he forgot, thank G-d, what he learned, at least he knows still the German letters and can recognize the difference between German and other scripts."[8]

The reaction of traditional Jewish society to the establishment of these schools was antagonistic. Nor did the authorities derive any satisfaction from the achievements of this school system. In 1806, during the reign of the next Austrian emperor, Franz I, the special schools for Jews were abolished. From then on, the government encouraged the Jews to integrate into the general educational system.

Herz Homberg was a consummate example of the activity of Austrian officialdom, which combined absolutist enlightened trends with a centralized system of administration, in which the government gave a monopoly to someone to run the school system, and he did whatever he saw fit. As we saw, Homberg was simultaneously a government-appointed official and a "representative" of the "native" society. He was very knowledgeable about the "indigenous" culture but also supervised it by virtue of his post as a censor on behalf of the government.

Homberg was also the man who gave the Austrian government expert advice before a tax was imposed on the lighting of Sabbath candles. This case, which was immortalized in the folklore of Galician Jewry and left its imprint on their collective memory for many decades after Joseph II's reign, was linked to the new taxes imposed by the Austrian government. The collection of these taxes, levied on the consumption of kosher meat (1784) and on the lighting of Sabbath and holiday candles (1797), was leased in a government tender to wealthy entrepreneurs. The candle tax was leased to Solomon Kofler, a Jew from Lwów, for a high price and a lengthy period. In Galicia, rumors spread that Homberg had been amply rewarded for his advice to the authorities. Every Jewish woman who lit Sabbath candles had to pay a certain sum. Agents of the Jewish leaseholder would enter homes on Sabbath eve to check who had paid and who had not, and if the homeowners could not present a receipt for payment of the tax, Kofler's agents would extinguish the candles. The Kofler case reveals something about the change in the state's attitude toward the Jews after the Polish partitions. It illustrates the combination of the trend to reform the Jews in the spirit of enlightened absolutism and the bureaucratic system, which had nothing to do with the hoped-for enlightenment.

As noted earlier, Joseph II was radical in his policy of separating state and religion and in integrating the autonomous bodies and corporative organizations into the framework of the centralized administration. His death in 1790 cut short the wave of enlightened absolutism in the policy of Austrian officialdom. A considerable number of these reforms, which had begun to be implemented in relation to Austrian Jewry, slowed in pace or were blocked. From then on, the Austrian government altered its policy toward the Jews and in the coming decades took a different direction. The officialdom became less enamored of the ideas of enlightened absolutism. The French Revolution of 1789 had an effect on the Austrian rulers similar to the one it had on the end of Catherine II's reign in Russia. They became apprehensive about reformist trends and had serious reservations about the ideas of the European Enlightenment. What Joseph II had regarded as desirable and beneficial was, from the 1790s, considered politically dangerous.

The Austrian administration continued, of course, to harass the Jewish population with restrictions and decrees, but now it showed no real interest in changing the face of Jewish society or "correcting" the traits of followers of the Mosaic faith. On the contrary, the Austrian government began to view the traditional population, which remained unaffected by the spiritual and political ferment that originated in France and Germany, as a kind of political ally. The talmudic scholars, Hasidim, and masses of Jews in the towns of Galicia did not seem to have any political aspirations; they did not wish to reform the existing state order, nor did they show any interest in societal change. During the French Revolution, the "conservative connection" between traditional Jewish society and the Austrian government began to take shape (and a parallel development took place later in Russia). Both parties now had common interests based on the understanding that the Jewish side would not endanger the ruling government or take any interest in changing it. The government, on its part, moderated its demands for cultural change in Jewish society and adopted a neutral position in the internal conflicts between the various factions in that society. For example, when a declared enemy of Hasidism, the preacher Israel Loebel, came to Galicia in 1798 and attempted to spread his ideas against the new religious movement, the authorities prevented him from doing so. The books he brought with him from abroad were examined by the Austrian censor, and the Hasidim managed to convince the officials in the districts that Loebel visited that he was a political element who was disturbing the public peace. At one place, the authorities demanded that he desist "from persecuting the Hasidim, who are God-fearing Jews."[9]

Despite Joseph II's resolute attempt to change the Jews and bring them spiritually and culturally closer to European culture, the majority retained their distinctive traditional character—strangely enough, with the support of the government. This was the background to a pathetic paradox that attended the emergence of the Haskalah movement in Eastern Europe. The Maskilim in Galicia who wanted to draw their coreligionists closer to European culture imagined that they were the loyal allies of the government. In their literary works, as well as in the memoranda that they submitted to the authorities, they presented themselves as the reformers of Jewish society, under the aegis of the Austrian state.

But Austrian officialdom, on both the local and imperial level, did not always see things in the same light. The bureaucracy was inclined to view the Maskilim as a dangerous political element. They were considered too radical by virtue of being associated with the European Enlightenment—not to mention the fact that their affinity for French or German culture exposed them to dangerous political influences from the West. This association between Jews and enlightened ideas was not to the liking of the Austrian government at the time of the Napoleonic wars and the post–Vienna Congress period (1815), which in old history books is generally denoted as "the period of the reaction." A considerable number of the ardent memoranda that the Maskilim sent to the offices of the Austrian government were filed in the archives with a brief accompanying comment to the effect that there was no point in angering the majority of the Jewish population and making them hostile to the government. For a while, the Galician Jews had to contend with the reforms of Joseph II, and then, even though the government was not inclined to adopt a favorable attitude toward them, they did integrate into the new political systems and also succeeded in maintaining the traditional character of their society.

We have to bear in mind that at this time, the Hasidic movement was spreading rapidly throughout the eastern part of the Austrian kingdom. The Hasidic *tzaddikim* were then the conservative forces in Jewish society, and the Austrian government, contrary to the hopes of the Maskilim, instead of persecuting the *tzaddikim* or restricting their activity, relied on their power as a moderating element that wielded influence over the large Jewish population. The Austrian government was apprehensive

about political unrest that might arise against the background of movements of religious awakening or ideological agitation in the areas
annexed from Poland. The major political element in Galicia, to which
we will return later, had been and remained the Polish aristocracy,
whose economic structure was based on the system of leaseholds. For
generations, the Jews were the economic allies of this aristocracy, and
any disruption of this relationship was apt to lead to the collapse of Austrian control, which largely depended on quiet on the Polish front. Galician Jewry's encounter with the Austrian government opened with a
short-lived radical attempt to change Jewish society, but in the end, the
government, the Polish aristocracy, and the major forces in Jewish society joined together to conserve the existing situation, at least until the
1840s.

The Austrian government's policy of conservatism after Joseph II's
reign was reflected in its attitude toward the estate economy of the Polish aristocracy. In the early nineteenth century, since the Austrian government preferred to keep Galicia as a primarily agricultural area, it did
not encourage industrialization. Administrative orders promoted the
development of the capitalistic economy in the more western regions
of the empire: Bohemia, Moravia, and the German-speaking regions of
Austrian. Galicia was intended to be a supplier of agricultural produce
to the developed areas; hence, the premodern estate economy maintained its character, and there was no movement from the village to the
large industrial city. Jewish leaseholders continued to run the alcoholic-
beverage industry on the estates owned by the nobles and to engage in
selling its products.

This planned backwardness of the region was added to another
change that severely damaged its economy: the fact that it was cut off
from all other parts of partitioned Poland. Galicia, which, prior to the
partitions, was a crossroads of international trade for all the neighboring
countries, lost its commercial preeminence in the first half of the nineteenth century, owing to the high tariff walls that divided it from them.
As a result of the economic gap between Galicia and Congress Poland
(Congress Poland was the autonomous part of Russian Poland) and the
Russian empire, modern transportation developed in the district at a
snail's pace, so Galicia was not flooded with imported industrial goods,
and the small local industry continued to prosper until the second half
of the century. The economic slump caused old, well-established trade
centers to decline. Cities such as Brody, which still had very large Jewish
communities in the mid-eighteenth century, shrank into medium-size,
even small, communities. Many Jews emigrated to the new economic
centers in Prussia and Russia (particularly to the provinces in the south
of the empire). Some communities that had enjoyed a high status and

prestige for centuries declined in the nineteenth century, while others gained in status. Lwów (Lemberg), the major Jewish community in eastern Galicia, retained its supremacy and even grew. In western Galicia, the major city, Kraków, remained the home of the largest Jewish community. As we shall see in the coming chapters, great changes occurred in the nature of Jewish life in these major communities.[10]

The year 1848 marked a turning point in the history of Galician Jewry, as it did in European history as a whole. In this sense, Galicia definitely belonged to the western part of Europe. That year, a wave of revolutions swept across western Europe, from France to Austria. In parallel, the Jews were the victims of a wave of pogroms. In the Russian empire, then under the police control apparatus of Czar Nicholas I, the "Spring of the Nations" had hardly any impact. Galicia, in contrast, entered a period of unrest, and its Polish aristocracy joined the political struggle that crossed the Austrian borders and encompassed the Prussian area. The 1848 revolutions brought to the surface the contradiction between a struggle for emancipation, to gain civil rights in a state, and the unique national demands of ethnic groups. The large Jewish minority in the Austrian part of partitioned Poland was not then regarded as a group worthy of receiving collective rights as a national unit. Jews largely still maintained corporative frameworks of identity, although these had been formally abolished by the central government. Representatives of the Jewish public wanted to preserve, as much as possible, the old frameworks of life, which depended on their ties to the Polish aristocracy. Those Jews belonging to the new bourgeoisie, who wanted to join the struggle for civil equality, had to decide between the imperial (German-Austrian) alternative or identification with Polish nationalism, both of which had played a role in the early days of the politicization of Eastern European Jewish society.

Here the great difference emerged between the political course taken by Russian Jewry and that of Austrian Jewry. These two demographic units, which until the end of the eighteenth century had been parts of one kingdom and for several decades had experienced an intensive encounter with an absolutist kingdom and enlightened absolutism, were beginning to move along separate paths of political modernization. In Lwów and Kraków, Jews participated in some military incidents and political events. The Jews' political status also began to change in Galicia, and their political activity took on a new, modern character, totally different from what it had been until then in Eastern Europe. The events of 1848 also threw the question of Jewish identity into sharper focus: Polish nationalism became a dominant force in the new political reality, and the "progressive" Jews were caught up in the growing tension between the imperial (German-Austrian) identity and the Polish identity.[11]

The problem was further exacerbated by the universality of the revolutions. Throughout Germany, including areas annexed by Prussia from Poland, the Jews' struggle for equal civil rights was coupled with their affinity for the German identity, language, and culture. So, while in Galicia, the Poles sought the support of the Jews for their political cause, in the Prussian area, the Jews of Poznań threw in their lot with the German government against the Polish nationalists. In Brody, in eastern Galicia, Jews wearing *kapotes* and *shtreimels* (Hasidic coats and hats) marched arm in arm with Polish aristocrats, singing: "We are brothers in adversity, hence our goal is the same." And in Krotoschin (Krotoszyn) in the province of Posen (Poznań), under Prussian rule, a Jew named Bines organized the defense of the town against the Polish rebels.[12] The decision of whom to support, the Germans or the Poles, was not a theoretical one, nor did it stem from abstract cultural considerations. For a large minority dispersed over a vast area with a mixed population of Germans and Poles, such a decision involved a risk. Poles could carry out pogroms against their Jewish neighbors (and there had been such precedents in the earlier uprisings), and the government was in the hands of the Prussians and Austrians who demanded the political loyalty of the Jews. This is what was written in the Jewish German-language newspaper *Allgemeine Zeitung des Judentums:* "At this time in Poland and Galicia, the Jews are identifying with the Germans. If there should be a schism between these two large parties, much grief is in store for both of them, and the Jews, even more than the Germans, are dispersed within these parts of Poland, the great majority of whose inhabitants are Poles, and they—the Jews—are totally defenseless. Countless victims are liable to fall."[13]

After 1848, the old legal situation was not restored. A new emperor, Franz Josef, ascended to the throne and ruled for decades, until World War I. After a period, lasting several years, of regression from the emancipatory trend, full equal rights were granted by law to the population. Franz Josef's reign is preserved in the collective memory of Galician Jewry as the time of a merciful monarch when the Jews enjoyed (from 1867) equal civil rights. At the end of the nineteenth century, in the eyes of many Jews, the kingdom of the exalted emperor figured as the absolute antithesis of the wicked Russian kingdom.

Chapter 7

"Brotherhood" and Disillusionment: Jews and Poles in the Nineteenth Century

Between 1772 and 1793, large parts of the Jewish population in the Polish-Lithuanian kingdom became the subjects of absolutist empires, but a sizable group of Jews still remained in the split country under autonomous Polish rule. In earlier chapters, we learned that the partitions of Poland did not happen overnight, nor was the abolition of Poland's political independence a one-time occurrence but rather a gradual process that lasted several decades. From the end of the eighteenth century to the first half of the nineteenth, certain areas in Eastern Europe that in the past had been part of the large Polish-Lithuanian kingdom continued to enjoy autonomous rule. Their borders changed from one period to the next, and the status of the Jews living in them changed, too. From 1815 to 1846, the part of western Galicia that encompassed Kraków and some of its surrounding villages was under Polish self-rule. The "Republic of Kraków" was within the Austrian area, but it was under the international control of the three powers that partitioned Poland, and in practice it had a separate legal status, and the status of the Jews living there also differed from that of their coreligionists in other regions of Galicia.

In the Russian empire, too, there were large regions of eastern and central Poland that enjoyed autonomy until the 1863 rebellion. During the Napoleonic wars, from 1807 to 1815, a political body known as the "Grand Duchy of Warsaw" was created in central and western Poland by Napoleon following his new partitions of Europe, and in it the Jews enjoyed a special status. In the history of Eastern European Jewry in the nineteenth century, there was, then, another context in addition to the Austrian, Russian, and Prussian. That was the context of Polish autonomy.

Poland was one of the first countries in Europe in which a "nationalist" movement, in the modern sense of the term, emerged. We have noted that in the Polish-Lithuanian kingdom, only the nobility was regarded as a "nation." Although at the end of the eighteenth century, there were some trends of integrating the townspeople into the Polish "nation," Polish nationalism, at least until the second half of the nineteenth century, was identified with the nobility, the social class that had possessed full political rights in previous centuries. Polish nationalism grew in strength under the impact of the partitions and, from time to time, made political or military attempts to change the political status of one or another region in the divided country. In this state of affairs, the Jews, who, on the average, made up 10 percent of the population in the Polish autonomous areas and were an influential element in the urban population, had a significant role to play. The participation or nonparticipation of the Jews in actively promoting Polish nationalist aspirations became an important factor in Jewish-Polish relations in the nineteenth century.

The Polish nobility, which enjoyed political autonomy in various parts of divided Poland, evinced, just as the Austrian or Russian government officials in these areas did, great interest in socially reforming the Jews and integrating them into the political system. In the first decades of the century, reformers among the Polish nobles acted according to the enlightened absolutist model, not with a Russian or Austrian orientation but rather a "Polish" one. This meant that the goal of these various reformers was to integrate the Jews into the Polish urban class, the same class that was destined to become part of the Polish "nation."

In pursuing this goal, they had a weighty problem, which we alluded to in previous chapters. For centuries, the relations between the Jewish townspeople and the Polish townspeople had been hostile. Moreover, the Polish urban class was not considered by the Maskilim, and certainly not by other Jews, as a cultural role model or as an objective of social integration. The urban Jewish population regarded itself as culturally superior to the Polish townspeople. The processes of their acculturation during this period in the cities of Poland did not originate with the creation of ties with the neighboring urban population, nor was the Polish nobility prepared to create social ties with a class inferior to it, certainly not with the Jews. The aspirations for closer relations between "Poles" and Jews were rather abstract, and both sides found it hard to form ties of a nontraditional character. The writer I. L. Peretz (1852–1915) acerbically described this situation in his memoirs: "'Arise, the dawn of the new day has arrived!' . . . But from what we could see in Zamość [the Gentiles] *hadn't* stretched out the hand of friendship far enough to be noticed."[1]

However, a specific group in Polish Jewry—the new economic elite in the large cities—was beginning to become acculturated, and identified with Polish nationalism and wanted to become part of Polish political and cultural life.

A test case for the notion of integrating the Jews in Polish urban society occurred in the first decades of the nineteenth century. It was an exceptional event in Eastern European history: an attempt to emancipate the Jews of the Warsaw duchy. In this political unit, established by Napoleon after his wars with Prussia, Austria, and Russia, the Jews gained full civil rights, similar to their legal status in France from the days of the French Revolution (the July 22, 1807, constitution). But there was a salient difference between France, in which tens of thousands of Jews lived during the revolution, and Poland under Napoleonic rule, with its hundreds of thousands of Jews. The large concentration of Jews in the cities and their role in the feudal estate economy made their political integration into the urban framework a complicated undertaking, one that was undesirable from the standpoint of the Polish nobility. And the Jews, who saw emancipation as a threat to their way of life, did not ask the Napoleonic rulers for full political rights. The communal bodies that primarily oversaw matters of taxation on behalf of the Polish state wanted nothing beyond a renewal of the institutions of autonomy in their old format, as they had existed in Poland from time immemorial. The enlightened Polish legislator was determined to carry out a comprehensive reform in the political status of the Jews, but owing to the opposition of more conservative circles in the Polish nobility, the resolutions relating to Jews in the 1807 constitution were frozen.[2] As a result, the status of Jews in the duchy was, at least in practice, similar to that of their French coreligionists in the Napoleonic era, since in France, the "infamous decree" had been proclaimed in 1808, suspending full civil rights for the Jews until they improved their economic behavior. Napoleon's attempt to grant emancipation to the Jews in Poland was an exceptional case at that time, unparalleled until the second half of the nineteenth century.[3]

With the end of the Napoleonic wars and the revised partition of the map of Europe, the area known as the Grand Duchy of Warsaw became in part an autonomous political unit under Russian rule, known as Congress Poland (Kongresówka). Now the Jews were under the rule of the Russian empire, but they were subject to a separate Polish set of laws. The status of Jews in Congress Poland differed from their status in the Pale of Settlement. Legislation with regard to Jews advanced at a different pace, since the Polish nobility—in particular, several magnates who held enlightened absolutist views, including statesmen from the Czartoryski and Potocki families—occasionally proposed programs for broad reforms in the status of the Jews and demanded the abolition of Jewish autonomy. Indeed, in 1821, twenty-three years before this happened in Russia itself, the rule of the *kahal* was abolished in Poland and replaced by an organization known as the "Congregational Board"

(Polish, Dozór Bóżniczy), intended to supervise religious affairs, similar to the organization installed after the partitions in Austria and Prussia. The Polish nobility was engaged by the complex issue debated at the time of the four-year *Sejm,* namely, how to integrate into the Polish urban class a large minority with a lifestyle that differed from that of the state population. The public debate on this matter was influenced, like others that preceded it in Eastern Europe, by the physiocratic school and other ideas from the legacy of the eighteenth-century enlightenment.[4] Furthermore, the planners took as their model the actions taken by the neighboring states in this regard, as well as the recommendations of Maskilim.

David Friedländer, a German Maskil who had for decades been active among the Prussian Jews, composed a memorandum in which he advised the Poles how to initiate reforms of Polish Jewry (1819).[5] The reforms that were brought for discussion during these years included programs for the reeducation of the Jews through a school system in the Polish language, a change in the socioeconomic stratification of Jewish society, and a demographic reshuffling by transferring "surplus populations" from one district to another as well as from the cities to agricultural settlements. These discussions began immediately after the Vienna Congress, 1815–16, but in the following years, too, the Polish nobility involved in political life carried on its intensive efforts to change the status of Jews in Polish society. Among other things, the autonomous Polish authorities took an interest in Hasidism, which was sweeping across the Jewish communities of Poland, and in its influence on the behavior of members of the "old faith."[6]

In November 1830, an uprising against Russian rule broke out. The Poles' attempt to use the weapons to overcome the superior military strength of the Russian empire ended in a blistering defeat. After the rebellion, the Russians greatly curtailed the Poles' autonomy, although they did not completely eradicate it. Centers of Polish cultural activity were hard hit, and consequently the Poles' ability to influence the systems of education and communication operating within the Jewish population was severely reduced. Owing to the curtailment of Polish self-rule, Russian influence on the Jews grew stronger. As the Polish nobility lost much of its political power, the traditional ties between the Jewish leaseholders and the estate owners weakened. Still, in these areas the separate status of the Poles was maintained, along with the special laws relating to Jews. The changes that occurred in the Vilna community are a good example of the social and cultural change produced by the defeat of the 1830 revolt. From the 1830s on, Russian cultural influence on the city greatly increased. The local group of Maskilim adopted a distinctly pro-Russian position, and the ties with Polish culture, so significant in the early decades of the nineteenth century, dissolved.[7]

After the defeat of the 1830 uprising, an industrial revolution began in several regions of Congress Poland, and we referred in previous chapters to the social, cultural, and economic changes that came in its wake. In western Poland, industrial plants were established, and a new Jewish bourgeois class was created, which invested capital in the factories and was actively involved in the capitalistic financial and commercial activity. We have noted that the processes of industrialization and the rise of the capitalistic economy occurred in Poland before they did in most parts of imperial Russia. As this economic change took place, circles in Jewish society that assimilated Polish culture and identified with the Poles' political aspirations accumulated more power. The trends of acculturation during those years were reflected in the activity of the Warsaw rabbinical seminary, established in 1826, to integrate Jewish and Polish culture.[8] Concomitantly, Hasidism gathered strength. These developments created the cultural reality that was typical of nineteenth-century Poland. On the one hand, there was a small elite of the affluent, the bourgeoisie, and members of the free professions who had assimilated Polish culture. On the other hand, the majority of the population retained Jewish patterns of life, and large parts of it became Hasidic communities. The Warsaw community, which attracted thousands of Jewish immigrants following the 1830 revolt, illustrates the societal change. A small group of *haute bourgeoisie* that had adopted Polish culture lived in that city, but the Jewish population constantly grew, with the addition of Hasidim who were immigrating to Warsaw from the towns to the south and the east. Similar processes were taking place in Kraków, which was then under Austrian rule but enjoyed broad autonomy. There, too, a Jewish bourgeoisie emerged that was assimilating Polish culture and identifying with Polish political aims. At the same time, a large Hasidic society, conservative in nature, gathered strength as a result of movement from the towns and villages to the city.

In the early days of Czar Alexander II's reign, an event occurred that put an end to the autonomy that the Polish nobility had enjoyed until the second half of the nineteenth century. When the new Czar took the throne at the end of the Crimean war, expectations heightened in Congress Poland for expanded autonomy and improved status for Poles in the Russian empire. After the political demonstrations of 1861 and 1862, Polish demands grew more extreme. Although in 1861, a political reform linked to the name of Count Aleksander Wielopolski expanded the Poles' political rights, an armed rebellion against Russian rule broke out in January 1863. This rebellion was a landmark in the relations between Poles and Jews. The Polish rebels turned to the Jewish population and asked for their support, and several groups in Jewish society identified with the Polish cause. Many sided with the rebels because of the centuries-old economic ties between leaseholders and communal leaders and families of the Polish nobility. The new elite from the bourgeoisie of the large cities, which had assimilated Polish culture and language, tended to identify explicitly with the Poles' political aspirations. Warsaw's Orthodox rabbi, R. Dov Ber Meisels (who had supported the Poles during the "Spring of the Nations," when he was the rabbi of Kraków), and the preacher Marcus Jastrow openly championed the Polish struggle and appeared together at mass demonstrations against Russian rule. After attending the funeral of the bishop of Warsaw, which turned into a mass demonstration, the two were arrested by the Russian authorities and sentenced to deportation from Russian Poland.[9] These two Jewish religious leaders found favor with the Polish public, and the Polish revolutionaries used them in the propaganda that it disseminated to Jewish society. Polish patriots distributed Rabbi Meisels's photograph in Warsaw, and when he was released from jail, he received 20,000 rubles raised from the sale of his picture—a gift of the Polish nation.[10]

Many Jews took part in the 1863 rebellion. Some assisted by providing money and supplies for the rebels, and some took part in the fighting against the Russians. Most of the Jewish fighters were members of the lower classes and residents of the provincial towns. We know that nearly two thousand Jews fought alongside the Poles in battle units (about a thousand of them from Warsaw). Jews filled important roles in the Polish government during the rebellion: Henrik Wohl and Mikołaj Epstein were active on the economic side; the Maskil Isaac Goldman (1812–88), a censor, translator, and publisher of Hebrew books, composed the revolutionary handbills that were distributed throughout the rebelling country; and a substantial part of the financing for the uprising came from wealthy Warsaw Jews.

Nonetheless, military units of the rebels struck out against the Jewish population in the towns and villages. Jews suspected of spying or aiding the Russian army were hanged; much Jewish property was looted, and large sums of money were confiscated from individuals and communities. After the uprising was quelled, about a thousand Jews were tried for their part in it. Several Jewish rebels were hanged in public in the Jewish streets of Warsaw, and Jewish fighters were among those tried and sent to Siberian exile. During the rebellion, a sense of brotherhood (*braterstwo* in Polish) prevailed among Polish patriots and Jewish supporters. Jews and Poles spoke of the common interests of the two nations aspiring to gain independence from the Russian oppressor. Contemporary Polish literature promised great things to the Jews if they would identify with the Polish objectives. A typical example is the handbill published by the rebels in Hebrew, in which the Jewish population was promised civil rights on the soil of independent Poland: "And now if the enemy leaves us to ourselves and his yoke is broken and removed from our necks, then you shall enjoy the benefits of peace, the fruit of your deeds, and you shall eat from the good of the land and shall have a memorial and a name in all the rights of the state, without measure, for the new government that will rise up in our lands shall not know any man according to his religion or his lineage but only by his homeland, for he is one of the children of Poland, and to Poland it will be said: this one was born here!"[11]

Yet with the failure of the uprising and the defeat of the Poles in their war against the Russian army, disappointment surged on both sides. The Poles' hopes for the rapid and complete integration of the large Jewish minority were dashed. On the Jewish side, the first voices of writers and thinkers were heard calling for the fostering of a separate Jewish identity, a kind of embryonic nationalism. In the 1863 uprising and in the short-lived "brotherhood," some historians find the roots of modern Polish anti-Semitism as well as the origins of the new Jewish nationalism that took shape during those very days in the wake of Jewish reactions to the Polish insurrection. Both Peretz Smolenskin (1840?–85), one of the fathers of modern Jewish nationalism, and David Gordon (1831–86), editor of the national Hebrew paper *Hamaggid*, disassociated themselves from Polish nationalism. Members of the Haskalah movement saw the failure of the Jewish-Polish brotherhood, which had existed during the rebellion, as proof that Jewish hopes to preserve their unique identity would not be answered by help from the Poles, but rather could be fulfilled only within the multinational empire.[12] Nearly sixty years before an independent Poland was reestablished, they keenly sensed how little hope there was for a unique Jewish existence within the modern nation-state.

From 1795 to 1863, the Poles and the Jews continued to maintain a complicated relationship within an autonomous Polish framework marked by the constant expectation of the reestablishment of an independent Polish state. This expectation was linked to the Poles' intentions to carry out comprehensive reforms in the legal status and socioeconomic situation of the Jews, similar to the ones carried out in the areas directly annexed to the neighboring powers. But because the Polish military rebellions ended in defeat and the Jews tried to adopt a neutral stance vis-à-vis the Poles and the partition powers, this possibility was never realized. After 1863, Polish influence over the Jews weakened in the Polish-speaking areas, and the Jews politically identified less with the Poles, as a widely influential, flagrant brand of anti-Semitism emerged at the close of the nineteenth century. In contrast, the Jews' cultural identification with the Poles persisted and even grew. These two ostensibly contradictory trends resulted from the gap between the strong cultural influence of the Poles on the Jews, and the loss of their political power in the areas where they had previously enjoyed broad autonomy.

We have seen, then, that there were four alternative paths to Jewish modernization that opened with the partitions of Poland. The paths taken by the inhabitants of Eastern Europe in the transition from a traditional corporative society to the reality of the modern era were largely determined by the geopolitical milieu—the Russian empire, the Austrian kingdom, the Prussian kingdom (about which we have spoken only briefly because the Jews in the areas annexed to Prussia seem to be more part of the history of German Jewry than that of Polish Jewry), and the Polish autonomy. The last exerted its influence on the Jews even when it lacked political independence. The Polish path had always existed, even during the long period (1793–1918) when there was no independent Polish state on the map of Europe. After World War I, when Poland again achieved its independence, the Polish path became a key factor in the history of millions of Jews. In the new Polish state, whose boundaries encompassed the regions of Congress Poland and also included parts of Ukraine and White Russia, the Polish alternative again became an influential path, albeit one fraught with tension, in the processes of modernization of the Jews. But this new phase in the relations between Jews and Poles, in a Polish nation-state, was brief, cut short by the German invasion of Poland on September 1, 1939.

Chapter 8

"My Heart Is in the West": The Haskalah Movement in Eastern Europe

> Who would have said to the Jews of Russia and Poland, a child will be born to a poor man of the common people, a copyist of the Scriptures in the city of Dessau, a Prussian city of little fame. And from him a light would go forth to the Jews of all the lands, and from the radiance before him a brightness would appear to the Jews of Russia and Poland, too, and a new light would shine upon them. And this is the man Moshe ben-Menahem [Moses Mendelssohn], from whom a new era began in the history of the children of Israel.[1]

In these flowery words, suffused with optimistic pathos, the Maskil Abraham Dov Baer Gottlober (1810–99) described the appearance of a movement that spread throughout the divided Polish-Lithuanian kingdom. The Haskalah, a cultural and social movement, modernist in character, first emerged in Eastern Europe during the period of the partitions and was closely linked to the political and social changes described in earlier chapters.

Members of the Haskalah generally claimed that their movement was born in Germany and from there spread eastward to the areas under the rule of the Polish kingdom. This is also suggested by Gottlober's ardent words. He chose to use images that were ubiquitous in the writings of the Maskilim; the messages of the Haskalah were often conveyed through concepts associated with "illumination." The light of the German Haskalah also shone upon Poland and evoked a quasi-messianic response (notice the nontraditional use that the writer made of the wording of the prayer "a new light will shine upon Zion"). It was the light of the European Enlightenment, a name, which in the various languages of Europe, is connected with light or the process of illumination. The members of the Haskalah, and Gottlober was no exception, agreed that a new era was unfolding with the appearance of their movement. In their view, human history, including that of the Jews, had taken on a new character from the inception of the Enlightenment, and the human condition was totally disparate from what it had been in the dark Middle Ages.[2] Until recently, scholarly historical literature has held that the Haskalah movement originated in Germany under special conditions that existed in the Berlin Jewish community in the last decades of the eighteenth century. Contemporary studies, however, have questioned the certainty of the idea that the movement was exclusively created in Western or Central Europe, and then spread from there to the east. Today we can definitely state that the Haskalah movement emerged simultaneously in several centers, some in Central Europe, some in Eastern Europe, and that the movement had its roots in the intensive contact between the two parts of the Ashkenazi diaspora: the Eastern European and the Central European parts of European Jewry.

The historiographic image of the Haskalah as a German product that was exported to Eastern Europe is perhaps one of the many results of the central role that German Jewry played in writing modern Jewish history. In eighteenth- and nineteenth-century Jewish culture, the terms *Westjuden* (Jews of the West) and *Ostjuden* (Jews of Eastern Europe) were in widespread use. The processes of modernization undergone by Eastern European society in general, and Jewish society there in particular, were regarded as the story of the spread of Western influence from the center of the continent to the east. The Polish *Ostjuden* were a passive object in this story, especially since the Maskilim were happy to adopt this image and tended to play down the original contribution to the birth of the Haskalah movement made by the communities of Poland and Lithuania. From a historical standpoint, the emergence of the Haskalah can be described as an all-Ashkenazi phenomenon that began on both sides of the line that divided Germany and the territories of the former Polish-Lithuanian kingdom.[3]

What was the social and cultural vision that members of the Haskalah cherished? The Haskalah movement, which in many senses was part of the eighteenth-century European Enlightenment, aspired to shape a new type of Jew who would be both a "Jew" and a "man." This pair of concepts—"Jew" and "man"—that the Maskilim of Eastern Europe used in their discourse concealed the unpleasant assumption that a member of the traditional Ashkenazi Jewish community, in its given cultural state (in particular, the Polish Jew, whose livelihood was linked to the Polish feudal system and who led the lifestyle typical of the *Ostjude*), was not a man. In the Maskilim's view, a Jew could turn into a man by adopting the values, moral criteria, cultural codes, fashions, and manners that came from Western and Central Europe. But the European model was not the only inspiration of the early Maskilim. Contemporary researchers, including Immanuel Etkes in his studies on the beginning of the Haskalah movement,[4] have pointed out that although the Haskalah was a branch of the European Enlightenment, it also drew upon an internal Jewish root: the rationalist philosophy of the Middle Ages, which led to internal reform based on immanent Jewish sources. In other words, the reform of contemporary Jewish society according to the principles of rationalist thought could be carried out on the basis of the Jewish tradition. Members of the Haskalah movement saw themselves as continuing a long-standing tradition that had been neglected by recent generations. They did not propose to abandon the classic texts but rather advocated a new reading of them. In this sense, the early Maskilim presaged, by several decades, the cultural path taken by the nationalist movement, which also suggested a new reading of the traditional texts, and argued, as did the Haskalah, for the continuity rather than the liquidation of the special Jewish identity. Moreover, the legacy of the past, which the Ashkenazi society had allegedly neglected, was, in their opinion, consistent with the most innovative ideas of the Enlightenment era.

Regardless of whether the external European element or the internal Jewish element from the medieval legacy of rationalism was ascendant in the Haskalah movement, it is impossible to understand its emergence without considering the change that occurred in attitudes toward the foreign ruler. The Maskilim regarded the modern centralized state as a historical innovation unparalleled in the history of humankind. The appearance of those they wrote of as "benevolent kings," rulers who acted in accordance with rational principles, opened a new historical era in which the ostracized, despised Jews would also be integrated as human beings in a reformed social order. The Maskilim did their utmost to instill in their coreligionists the notion that the transformation of the Jew into a loyal subject of the modern centralized state was consonant with the principles of rationalist thought (which, as noted earlier, originated both in the Jewish heritage and in the European Enlightenment). The history of the Haskalah movement is closely linked to the transformation of the European state into an "enlightened" absolutist kingdom.

Hence, the chronology of the Haskalah's development is linked to the history of the Polish partitions and to the various stages in the active intervention of the Russian, Austrian, and Prussian authorities in the internal life of the Jews. The centralized state, which throughout the eighteenth century adopted significant parts of the social and cultural platform of the European Enlightenment, desired, as did the Maskilim, to make the Jew a "man": namely, to turn the Jew into a European in his way of life, his behavior, and his culture. Here, the paths of the Maskilim intersected with those of the Austrian, Prussian, or Russian government official. The Maskil, who served as a kind of cultural agent of the empire, and the official, who searched for ways to effect the integration of Jews into the new political setup, shared the same ideological tenets. Their goals were not identical, but there were enough points of contact to enable the Maskilim to identify with the imperial government.

In the political reality that prevailed in the multinational empire, with its vast Jewish population, the course taken by the Maskilim seems like an attempt to offer a Jewish identity that would be an alternative to the traditional one. This identity would combine citizenship in a centralized state with the preservation of the unique religion and culture. The Maskilim wanted to separate the "political" from the "cultural." They left the political to the imperial administration, while they developed and disseminated the culture through their literary creation (poetry, prose, drama, translation, scientific research, and journalistic writing) and their educational activity (schools). They fostered the linguistic uniqueness of Jewish culture (a renaissance of the Hebrew language) and strove to revive elements of cultural identity from the religious heritage (historical and philological research, the study of all branches of halakhic literature). In their cultural work, the Maskilim created, wittingly or not, a different definition of Jewish society in the Eastern European empire: no longer the religious-corporative identity of the premodern autonomy, as it had existed in the Polish-Lithuanian kingdom, but a linguistic-cultural identity within a multinational empire. In this sense, the Maskilim in Eastern Europe were part of a historical phenomenon that can be defined as Jewish "proto-nationalism."

The buds of the Haskalah movement appeared in Eastern Europe as far back as the 1770s. This historical fact deserves attention because the partitions of Poland took place in the very years when the first groups of Maskilim were forming in Berlin, the capital of the Prussian kingdom, and in Königsberg in eastern Prussia. Königsberg, which became the center of Haskalah second in importance after Berlin, is much farther east than many communities in the Polish kingdom, so that one of the centers of the German Haskalah actually sprang up deep inside Eastern Europe.[5]

The harbingers of the new phenomenon in Eastern Europe were members of two social groups who rallied around a common social and cultural platform: members of the economic elite, who maintained close contacts with aristocrats and high government officials; and intellectuals whose interests extended far beyond the pages of traditional religious texts. The second group included Jewish physicians who had attended universities in Italy or Germany and returned to their countries of origin. In the last decade before Poland's loss of independence, there were Jews in Vilna who took an interest in philosophy, Hebrew grammar, and the sciences and also closely followed the political and cultural changes in France and Germany (these were the days of the French Revolution). They were not yet part of the Haskalah movement, which began several years earlier in Berlin and Königsberg, but they were akin in spirit to some of the founders of the German Haskalah, kept in touch with them, and read their writings. R. Yehezkel Feivel, the Vilna community's *magid* (a preacher who delivers sermons on the Sabbath and on Jewish holidays), perused the books of Moses Mendelssohn and Naphtali Herz Wessely. The sons of the wealthy Vilna Jew Eliahu Ben Zvi Pesseles, cousin of the Vilna Gaon's father, paid in advance the printing costs of Mendelssohn's *Bi'ur* (a German translation and commentary in the spirit of rationalism).[6] *Hame'asef*, the periodical of the Berlin Haskalah, had a considerable number of subscribers among the Jews of Vilna. R. Solomon Dubno (1738–1813), a publisher and bookseller who tutored Moses Mendelssohn's children in Berlin and was actively involved in the publication of the *Bi'ur*, settled in Vilna in the early 1780s and enjoyed the patronage of R. Joseph, son of Eliahu Pesseles.[7] A physician of the Vilna community, Yehudah Halevi Hurwitz (1734–97), was in close touch with Mendelssohn and Wessely.[8] Other physicians in the city served in the Polish royal court (Vilna was one of the capital cities of the kingdom) and engaged in the sciences and matters relating to the social reform of Polish Jewry.

In Shklov in White Russia, members of a similar circle combined financial success and association with the non-Jewish high society with a new type of cultural openness. This town, which was already within the Russian empire after the first partition in 1772, was home to several financial entrepreneurs who amassed fortunes from their dealings with the new government.[9] In a number of cities, Jews participated in the cultural activity that emanated from Mendelssohn's circle in Berlin (by subscribing to *Hame'asef* or paying in advance to acquire volumes of the *Bi'ur* project). But one can speak of the Haskalah as a real movement only several decades later, in the 1820s and 1830s. In the broad social sense, the Haskalah spread throughout Eastern Europe in a distinct form when the Maskilim began to view themselves as part of a group that could be identified by singular characteristics. In Austrian Galicia, this happened in the second decade of the nineteenth century, and within the Russian empire, in the early days of Czar Nicholas I's reign.

Unquestionably, it was the link that the Maskilim attempted to create with the imperial government that made the Haskalah a distinct social movement. This was a link of a new sort, unknown until then in the traditional society. It was not based on loyalty according to the principle "raise a prayer for the well-being of the kingdom" but on ideological identification. In their case, the authority of the state supplanted the age-old ties between the Jewish community and the Polish aristocracy.

Local loyalty was replaced by loyalty to a remote ruler, seated in a hidden imperial capital (they supposedly joined an "imagined community" of subjects of the centralized state). This explains why the Maskilim's activity bore an international character. Jews in Austrian Galicia collaborated with Jews in Russian Poland and in the German kingdom of Prussia to achieve new cultural and social goals. Without deliberately intending to, the Maskilim were perpetuating the premodern unity of the Ashkenazi community beyond the new political boundaries that the powers had drawn on the map of Poland. The international character of the Haskalah was already evident at the time of the partitions, in the biographies of the Maskilim and in the locations where they were active.

Mendel Lefin (1749–1826), writer, translator, and social reformer from Satanów in Podolia, embarked on his path in Podolia, then under Polish rule (under the patronage of Adam Czartoryski). He spent time in Berlin in Mendelssohn's milieu, and during the debates in the Polish four-year *Sejm*, he was one of the drafters of proposals to reform the status of Polish Jewry. Several years later, he was involved, together with his Polish patron, in the activity that preceded Czar Alexander I's legislation relating to the Jews (1804). During this time, he resided in White Russia, under the aegis of the Jewish tycoon Joshua Zeitlin, who assembled a kind of academy of scholars and Maskilim in his private estate at Ustye. The last stage in his Maskilic career took place in Galicia under Austrian rule, where he collaborated with Joseph Perl and the members of his group. In all the countries where Lefin spent time during his long life, his aims were similar and the methods he used to encourage the integration of Jews into the state on a rational basis were the same. He wrote books, distributed translations of scientific material from European languages, popularized key texts from the Jewish heritage (by translating them into Yiddish), and submitted memoranda to the various authorities.[10] All these actions were taken to achieve two aims, which were appropriate for any land and not connected to a specific country. These aims were the moral and social reform of Polish Jewry and their integration into the new political order.

Unlike later nationalist movements, the Maskilim did not aspire to integrate the Jews into a nation or to link them to a specific ethnic group. They were thinking of a "kingdom," not a "nation." Loyalty to a kingdom was not necessarily linked to identification with a specific ethnic group. This universalism may explain why the Haskalah movement in Eastern Europe was for decades distinctly German in character, although one might have expected support for a Russian state or for the Polish political alternative to be linked to the Polish or the Russian language and culture. The Maskilim were in the "pre-national" phase as far as their political identification was concerned. They identified first with the state (headed by the absolutist ruler), not with the nation (the dominant ethnic group in the country) and hence could identify themselves as "Jews" in an era in which the corporative identity had been weakened.

Beyond the abstract identification with an "imagined community" of subjects, the Haskalah was also a real-life social phenomenon in the sociological sense. The Maskilim of Eastern Europe generally formed small groups. Sometimes these were made up of a few people, one from a city or two from a town, who never met but corresponded with one another, subscribed to a newspaper that spread the message of the Haskalah, or sent memoranda to the authorities. For example, Joseph Perl in Galicia (under Austrian rule) and Isaac Baer Levinsohn (Ribal) submitted memoranda to the Austrian and Russian authorities, respectively, suggesting reforms of their coreligionists during the reign of Czar Nicholas I.[11] Sometimes the Maskilim founded groups that drew up a common platform or manifesto. However, these groups were far less cohesive than the Hasidic communities or the *hevrah* (a society that flourished at the time when the formal Jewish autonomy was declining). This lack of cohesion was part of the fragmentary, weak nature of the Haskalah movement. Hasidism became a mass movement in the first half of the nineteenth century with hundreds of thousands of believers throughout Eastern Europe; the Haskalah, although it had the distinct features of a movement, was until the mid-nineteenth century limited to several hundred supporters and sympathizers.

Every reader of history books has the impression that the Haskalah movement was the major stream that led to change in Jewish society. Present-day Orthodoxy reinforces this erroneous image and "blames" the Haskalah for nearly every change that occurred in Jewish society in the last two hundred years.[12] What changed Jewish society was the process of modernization; the Haskalah was not a cause but rather an effect of modernization. Moreover, the emergence of this movement was one possible response of Jewish society to the other processes of modernization: the decline of the feudal economy and the rise of capitalism; the dissolution of Jewish autonomy; the increased involvement of the centralized state in the internal life of the Jews; and immigration and urbanization. All these—not the Haskalah—undermined the foundations of traditional Jewish society. However, the enemies of the Haskalah and the Maskilim themselves, for opposite reasons, made the claim that the Haskalah was a hugely influential movement that engendered the transformations that occurred in Jewish society in the nineteenth century.

In what sense was the Haskalah in Eastern Europe one of the responses evoked in Jewish society by modernization, and not merely one of the many causes of this process? One could say that the Maskilim of Eastern Europe sought to protect Jewry from the drastic changes introduced in the modern era by accepting them in a controlled, moderate fashion. We have noted that the Maskilim did not want to see Jewish society disappear, nor did they aspire to bring about the disappearance of the Jews as individuals. Many of them regarded the rapid and uncontrolled acceptance of the processes of change as a danger to the future existence of Jewish identity.

What they wanted to do was to "reform" the Jews. The image of the future society that the Haskalah wanted to mold had been and remained a society of "reformed Jews," not one of "non-Jews" integrated into a universal society. If we take a broader view of what happened in Eastern Europe in the mid-nineteenth century, the Maskilim were not very different from the Orthodox, who hated them and whom they hated in return. The Orthodox, too, were seeking to continue the existence of Jewish society under the new conditions created by the breakdown of the traditional Jewish frameworks. The Maskilim took an "optimistic" approach—namely, that the political, social, and cultural changes linked to the appearance of the modern era seemed to be fundamentally good, and they proposed ways to partake of these changes while strictly adhering to those Jewish values worthy of preservation. The Orthodox made a similar claim but with a change of emphasis, and we will refer to that in the coming chapters. The Maskilim in Eastern Europe were, in a certain sense, the forefathers of all the major Jewish movements of conservatism of the end of the nineteenth and the beginning of the twentieth century. It is no coincidence that a straight line leads from the Haskalah to the beginning of modern Jewish nationalism (contrary to what you would read in the old type of Zionist historiography).[13] Jewish nationalism did not rebel against the Haskalah. Rather, it carried on the Haskalah's concepts and gave them a nationalist slant.

The conservative character of the Eastern European Haskalah did not protect it from the fierce opposition of those who were more conservative. As the movement began to gain a place for itself in Eastern European communities, the opposition of broad segments of the traditional society to its social and cultural activity heightened. To the members of the traditional society, the Maskilim seemed to be collaborating frequently with the imperial government. For example, when the Jews of Russia were obliged to serve in the military, by order of Czar Nicholas I, the Maskilim encouraged the conscription in their literary works and supported it for ideological reasons. The efforts of a Maskil from Kremenets in Volhynia, Isaac Baer Levinsohn (Ribal), to persuade the Russian government to supervise the printing of (Hebrew) books, or the sharply worded anti-Hasidic memoranda submitted to the Austrian authorities by the Galician Maskil Joseph Perl from Tarnopol, hardly evoked any affection for the Haskalah. The Maskilim were perceived as informers, and their actions were seen as a betrayal of the accepted social values. In addition, they were considered a serious threat to the religious world of the traditional society. The traditional leadership, the Hasidic *tzaddikim* as well as the Lithuanian scholarly elite, tended to accuse them of various halakhic and moral offenses and felt that the Haskalah showed signs of being a religious reform movement. They were less apprehensive about the Maskilim's social and political activity than they were about the religious dangers it concealed.

Although the Haskalah movement had a universal character, it also had local characteristics that differentiated between Maskilim in different areas of partitioned Poland. Earlier I referred to the Maskilim in Galicia, in Podolia, in Volhynia, and in Lithuania, all of whom adopted different means of disseminating the Maskilic message and putting it into practice. In the different areas, the processes of modernization that the Maskilim coped with moved at their own pace and had a unique nature stemming from the special conditions in each locale. The tactics employed by the Maskilim and the results they produced also differed. The attitude of the Maskilim toward Hasidism provides a telling example of the difference between one area and another. The Galician Haskalah, which was distinctly rationalistic in nature, placed an emphasis on its struggle against Hasidism. It is not surprising that the leading Maskilim in Galicia, the authors Joseph Perl and Isaac Erter, devoted a considerable portion of their writing to scathing parodies and satires of the Hasidic movement.[14] In this sense, the Haskalah in Lithuania had a totally disparate character. Although the Lithuanian Maskilim advocated a platform similar to that of the Galicians, their activity was not centered on vigorous opposition to Hasidism. Instead, they focused on the argument that the traditional Jewish society as a whole, not merely part of it, was deficient and in need of reform. In the Polish Haskalah, in the autonomous regions of Poland, there were diverse shades of opinion and different emphases.[15]

The position taken by Eastern European Maskilim on the issue of language was particularly innovative when it came to premodern Ashkenazi society. In Jewish communities in the Polish-Lithuanian kingdom, as elsewhere in the diaspora, a state of bilingualism (diglossia) prevailed until the modern era. The language of spiritual creativity, of the halakha, and religious ritual was the "holy tongue" (Hebrew in its various levels and Aramaic). The vernacular (the language of speech and everyday life) was Yiddish. The Haskalah movement, which simultaneously advocated the integration of the Jews into the state and the preservation of Jewish identity, was in favor of linguistic dualism, but it wanted to change the two elements in that dualism. On the one hand, it strove to revive biblical Hebrew, which the Maskilim viewed as part of the process of culturally reforming Jewish society. The revival of the biblical language and its expanded use in literary and scientific writing meant a return to the ancient cultural language, which had allegedly been corrupted by, among other factors, foreign languages such as Aramaic and the depletion of the rabbinical language in the Middle Ages.

On the other hand, the Jews were exhorted to learn the language of the state (the imperial language): Russian in Russia, Polish in autonomous Poland, and German in the Austrian kingdom.[16] The vernacular did not occupy a legitimate place in the Haskalah's linguistic vision of the future. Yiddish, the spoken language of Ashkenazi Jews, was regarded as a garbled dialect that bore witness to the miserable cultural state of its speakers. Nonetheless we find that the Haskalah movement did use, often against its declared will, the language that Maskilim had described as the greatest perversion of Jewish society, which was a sign of that society's deterioration. They even thought that the persistent use of Yiddish was a political act taken against the authorities of the centralized state. They averred that the Jewish dialect, the code language of the lowest class of Jews (who concealed their improper business dealings) and a language used by thieves and smugglers, had to be eradicated before adopting the use of the state language: German, Russian, or Polish, depending on the place and the ruling government. But if they wanted to speak to the broad Jewish population, the Maskilim could not address them in Hebrew or in the language of the state; Yiddish was the only possible language of communication with the lower social classes. Moreover, it was the language of speech and writing for Jewish women. And since it was impossible to avoid using Yiddish, the Maskilim wrote comedies, satirical poems, and even published newspapers containing articles on popular science in Yiddish. The Maskilim had no other choice but to use that despicable language to persuade the Jewish population to change its culture and to stop using that same despicable language. So the Maskilim became the sire of modern Yiddish literature, because they used that language in order to abolish its use.[17]

The Haskalah movement in Eastern Europe introduced a new dimension into communication. The Maskilim were the first to use the press as a channel for exchanging views and disseminating ideas. One of their major vehicles was a periodical they printed, which was distributed widely and published regularly, either as a monthly or a weekly. By the end of the eighteenth century, *Hame'asef*, the organ of the Berlin circle of Maskilim, had a readership in some of the large communities of Poland and Lithuania. In the following decades, a network of written communication spread over the territory of Eastern Europe, linking a readership in Jewish languages (Hebrew and Yiddish) and in the state languages (German, Russian, Polish). The regular readers of the Haskalah periodical became a supra-local community of Jews who shared the same ideas, literary taste, and ways of spending their leisure time. In their use of the press, the Maskilim were adopting a distinctly European means of communication but were also creating a tool that reinforced their readers' special Jewish ties. Their readers altered their traditional reading habits by moving from the canonical religious text (a page of Gemara, a book of ethics, or a kabbalistic-Hasidic text) to the pages of news, science, and literature columns, and poetry in the Maskilic newspaper.

The Jew in Lithuania or Galicia who underwent this kind of cultural transformation accepted, consciously or otherwise, the values of the bourgeois culture of Central Europe. He became a partner in the educational project of the German Enlightenment (*Bildung*) because of the reading material that the newspaper supplied him and the role that the new means of communication played in his social and cultural world. In the press, we can also see the great discrepancy between the Maskilim's aspiration to be counted among the loyal supporters of the centralized state, and the opposition of the state, or at least the indifference of its bureaucratic apparatus. In many cases, the government censor, either the Russian or the Austrian, was not eager to permit the Maskilim to publish a newspaper, particularly since they believed that a newspaper of this kind, Western in its character and adhering to liberal views, would cause political damage to the state. In Russia, some cases dragged on for years, in which various Maskilim (for example, the Maskilic circle of Vilna) repeatedly requested permission to publish a Maskilic paper. The authorities refused time and again, and the newspaper was never published. In the end, a large part of the Maskilic propaganda that they hoped to disseminate through the press reached its readers through literary works or various other types of writing. In the absence of a government license to publish a newspaper, printed books served as an alternative form of written communication.[18]

Haskalah literature in Hebrew, Yiddish, and in the state language was strongly linked to the movement's social and political aims. Many Maskilim thought of literature principally as a tool, rather than as a form that had an aesthetic, cultural value in itself. A large part of the poetry and prose of the Haskalah can be defined as militant literature. It engaged in depicting the flaws in traditional Jewish society, sometimes by exaggerating them in a grotesque manner.[19] Several Maskilim writers adopted another method, that of presenting ideal, rather naive, models of a future Maskilic society, one that had never existed in reality.[20] Paradoxically, it was the Maskilic caricatures, those distorted, ludicrous depictions of traditional Jewish society, so desperately in need of thoroughgoing reform and supposedly crying out to adopt the European model, that have provided us with invaluable historical material. How to explain this amazing fact? The Maskilim's interest in documenting everything, even in a caricatural, distorted manner, led them to obsessively collect ethnographic material on the Eastern European society they aspired to change. As a result, historians researching Hasidism, Lithuanian scholarship, or other economic and social phenomena in Eastern European Jewish society rely on the Maskilim's documentation.[21] Of course, they constantly endeavor to separate the exaggerated and distorted part from the factual part. In this ethnographic obsession of the Haskalah, as in the case of the use of Yiddish, there was clearly an element of nurturing an alternative identity. Without intending this from the outset, the Maskilim in Eastern European communities contributed to the documentation of the traditional world of customs, which they so greatly desired to eradicate. From a cultural and social standpoint, the Maskilim, using innovative tools, preserved the collective heritage. In this sense, they were the first shapers of a new national identity in Eastern Europe.

Chapter 9

"The Days of Springtime": Czar Alexander II and the Era of Reform

When Czar Alexander II ascended to the throne, Eastern European Jewish society, especially in the Russian empire, was transformed. Alexander's reign began with the death of Czar Nicholas I, inscribed in the history of Russian Jewry as a hater of Jews who issued oppressive decrees affecting the Jewish people. The Russian government's policy on the Jewish question was not directly related to the young czar's attitude toward the Jews. The changes that the new ruler made affecting the status of Jews stemmed primarily from the wide-ranging changes he wrought in his predecessor's methods of governance. The new czar was crowned in the last days of the Crimean war, in which the Russian empire had been embroiled from 1853 to 1856. This war, fought on the southern frontiers of the country, exposed the great weaknesses of the Eastern European power and its economic inferiority and affected the empire's political status and military power. The reform introduced in the wake of the war was intended to narrow the gap between Russia and the European powers. The influence of Western political, organizational, and economic models grew stronger, heralding a great shift in the history of the Russian empire and the short history of Russian Jewry in the modern age. The changes in Jewish society during Alexander's reign (1855–81) were connected to the processes that had begun in Jewish society even earlier, which we referred to in previous chapters, as well as to surprising new developments relating to the Jews of the empire during this period.

In the first years of Alexander II's reign, far-reaching reforms that centered on the abolition of serfdom were introduced. The peasants in Russia, the largest social class in the state, were now freed from the shackles of serfdom and the feudal system was abolished. Moreover, many appreciable changes affecting the relations between subject and government and concerning local and regional government were introduced. Another significant development was the radical shift in the economy: the Russian empire shifted rapidly from a primarily agricultural feudal economy, a monopolistic centralized system, to an era of capitalism and industrialization. These changes, not introduced specifically for the Jewish population, nevertheless had a dramatic effect on Eastern European Jewish society, since in the first half of the nineteenth century, a considerable proportion of the Jews were still linked to the feudal estate economy. Hundreds of thousands of Jews earned their livelihood from the old leasehold system, in various areas of manufacture in the villages. The Jewish shtetl, established as part of the estate economy, depended on the feudal system that existed until 1861. The abolition of serfdom demolished the economic foundation for the maintenance of the traditional way of life in the Pale of Settlement. Thousands, perhaps even hundreds of thousands, were uprooted from the estate economy and forced to seek new sources of livelihood. This swift upheaval led to a thoroughgoing reshuffling of Jewish society.

The administrative changes also eroded the last vestiges of Jewish autonomy, which had been formally abolished in 1844 by Czar Nicholas I's ukase annulling the *kahal*. Now the Jews became much more integrated into the systems of the Russian administration, which hastened the entry of many Jews into various academic, professional, and economic fields throughout the empire and made them independent of the internal forces of Jewish society.

The rise of the capitalist economy and the growth of modern industry had an impact on all these changes. Jews who had been ejected from the crumbling feudal estate economy but were independent of the local Jewish community and could move freely found their place in the new economic systems. For the first time in the modern history of Eastern European Jewry, a Jewish proletariat—namely, a Jewish working class of wage earners in various types of industrial plants in the Pale of Settlement—was evolving. In parallel, a new class of Jewish bourgeoisie was taking shape and taking an active part in the economic spheres now opening to Jews in Russia with the rise of capitalism. Significant changes also included specific reforms intended only for the Jews, which we will discuss in the following pages.

The momentum of the reforms was halted in the second half of the 1860s. The 1863 Polish uprising aroused the fear that too-radical reforms might encourage the rise of national movements among the peoples of the empire and revive separatist tendencies, namely, demands by national ethnic groups for separation from the Russian empire. At the same time, the Russian government continued its vigorous policy of imposing imperial Russian culture on the western areas. The Russian educational system was greatly expanded, and the use of local languages was restricted. The Jews were regarded as a useful element in spreading Russian culture to the western regions, so the local administration adopted a sympathetic attitude toward them. Still, the situation in relation to the Jews was problematic because at the time, the implementation of reform had been halted. The reforms introduced at the end of the 1850s and the early 1860s intended specifically for the Jews enabled several select groups of Jews to leave the Pale of Settlement and become integrated into economic life in all parts of the Russian empire; but the cessation of the reforms halted the process when the majority of the Jews were still in their old situation, namely, unchanged from the situation that existed in the 1840 and 1850s.

Most of the government's reforms relating to the status of the Jews stemmed from the desire to encourage economic activity that would be beneficial to the Russian economy or from the intention to use the Jewish population to disseminate Russian culture. Those capable of contributing to the growth of a modern financial economy, of establishing industrial plants and introducing modern methods of production, were regarded as beneficial from an economic standpoint. For this reason, the Russian legislator focused on several select groups and enabled only them to emigrate from the western provinces. Typical Jewish occupations, such as retail commerce, peddling, or the traditional trades (shoemaking, tailoring) were not thought worthy of encouragement. Hence, most Jews in the Pale of Settlement remained in their previous state, unable to leave the crowded, poor areas of the western empire.

One of the most significant changes wrought by the reforms specific to the Jews was the abrogation of restriction to the Pale of Settlement for the Jewish economic elite. Jews belonging to the upper class of merchants, members of the first guild—namely, people with a very high income of more than 50,000 rubles a year—were exempted by law on April 3, 1859, from all the restrictions and could settle as they pleased in all parts of the empire. This change was introduced by the government out of its desire to encourage the commercial and financial activity of wealthy Jews. Another reform linked to the government's desire to encourage Jews regarded as beneficial was the granting of rights of residence in all parts of the empire to graduates of the Russian educational system. Although in 1804, Russian educational institutions, from elementary school to university, had been opened to Jews, it was only now, nearly sixty years after the reforms of Alexander I, that education became a preeminent economic factor in Jewish society. This is the wording of the November 27, 1861, law: "Jews possessing certificates of the learned degree of Doctor of Medicine and Surgery, or Doctor of Medicine, and likewise of Doctor, Magister, or Candidate of other university faculties, are admitted to serve in all government offices, without their being confined to the Pale established for the residence of Jews.

They are also permitted to settle permanently in all the provinces of the Empire for the pursuit of commerce and industry."[1]

This meant that Jews holding academic degrees were also exempt from the restrictions of the Pale of Settlement and could reside wherever they pleased in the Russian empire. This created great demand on the part of Jews to receive secondary and higher education. Many students streamed to the institutions of learning, motivated by the desire to advance economically. Within a few years, the Jews, from being a small minority within the student body in these institutions, became a group whose numbers were far out of proportion to their percentage in the general population. While they constituted less than 4 percent of the inhabitants of imperial Russia, in 1880 they formed about 6.8 percent of all university students. In the Russian secondary schools at the time, 11.5 percent of the students were Jewish.[2] It was not the government decrees that led the Jews to flock to Russian schools; they had done very little during Nicholas I's reign to draw the Jews any closer to Russian culture by coercive means. Rather, it was the economic opportunities made available through the school system and institutions of higher learning. This showed that Jewish society changed more rapidly when the government did not try to coerce it into doing so, but was more forthcoming and offered them economic benefits.

Another reform linked to the Russian government's aspiration to make the Jews more economically effective freed Jews in preferred occupations from the restrictions of the Pale of Settlement. A new law (June 28, 1865) stated that Jews who were certain types of artisans—technicians, mechanics, and, among others, experts in the manufacture of alcoholic beverages—could also reside anywhere in the Russian empire. Many Jews took advantage of these exemptions, and other Jews began to acquire certificates confirming that they were engaged in these sought-after occupations. This was because the legislator worded the law as follows: "Anyone wishing to use this permit must produce a certificate affirming his rank as an artisan or an apprentice from one of the cities in order to obtain a passport . . . or certificates from owners of factories and industries approved by the Police, in whose plants they have learned or been employed in this profession, attesting to their professional ability."[3]

In Russia in the second half of the nineteenth and the early twentieth century, Jewish literature depicted characters who were not necessarily engaged in these occupations but had managed to acquire documents certifying that they were tradesmen or artisans. In this way, many Jews were able to settle outside the boundaries of the Pale.

The reforms of the 1850s and early 1860s led to the formation of a significant class of Jews who had left the Pale of Settlement and settled in the large and medium-size cities of the Russian empire. The members of this group, about 60,000 Jews, spoke Russian instead of Yiddish and adopted the lifestyle of the non-Jewish bourgeoisie. Although this class represented a minute percentage of the millions of Eastern European Jews, it was the most modern, most "European" sector of Jewish society in the Russian empire. From its ranks came Jewish scientists, writers in the Russian language, political activists in various Russian movements, and later, the founders of the modern Jewish nationalist movement, who emerged not from the traditional society in the Pale of Settlement but from the new Jewish bourgeoisie or the new Jewish intelligentsia that sprang up alongside it.[4]

The reform in the law of military conscription engendered another important change in the status of the Jews. During the reign of Nicholas I, the law required the Jews to provide a quota of *cantonists*, namely, boys from the age of twelve for pre-military education. In addition, a double quota of eighteen-year-old men for twenty-five years of military service was imposed on the Jewish communities. Alexander II abolished that harsh, terrifying decree by applying the same rules of conscription to the entire population, including the Jews. From 1874, the Jews would serve like all others, for a few years. They would be drafted in the framework of a universal system of conscription and would no longer be victims of the relentless Jewish apparatus that had abducted children and young men to fill the special quota imposed on the Jews.

Jewish society viewed the days of Alexander II's reforms as a springtime. The Maskilim, who believed their greatest aspirations were being realized, were overjoyed to see the government of the merciful czar doing its best to improve the lot of its Jewish subjects. To them, it was clear and unambiguous: the great moment had arrived when Russia was becoming an enlightened Western state in which the Jews would be loyal, desirable citizens.[5] This is what the poet Judah Leib Gordon, an ardent Maskil and great Russian patriot, wrote in 1864:

And now there is no city nor any province where the young men of Israel cannot draw cold, flowing waters, defiantly and without shame. You will find thousands in the secondary schools, hundreds in the universities, and scores of specialist physicians in government service! . . . How many of our young men will you now find wielding the pen of an author, fluently speaking the language of the land or German and French, and all of them of this new generation, creations of the last decade; how many noble, wealthy Jews will you find now regarded as dignitaries by the government, Jews in their hearts, but in their appearance, clothing, and manners—like Europeans. Now we can remain calm and rely upon the Almighty, for there is great hope for our future.[6]

The Maskilim were not the only ones to feel this way. Many members of the traditional society at first regarded these reforms favorably, believing that they were a clear sign that the new reign would be merciful. However, when the processes of change began to intensify in the traditional milieu, as we shall see later, they began to sense the threat of tolerance and the dangers posed by the openness of the surrounding society toward the Jews. The world of traditional Jewish society and its values now had to compete freely with the temptations of a foreign culture that also offered attractive social and economic change. This new openness, which seemed to be part of the move toward full emancipation in the future, hastened the dissolution of the old frameworks. It gave rise to an unfamiliar cultural reality that was developing at a rapid pace and prompting a momentum of acculturation, which decades of ukases by the previous czarist rule had been unable to achieve. It is not surprising that the cultural threat to traditional values provoked a strong Orthodox reaction in the first decade of Alexander II's reign.

An example of the far-reaching cultural change that these reforms engendered in Russian Jewish society, one noted with regard to the Haskalah, was the development of a modern network of communication in the form of the Jewish press. The press is a modern phenomenon that developed in the centers of the capitalist economy emerging in the large European cities, and the Jewish press developed in a similar context: commercial newspapers that were published in Amsterdam, as far back as the late seventeenth century. This new medium of communication supplanted traditional forms of writing and existed outside the old social frameworks. It was one of the major forms of expression for the Maskilim of Germany. In the 1780s, the periodical *Hame'asef*, which disseminated the message of the Haskalah movement in Central Europe, had many subscribers in Jewish societies in Eastern Europe. In the early nineteenth century, the Maskilim in Galicia also spread their message in German in the Bohemian periodical *Sulamith* and in Hebrew in *Bikurei ha'itim*, which were published in Central Europe.

. The press, then, was one of the major modes to give expression to modernization in Ashkenazi Jewish society. It was an appropriate vehicle for this purpose, owing to its ideological content and because it was a modern phenomenon from a social standpoint and disseminated new forms of writing. The Jewish press addressed a new type of readership. These were readers who spent their leisure time differently from the religiously observant reader of the old community. Alexander II's reforms considerably reduced the strict censorship that had been in force during his predecessor's reign. It became possible to establish Jewish periodicals in various languages, designed to meet the new cultural needs of a changing society. The changes introduced in the press in the Russian empire after 1856 can serve as a mini-sample of every social and cultural development in Jewish society in general. Within a few years, Jewish newspapers began to appear in three languages: in Hebrew, the sacred language that became a modern language of culture; in Yiddish, the spoken language of millions; and in Russian, the language of the state.

The Hebrew newspaper during Alexander II's reign was a direct continuation of the earlier periodicals of the Haskalah movement, but it was marked by the intensified secular use of the language of the Holy Scriptures. The newspaper *Hamelitz*, edited and published by Alexander Zederbaum, which first came out in Odessa in 1860 and then moved to Saint Petersburg, was the most prominent Hebrew newspaper published in the Russian empire for several decades. Introducing itself to its readers as an intermediary between the Jews of Russia and their government, it was the mouthpiece of a Maskilic readership and later was used by modern Eastern European Jewish nationalism to convey its messages. In the following years, Hebrew newspapers appeared in Vilna, Warsaw, and Saint Petersburg.

Another newspaper, although it was published across the border, was an inseparable part of the new system of communication in the Russian empire: *Hamaggid*, which began to appear in 1856 in Lyck, on the border between eastern Prussia and Russia, but was addressed to readers on the Russian side. Readers of *Hamelitz* and *Hamaggid* received international news, only a few days old, editorials of political commentary, articles on science, and Jewish material written specifically for the paper or copied from Jewish publications abroad. The modern secular use of Hebrew was now widespread and accepted. In addition, the horizon of culture and Jewish consciousness was expanded to include material from the outside, since the Hebrew newspapers translated a considerable amount of material from the general press—in particular, the German and the Russian—and provided it to the Jewish reader who was not fluent in foreign languages. The Hebrew newspapers were also a forum for ideological debates between various streams, and turned controversies of a local character into matters of nationwide interest. The conflict between Hasidim and Maskilim, conservatives and modernists, moderate Maskilim and radical Maskilim was largely waged on the pages of the Hebrew press.

The second language in which the new press began to appear was Yiddish. We have discussed the attitude of the members of the Haskalah movement toward Yiddish: from the second half of the eighteenth century, they regarded it as a flawed, degenerate language that ought to be banished from Jewish culture.[7] But in the absence of any other linguistic means of influencing the lower classes and disseminating their ideas, the Maskilim realized that they had to turn to Yiddish. So, while clearly demonstrating their disinclination to use that language, they wrote in it—Maskilic comedies, anti-Hasidic satires, biting humorous poems—

sometimes preferring to remain anonymous. In Russia during Alexander II's reign, Yiddish was still the major, if not the sole, language in which the new cultural elite could communicate with the masses of Jewish society.

In the early 1860s, Alexander Zederbaum, publisher and editor of *Hamelitz*, began to publish a newspaper in Yiddish, *Kol mevasser*. This newspaper was a consummate Maskilic organ intended to educate the Jewish masses and to disseminate knowledge, in keeping with the spirit and taste of the Maskilim. It contained popular scientific articles in Yiddish (for example, on electricity) and editorials advocating social and economic change in the spirit of the Haskalah. And it was in *Kol mevasser* that modern Yiddish literature began to evolve, intended primarily to criticize the flaws and foibles of traditional society and to suggest solutions for its problems. A distinguished list of writers began their writing careers in modern Yiddish literature by publishing their work in *Kol mevasser*. Shalom Yaakov Abramovitch, better known by his Yiddish pen name, Mendele Moykher Sforim, published his Maskilic writings in that paper, as did Abraham Baer Gottlober, Judah Leib Gordon (the great Hebrew poet of the Haskalah who despised Yiddish)[8] and Isaac Joel Linetzky. The Yiddish press was not only an incubator for new literature in the language of the common people; it also filled an important cultural function by cultivating modern reading habits among Yiddish speakers.[9]

The appearance of a Jewish press in Russian, the imperial language, marked a more significant phase in the processes of acculturation. It was the realization of a pivotal Maskilic aim: acquisition of the language of the state. Here, as in the case of Hebrew and Yiddish, Odessa was first, and Jewish newspapers in Russian began to appear in that commercial and multicultural city on the shores of the Black Sea. Many Jews in Odessa had gained fluency in Russian even before the reforms of Alexander II, and the city had a Jewish intelligentsia who regarded themselves as part of the Russian cultural world and tried to disseminate their pro-Russian views. From 1860 on, a wide variety of Jewish newspapers began to appear in Russian—dailies, weeklies, and monthlies. They had a politically liberal orientation and also addressed Jewish cultural issues and printed the literary works of Jews who were beginning to write in Russian. This press gave explicit expression to the way in which the Jewish bourgeoisie, created in the era of Alexander II's reforms, wished to integrate into Russian culture, and also dealt with the issue of political rights.

In these newspapers, there were the first manifestations of the *Wissenschaft* in the Russian language, namely, scientific-scholarly writing on Jewish history, literature, and culture. All the members of the *Wissen-*

schaft in Russia, including the historians Elijah Orshanski and Simon Dubnow, began their careers by publishing scientific or popular articles in the Russian press. The major political issues that concerned the Russian Jewish intelligentsia were discussed on the pages of these newspapers. For example, the 1863 Polish uprising against the Russians aroused a debate that lasted several years (parallel to a similar debate in *Hamaggid* that led its editor, David Gordon, to write an essay in the spirit of Jewish nationalism, entitled "In Peace and Tranquillity Shall You Be Redeemed.")[10] The question of whom the Jews should support—the Russians or the Poles—was discussed in a distinctly pro-Russian spirit.

A high point of the debate was the serial publication of a novel in Russian entitled *Hot Times*, by the Vilna writer Lev Levanda, in the periodical *Evreiskaia biblioteka* (1871–73). Its message to readers in the Pale of Settlement was that it was politically expedient to identify with the Russian state rather than to support the aspirations of the Polish nationalist movement. Levanda was well versed in Polish literature and reacted to it in his writing in Russian in the Jewish press.[11] Later, he became a founder of the Hibbat Zion movement. In the 1860s and 1870s, Leon Pinsker, known mainly for his work *Auto-emancipation*, written in the wake of the 1881–82 pogroms, contributed regularly to the Jewish press in Russian and wrote many ardent pro-Russian articles.[12]

The Russian Jewish press introduced Jewish society to its non-Jewish readership and revealed unfamiliar sides of its culture to them. The dialogue between the Jewish and the non-Jewish press often took on an acerbic, brash tone. The Jewish press in Russia was active on a two-pronged front. From one direction, it reacted to what was written in the liberal wing that aspired to the massive integration of the Jews. On the other side, it had to cope with the anti-Semitic writings that grew more numerous and more strident in the 1870s, and to come to the defense of Jewish society that was severely attacked from time to time.

The growth of a Jewish press was an expression of the significant change that took place in Jewish society in the Russian empire in the 1860s. The social and economic changes also left their mark on culture and communications. New, unprecedented reading habits and modes of organization reflected the new social map that supplanted the old order. The newspaper filled the place of the federative organizations that had existed in the premodern society and strengthened corporative ties that had been undermined. It was an alternative point of identification whose geographical distribution enabled widely separated Jews to feel nearer to one another.

The Jewish press also played a role in creating public opinion, which altered the political and cultural power play within Jewish society in all respects. It was no coincidence that the traditionalists, who wanted to preserve the old values, recognized the influence of the new medium and adopted it as another device in the campaign that they were waging to defend their world. In the early 1860s, Rabbi Israel Salanter began to publish a halakhic journal called *Tevunah*, in the city of Königsberg.[13] A few years later, the Orthodox circle that had formed in Lithuania began using the newspaper *Halevanon* in their struggle against the Maskilim.

In the coming decades, the press would play a key role in the politicization of Eastern European Jewish society and in the formation of mass movements based on a wide range of differing and competing ideological platforms. These developments began, albeit in an embryonic form, with the first appearance of *Hamelitz, Kol mevasser,* and *Sion* in Odessa. The large-scale, widely circulated Jewish press of the twentieth century is a direct outgrowth of the means of Jewish communication that began during the era of reform in the Russian empire.

Chapter 10

Between Two Extremes: Radicalism and Orthodoxy

The era of reform wrought many changes in the Jewish society of the Russian empire. One of the most striking was the creation of a new social class, previously unknown in Eastern Europe: a Jewish proletariat. The emergence of a Jewish working class gave rise to social, political, and cultural developments that left a significant imprint on the Jewish world for many decades. The large political streams of the early twentieth century (including Jewish labor parties and socialist Zionism), literary works in Hebrew and Yiddish, and radical-national historical scholarship all had roots in the change engendered by the proletarization of Eastern European Jewry. In addition, an influential branch of modern Jewish cultural discourse developed in the radical-messianic environment that emerged from within this new, unprecedented socioeconomic stratum in Eastern European Jewish society. Radical secularization and an obsessive aspiration to reform the world, which until then had been the hallmark of a small number of Jewish intellectuals in Germany, now characterized circles, movements, and political parties in Eastern Europe. However, as the American Jewish literary scholar David Roskies wrote, "It required great homiletic skill to recast the concepts of surplus value, class conflict, and alienation of labor into recognizably Jewish terms."[1]

By 1880, the traditional Jewish language of symbols had been absorbed into the revolutionary-partisan vocabulary of the Russian opposition intelligentsia. The left-wing (or liberal, in American parlance) Jewish discourse was part of the political message of the future brought to the United States and Palestine by Eastern European immigrants. Some then (and still do today) regarded this discourse as the greatest internal enemy of the Jewish people, one that undermines the foundations of Jewish society, weakens its resilience, and cuts it off from the tradition.

I have mentioned that masses of Jews were ejected from the estate and town economy that rapidly crumbled with the abolition of serfdom in

1861 and the results of the 1863 Polish uprising. These were the residents of towns and villages whose families had been linked to the feudal economy for hundreds of years (many generations before the Polish kingdom lost its political independence) and had engaged in various trades, all connected with the peasants, farm produce, and forestry products. These Jews now had no means of livelihood and were forced to integrate into economic systems that began to spring up in Russia with the rise of modern industry and the development of the capitalist economy from the 1860s.

In the first half of the nineteenth century, an average Jewish family was still linked to some leasehold, to the assets, or to the estate of a Polish noble in a town in the Pale of Settlement. By the 1850s, that family often lost its association with the estate economy. In the 1860s and 1870s, the sons of that family scattered in all directions, some immigrating to cities such as Kiev, Odessa, or Warsaw, some moving to medium-size towns that had become, in the wake of the economic change, large cities, such as Berdichev in Ukraine. Later they turned westward and settled in London, New York, or Philadelphia. That was the story of hundreds of thousands of men and women from Eastern European Jewish society, who within less than two generations, from the middle of the century to its end, lost their traditional economic infrastructure. Those same hundreds of thousands, propelled by financial distress, moved to the big cities or traveled across the sea, also to the big cities. Those whose economic situation worsened became part of the proletarian class and made their living as wage earners in the factories and workshops that sprang up during the industrial revolution in the cities of Eastern Europe and to the west, as well as in the cities on the East Coast of the United States.

This change in Eastern Europe began earlier, as we saw in previous chapters, during the reign of Alexander I. Industrial plants producing textiles, metal, and foodstuffs were established mainly in the Polish districts of the Russian empire decades before the flourishing of industry in Ukraine and White Russia.[2] Jewish entrepreneurs played an important role in establishing factories in Warsaw, Lodz, and Białystok, and in these cities there were already Jewish factory workers. However, the massive industrialization was stepped up in the 1860s and 1870s. This socioeconomic upheaval was not peculiar to the Jews. The proletarization of premodern society was an indivisible part of the industrial revolution that began in Europe in the second half of the eighteenth century and intensified in the nineteenth century.

What were the unique features of the proletarization of Eastern European Jewry? First, in the society in general, this process affected peasants who had become hired workers in factories. In the case of the Jews, those affected were not liberated serfs but leaseholders or tradesmen, shop-keepers, and peddlers from the town who were reduced to the proletarian class. Consequently, the social decline among the Jews seemed much more significant economically and from the standpoint of class consciousness. The Jews, historically tied to the city and its culture, even when they became propertyless daily workers, revealed a great capacity for social mobility. They moved with relative ease from one economic class to another, which may explain why the Jewish proletariat did not remain in existence for more than one or two generations, whenever conditions enabled them to rise on the economic ladder.

Another feature typical of Jewish workers was their tendency to concentrate in certain fields. This was true not only of the Eastern European Jewish proletariat but also of Jewish immigrants, particularly to the United States. Polish or Ukrainian peasants, who moved from the village to join the ranks of the urban working class, either in the cities of the Russian empire or the industrial areas of Pennsylvania, earned their living primarily in heavy industry—steel mills and metal-product plants. In contrast, the Jews, for various reasons, worked primarily in the "light" industries—food plants, textile factories, or sewing workshops, and in the manufacture of ready-to-wear clothing. The textile industry, historically a major component of the industrial revolution, attracted thousands of Jewish workers—men and women—in the Russian empire as well as in the crowded sweatshops of New York's poorer neighborhoods. In the 1860s and 1870s, a Jewish working class emerged in various fields: in the big cities where a large textile industry developed, such as Białystok in the northeastern district of Poland or Lodz west of Warsaw; in the food industry—for example, in the sugar plants of the Brodskii family in Kiev; or in the cigarette factories in Vilna.[3]

The reason Jews concentrated in the textile industry may be that many of that factories were established by Jewish entrepreneurs in cities where there was already a large Jewish population, or perhaps because tailoring, shoemaking, furmaking, and other branches of clothing and shoe manufacture were popular occupations in Jewish society on the eve of the industrial revolution. In the early stages of these industries, artisans worked in small shops, often bringing their tools with them, and later women brought their sewing machines to their place of work. The transition to mechanized mass production adversely affected Jewish artisans who worked in their own workshops, forcing many of them to abandon traditional means of production and seek their livelihood in the new workshops and factories.

There was another side to the proletarization of Jewish society, which we have described in an earlier chapter: the emergence of a Jewish bourgeois class. From the other end of the new social map in Eastern Europe, a class of Jewish capitalists began to coalesce: entrepreneurs, builders of industrial plants, bankers, and merchants. This phenomenon, like the emergence of the proletariat, did not commence in the period of Alexander II's reforms; but during those years, its pace greatly accelerated and its dimensions greatly expanded. Until the abolition of serfdom in the Russian empire, a Jewish entrepreneur would have had a hard time establishing an industrial plant because he was dependent on the nobility that owned the land and controlled the supply of raw material (lumber, iron, and coal mines), the sources of energy (rivers, coal), and the labor force (the serfs).

Indeed, the inception of Jewish industrial entrepreneurship in Eastern Europe was linked to various types of partnership between a Jewish entrepreneur, who raised the capital, and a Polish nobleman, who supplied all the rest. When the economic restrictions of the feudal system were lifted, new opportunities opened to Jewish entrepreneurs, and they began to initiate the establishment of various enterprises, particularly in the food and textile industries. The Brodskii family founded plants for the manufacture of sugar, and the Wissotsky family specialized in marketing tea throughout the empire. Moreover, Jewish entrepreneurs entered new fields not yet taken over by more well-established capitalists.

The role played by Jews in building railway lines is worthy of special mention. The railway, which clearly signaled the penetration of the industrial revolution into the Russian empire following the reforms, connected the centers of industry to markets and drastically shortened distances. The traditional fairs lost their economic value, and the appearance of the new means of transportation made various fields redundant. In his poem "Kotzo shel yud" (The tip of the yud), written in 1875,[4] Judah Leib Gordon, the Vilna poet of the Haskalah, attested to the enormous impact of the railway on Jewish occupations in the sixties. The wealthy father of the poem's heroine, Bat Shua, loses his livelihood when the railway line is laid in the Vilna district, while her lover supervises the construction of the line and later becomes an independent contractor in this field. This is how the poet describes the economic and social upheaval wrought by the laying of the railway and telegraph lines in Vilna in the 1860s:

In those days R. Hefer, the rich father, saw
the great hand that humbles the haughty and high,
. . . a fiery chariot and horses of fire
flying past with a fearful noise of alarm.
Not since Elijah was such a thing heard,
raised up in a storm on a wind from the east.
By their side in the wind is a chaotic line,

which carries the sound, speeds missives along.
And in a chariot of fire the passersby speed;
these pathways of doom were laid all round the town
although to Ayalon [Vilna] they had not yet come near.
But the steeds have all gone, and the king's royal stud,
and with each passing day the horse riders abate.
Day by day Hefer dwindles; his purse grows more thin,
the stables deserted, the horses all sold,
the travelers' fares gone with the price of the feed.
Four horses alone remain in the stable
in time of old age to give bread in a pinch.[5]

The rise of the capitalist economy in Russia led to the development of banking and the flourishing of stock exchanges in the big cities of the Russian empire. From the 1860s on, many Jews were active in finance, in banking and in the exchange. The Kiev stock exchange is immortalized in *Menahem Mendel*, a work by Sholem Aleichem (Shalom Rabinowitz, 1859–1916).[6] The stock exchange of Yehupetz (the fictional name of Kiev, the big city to which the town Jew travels) is a caricature of the Kiev exchange in the 1880s and 1890s; and the author himself invested a large sum on the stock exchange that he had inherited from his father-in-law—and went bankrupt in the early 1890s. The author's biography, as well as the ups and downs in the fortune of his protagonist, are linked to an economic feature of contemporary Jewish society: the decline of the shtetl economy and the entrance of Jewish emigrants, uprooted from the town, into the city, into the heart of the new financial economy. Jews played a leading role in the activity of stock exchanges in the commercial and financial centers of the empire. In Odessa, the large port city that attracted thousands of Jewish immigrants from the rapidly declining shtetls in the northern part of the Pale of Settlement, Jewish investors were actively involved in the grain exchange. During its early years (when it was published in Odessa), *Hamelitz*, a Hebrew organ of the Haskalah movement, printed the rates of the grain exchange.

In Odessa, which was the major port for the export of grain crops of Ukraine, the economic initiatives of Jewish immigrants were coupled with the social and political aspirations of the Haskalah movement.[7] But at the very time when a class of wealthy capitalists was emerging in the city, masses of Jews lived in crowded, appalling conditions in the slums of Odessa. Violence, crime, and prostitution in these poor neighborhoods existed in stark, bitter contrast to the wealth and opulence of the homes of the entrepreneurs and financiers.

The polarity between a Jewish proletariat and a rising Jewish bourgeoisie was part of the great socioeconomic change that broke down the traditional frameworks of life in Eastern Europe, which were overturned by the thriving capitalist economy. In these new conditions, socioeconomic mobility enabled capable, energetic financial entrepreneurs to rise within a few years from poverty and anonymity in traditional Jewish society to great wealth and political and economic influence. The traditional elites underwent a complete reshuffling; the prestige of the Eastern European rabbinate declined drastically in the second half of the nineteenth century. The scale of values from the far-off days of the Polish-Lithuanian kingdom, according to which family lineage, wealth, and talmudic scholarship went hand in hand, lost its place in Jewish society. By listening again to Gordon's description of the upheavals of the 1860s in his poem "Kotzo shel yud," we get a sharply focused picture of the change. The rich Jew of the old generation, who loses much of his wealth but adheres to the values of traditional society, marries his daughter to a scholar well versed in the Talmud. He supports the young couple for three years, in keeping with the traditional custom. But in view of the economic changes in the Russian empire, the propertyless scholar is unable to support his family because

What can a talmudic scholar do who lacks general knowledge?
He cannot be a tax collector without knowing the state language.[8]

Hence the penniless scholar follows the route taken by thousands like him: he goes overseas (to England, the heart of the industrial revolution) and earns his living as an itinerant peddler.

One of the most important developments in the social history of Eastern European Jewry in general, and in the Russian empire in particular, was the appearance of radical political movements that grappled with the social and economic changes I have just described. At first, the political movements that proposed solutions for the problems of the Jewish proletariat linked the political salvation of the Jews in the Russian empire—namely, the granting of equal rights—to an improvement in their economic situation.

In other words, the early Jewish socialists assumed that the specific problems of Jewish workers would automatically be solved if and when an overall political change occurred in the Russian regime. Historically, the major radical-political activity of Eastern European Jews belongs to a period later than the years we are speaking of, but Jewish political radicalism relating to the Jewish proletariat began in the last years of Alexander II's reign. This activity was carried out primarily by Jewish intellectuals who were concerned by the appalling living conditions of Jewish workers in Vilna and other Lithuanian cities. The process of radicalization that the Haskalah movement underwent in the 1870s was one

reason for the relationship that developed between groups of this intelligentsia and the working class. The Maskilim began to adopt a more critical, hostile attitude toward the Russian government. Moreover, the
younger Maskilim, who had been exposed to the Russian political literature of the 1860s, imbibed ideas, modes of thought, and political concepts from the oppositional wing of the Russian intelligentsia. This was
yet another manifestation of the acculturation of Jews to the imperial
culture. These Maskilim, as well as Jewish students who had had no connection with the Haskalah and its literature, developed the sense of duty
toward the toiling masses that was central to Russian revolutionary movements at the time. These young men directed a considerable part of
their dissatisfaction toward the Haskalah movement itself, which in their
view was outdated, too traditional, and had no relevance to the real
problems of the Jewish masses. Some of them were in touch with Russian
or Ukrainian revolutionaries and adopted the idea that Russia's conver-
sion into an industrialized capitalist society had to be halted. They internalized the idealized image of the exploited peasant and believed in the
establishment of a utopian-cooperative society of peasants and artisans
(agrarian socialism). In the revolutionary movements that Jews wanted
to join, they came up against the grim fact that the Russian and Ukrainian revolutionaries refused to consider the possibility of a Jewish proletariat, since they identified the Jews as one specific social class. It was
from this ideological tension—between willingly relinquishing any link
to the specific problems of Jewish workers and recognizing the need to
deal with the proletariat of their own people—that the first buds of "Jewish socialism" grew.

A particularly intriguing figure, a man several decades ahead of his
time insofar as the development of Jewish radicalism, was the author and
political thinker Aaron Samuel Liberman (1843–80), who was known as
the "first Hebrew socialist."[9] He began his intellectual career as a Maskil
in Lithuania in the 1860s and, like other Maskilim during the "days of
springtime," he lauded the reforms of Alexander II. In the early 1870s,
influenced by the radical streams of the Russian revolutionary movement, Liberman adopted a distinctly socialist position, and from the
mid-1870s began to publish his views in the Maskilic press in Eastern
Europe, including in *Hashahar*, Peretz Smolenskin's monthly. He took a
strong interest in the appalling economic conditions of Jewish workers
in Vilna and other Lithuanian towns and reflected on the need to make
them aware that they were an exploited class and ought to take their
destiny into their own hands. As a result of his political activity, Liberman was in constant danger and, fearing the czarist police, was forced
to leave the Russian empire. He moved to London, where he met up
with a circle of Russian and Ukrainian socialists whom he joined in pub-

lishing a revolutionary Russian-language newspaper, to which he contributed articles about the Jewish proletariat in the Pale of Settlement.

At the same time, Liberman sought ways to bring the message of socialism to his own people, so after moving to Vienna, he began publishing a Hebrew-language paper, *Ha'emet*, the first Hebrew socialist newspaper. Liberman wrote articles in *Ha'emet* in the spirit of socialism, in the hope of influencing the political consciousness of members of the Jewish intelligentsia in Eastern Europe, that negligible minority that could read and understand a Hebrew text. Who were the readers to whom Liberman addressed his articles? They were yeshiva students, rabbis, and members of the Jewish bourgeoisie who had received a Hebrew education. The radical Maskil called upon these readers to recognize the plight of the Jewish proletariat and, as members of a highly conscious intelligentsia, to show their concern for the fate of the exploited workers. This revolutionary tactic reflected prevalent views of the Russian intelligentsia at the time: the intelligentsia's duty to become politically involved and its responsibility for the fate of the masses. *Ha'amet* was written in Hebrew not because Liberman viewed it as the national language but because he needed to create a channel of communication with the Jewish cultural elite. In this sense, he gave faithful expression to the position of the radical Maskilim, who believed that Hebrew ought to be used for purely practical reasons, not because of its cultural and national value or to ensure its future. This view is consistent with that of the radical Maskil Abraham Uri Kovner (1842–1905)[10] in 1865: "Our authors must not imagine they will create a living literature in the Hebrew language for all eternity, for that will never be. But by using the Hebrew language or the spoken language [Yiddish] they will arouse the desire and interest of the Jews for learning and science, which they will find only in the living languages, where they can quench their thirst for wisdom and knowledge."[11]

Paradoxically, Liberman's and Kovner's use of Hebrew was a sign of cultural continuity. Without intending to, the radical Maskilim and the early socialists created an infrastructure for the revival of a secular national culture of the ethnic group they belonged to. Liberman, in *Ha'emet*, continued the tradition of the Haskalah literature that used various traditional literary forms to convey innovative messages.

Liberman led a checkered life. His life story reads like those of other Russian Jews of his generation who, in search of redemption in the time of Alexander II, tried a variety of alternatives all linked to the crisis that affected Jewish society. The first Hebrew socialist, a revolutionary wanted by several police forces in Europe, was a married father who abandoned his family and wandered among the capital cities of the world, driven by a sense of mission. After passing through London, Vienna, and Berlin, he traveled to the United States on a desperate journey to follow a woman who did not return his love. In 1880, he took his own life, at the age of thirty-seven, in Syracuse, New York. His life story affords us a glimpse into the radical change that occurred in Eastern European Jewish society, a change that gave rise to the figure of a Jewish revolutionary, an advocate of the great revolution that would alleviate the suffering of the Jewish proletariat. This revolution was not meant to take a national Jewish direction, but was rather to be achieved through the integration of the Jewish workers into the proletariat of the Russian empire. Liberman was not alone in his socialist views. In the 1870s, other members of the Haskalah movement espoused similar positions and published articles in a socialist spirit in the contemporary Hebrew press. Some of them, including a Maskil from Kiev, Judah Leib Levin (Yehalel, 1844–1925), became within a few years the founders of the new Jewish national movement.

The rapid changes that began in the 1860s gave rise to a different type of reaction in the traditional society. The members of this society, unlike the radicals, did not engage in revolutionary activity to reform man and the world but entrenched themselves in a conservative position. Scholars of Jewish history now call a reaction of this type "Orthodoxy."[12] It was diametrically opposed to the radical approach adopted by Liberman, who advocated destroying the old frameworks and called upon the Jews to break out of the restricted Jewish world in order to cure the economic and social ills caused by the vicissitudes of Alexander II's reign.

In contrast, the conservatives sought to shore up the walls of traditional society. The rabbinical elite in the Pale of Settlement began to adopt a defensive position, the earliest public manifestations of which appeared together with the first buds of Jewish radicalism. But this new defensive posture was not a reaction to radicalism, which was still marginal at the time and exerted scant influence on the public. Rather, it was engendered by a wide variety of elements in Jewish society as well as in the general society, which the first members of Eastern European Jewish Orthodoxy identified as enemies of the traditional world. For example, the social, cultural, and educational programs of the Haskalah movement, which resonated strongly in the time of Alexander II, aroused harsh counterreactions by the defenders of tradition.

Historically speaking, one could argue that the Orthodox made a mistake in identifying the great enemy threatening the continued existence of traditional society. The real threat to the old world of values, which finally destroyed the traditional frameworks in Jewish society, did not come from within; it was not the Maskilim who undermined the foundations of Jewish society, nor was it the members of the Jewish national movement who appeared later. As we learned in earlier chapters, the traditional society's death knell was sounded by the social and economic changes that occurred in the 1860s and 1870s. These changes unsettled hundreds of thousands of Jews and within days destroyed centuries-old social structures. They uprooted Eastern European Jews from their premodern feudal way of life in the shtetls and provincial towns and propelled them into large, cold, and impersonal cities or sent them overseas to places where old traditional frameworks had lost their meaning and no longer had any social or cultural viability.[13] The destruction of the feudal system was the great enemy of the traditional Jewish society. But the Orthodox circles, writing in the way that typified the defenders of tradition, were unable to define as their "enemy" a socioeconomic process that they could not battle face-to-face. It was difficult for the Orthodox to arrest the changes of time; they were incapable of restoring the old political order from the days of the Polish kingdom. And certainly the rabbis and laymen active in the Jewish community were unable to withstand the destructive force of rising capitalism. It was much easier to focus their sense of threat on a known, familiar personality or group. Hence, they blamed the Haskalah movement and its branches for the crisis.

The "enemy" was sometimes identified as the creators of the new Hebrew literature; thus the poet Judah Leib Gordon, who criticized the deplorable influence of the rigid religious laws on Lithuania's Jews, became a symbol of the danger concealed in Maskilic criticism.[14] The same was true of Moses Leib Lilienblum, who dared suggest to the rabbis of Lithuania that they ought to adapt the demands of halakha to the conditions of the modern era. Lilienblum wrote: "We have come upon fine times and here we are following the life of the land, to live like all other men, and that will require many changes in our lives, and you will stand against us as if nothing at all had happened. . . . Why do you not remove some of the many restrictions from us, those added by the more recent rabbis, which lay heavy upon us like the sand upon the shore?"[15]

The response was not long in coming. The brave young man who had dared to publicly air his opinion about the need to adapt the Jewish religion to the era of reform in Russia was ostracized and excommunicated in his city. In a letter to his friend the poet J. L. Gordon, he described the harrowing experience:

On the festival of Shavuot, a meeting was convened in the home of the community rabbi for the purpose of depriving me of a livelihood and driving me from the town. The government-appointed rabbi informed me the day after the festival that the leaders of the town had resolved to write a letter of slander about me to the governor of the province in Vilna. . . . All my acquaintances have distanced themselves from me. I cannot come to their homes nor they to mine, for fear of their parents. If I should come to the house of prayer, I am regarded as one of God's accursed; no one greets me, nor am I allowed to join a minyan of ten for prayer. When I walk in the town streets, I am surrounded by a flock of boys yelling at me: "Heretic! Apostate!"[16]

Later the Orthodox also identified all shades of Jewish radicalism, from socialism to nationalism, as an enemy. There was no correlation between the events in Jewish society that had led it to change and the reaction of Eastern European Orthodoxy, which directed its struggles against personal or group targets. Even if at times, Orthodoxy did defeat the "enemies" of tradition (and, in many cases, such as that of Lilienblum, it did gain local victories over people or small groups), it could do nothing to arrest the momentum of capitalism, to halt industrialization, or to stop the dissolution of traditional frameworks. No one in Eastern Europe could have done so at that time, not even the radical movements, whose members believed that the course of progress could be halted by preserving the premodern agricultural economy and preventing industrialization and urbanization. The philosophers whose writings inspired the members of these movements sought to deter the modernization of the Russian economy by means of agrarian socialism. While the radical movements in Russia engaged in political activity (albeit in the underground), the Orthodox in the Pale of Settlement did not become politicized then, in contrast to their counterparts in Galicia, who succeeded in joining Polish conservative circles, which aided them in their struggle against the Jewish liberals. In historical scholarship, the development of the Orthodox reaction in the Russian empire is generally identified with the great controversy in Lithuania in the late 1860s and early 1870s that revolved around the proposals for religious reform.

Moses Leib Lilienblum, who was influenced by the ideas of the Haskalah movement, published a series of articles in the Hebrew press at the end of the 1860s, calling for very moderate changes in the halakha to adapt the strict observance of religious rules advocated by the rabbis of Lithuania to modern life. In the second half of the 1860s, there was a famine in Lithuania, caused by a bad grain harvest in the region. The poorer classes suffered greatly, and many Jews died of hunger. In the nascent Jewish press, voices were heard calling on the rabbis to alleviate the people's distress by revoking, at least temporarily, some of the more severe halakhic restrictions. One proposal was that because of the food shortage, the Lithuanian Jews should be permitted to eat pulses during Passover, in accordance with the Sephardic custom, as a substitute for grain, which was in such short supply. Lilienblum, a Lithuanian talmudic scholar, approached the issue of religious reform from a halakhic standpoint and proposed exemptions on the basis of rabbinical authority. Shortly thereafter, he again published a series of articles: *Additions to the Ways of the Talmud.* This time, he adopted a more extreme position and referred to the Oral Law as a human creation that had developed throughout history: "The Talmud in general . . . is the creation of very wise men who understood the spirit and ways of man . . . The Talmud is a compilation of various opinions and permits one person to differ in his views from another. . . . Hence, it contains opposing views in matters of faith as well as in matters of practice."[17]

A group of rabbis from the Lithuanian scholarly elite was enraged by the Maskil. Although some rabbis agreed that there was some basis for adapting the halakha to the spirit of the time, it was the conservative position, which venerated the existing situation and rejected any possibility of modifying the halakha, that won. Lilienblum also adopted a more extreme approach, abandoning the issue of halakhic reform. The controversy that raged around his *Ways of the Talmud* was a significant milestone in the history of Russian Jewry, underscoring the intensity of the inevitable antagonism between two uncompromising extremes. It should have been feasible for the Maskilim and the rabbis to cooperate, since many of the former, including Lilienblum, did not seek at first to uproot Jewish tradition and many rabbis accepted the Maskilim's views about the need to reconcile faith with the changing times. But both sides entrenched themselves in extreme positions. All those who proposed reforms to the halakha were ostracized and ousted from traditional Jewish society. Lilienblum, forced to flee from his home in Vilkomir, moved to Odessa, where he became a radical Maskil. Later, in the wake of the 1881 pogroms, he joined the Hibbat Zion movement as one of its leaders and never returned to the world of Lithuanian religious scholarship.

These two extremes, engendered by the reforms of Alexander II and the social and economic changes that came in their wake, reflect the two opposite alternatives in the Jewish politics emerging in Eastern Europe. Between the two—the secular, radical pole, and the defensive, conservative Orthodox—was a wide variety of other responses to modernity, responses that turned contemporary Jewish society into an impassioned public, replete with ideological and political tensions. It seems that the primary concern of millions of Jews in the Russian empire in the 1860s and 1870s was not matters of the spirit, but the bread on their table or, as the first Jewish socialist, Aaron Samuel Liberman, called it, "the question of the knife and fork."

Chapter 11
The Conservative Alliance: Galicia under Emperor Franz Josef

What happened in the Austrian part of Eastern Europe in the decades when enormous changes were taking place in the Russian empire? In the 1860s and 1870s, political developments in this region, known as Galicia since the first partition of Poland in 1772, were different from the events in the Russian empire during the reign of Alexander II. As we learned in earlier chapters, two historical phenomena combined to differentiate Galicia from other regions. On the one hand, it had a Jewish society so similar in its culture, language, way of life, and economic infrastructure to the Jewish society across the border that they seemed to be the same society. On the other hand, from 1848 on, different political processes than those of the Russian empire affected the Jewish society in Galicia. The 1840s and 1850s marked the height of Czar Nicholas I's conservative policy in Russia, while in the large urban centers of Galicia, the 1848 revolutions engendered a political awakening and social activity. Although constitutional reforms were halted in the first decade after the "Spring of the Nations" revolutions, the emancipatory process was renewed at the end of the 1850s, and these trends finally came to fruition in 1867, when equal rights were proclaimed for all the empire's subjects, including the Jews.[1]

In Galicia, Jews were granted equal political rights in 1868, so that the Jews on the Austrian side of the border were integrated into a parliamentary political system and rapidly adjusted to all aspects of modern politics. This was a significant difference that greatly influenced the separate development of Galician Jewry. This is an interesting case study of comparison between two societies, which until a certain point had been one society, but underwent disparate political changes. What was the role of the modern state in shaping the similarity and the disparity between different communities in the era of modernization? What was the historical difference that stemmed from a different political background? The historian examining the history of Galicia and comparing its history in the second half of the nineteenth century with that of the Pale of Settlement in Russia may also wonder why, despite the fact that Galician Jewry gained full equal rights in 1868 and had different political status from that of Russian Jewry, similar socioeconomic and cultural processes took place in these societies, making it seem as if emancipation had no effect on the difference between the two.

The similarity between the Jews in the Pale of Settlement and the Jews of Galicia across the Austrian border was greater than the similarity between the Jews of Galicia and the Jews of Bohemia, who lived within the same kingdom. Scholars, including the historian Israel Halpern (1910–71), have already noted that the political boundaries dividing the different parts of Eastern European Jewry did not prevent any of the social and cultural processes in the region from crossing from one state to another. The demographic structure of Jewish society on both sides of the Austrian-Russian border was similar. Both countries had a large Jewish population, numbering about 10 percent of all the inhabitants. In 1857, there were 448,973 Jews in Galicia (out of a total of 4,632,866 inhabitants), and in 1880 there were 686,695 (out of 5,938,461). In the Russian empire, Ashkenazi Jews numbered 2,350,000 in 1859 and 3,980,000 in 1880, and in the various parts of the Pale of Settlement and the Polish kingdom they formed a similar proportion of the entire population as Galicia's Jews. A considerable number of the Jews in Galicia lived in towns and in small and medium-size cities, but there were two large communities in big cities and a rapidly growing population of immigrants from the provinces to Vienna, the capital of the kingdom.

The Polish estate economy continued to exist in Galicia, and a large number of Jews were linked to the leasehold economy, just as they had been in other parts of Eastern Europe before the abolition of serfdom. The relationship between the Jewish population, the Polish aristocracy, and the Ukrainian peasants in eastern Galicia was structured on a basis very much like its counterpart on the Russian side. This may explain why most of the Galician Jews clung to the traditional way of life, and their reaction to the innovations introduced where they lived in no way differed from that of their brethren in Podolia, White Russia, or Lithuania.

The Hasidic movement that emerged in Podolia in the mid-eighteenth century flourished in Galicia. It grew in strength in the mid-nineteenth century and succeeded in maintaining its power in the second half of the century, notwithstanding the fact that some Hasidic *tzaddikim* guided their flock of believers from the Russian side of the border. An intriguing case, mentioned in Chapter 4, is that of the influential *tzaddik* R. Israel of Ruzhin, a Russian subject who, after getting into trouble with the law in the Russian empire, fled to the town of Sadagora on the Austrian side. He became a respected Austrian citizen, and his family amassed wealth and property in their new country. As a consequence, a large number of R. Israel's followers were on the Russian side of the border but continued to maintain social and religious ties with him, and later with his successors.[2]

Although the Haskalah movement in Galicia, the avowed enemy of Galician Hasidim, had some characteristics peculiar to the Austrian area, it also maintained close ties with its adherents on the Russian side. Works written by Maskilim were read on both sides of the border, and the literary discourse, as well as the social and cultural criticism, was shared by all members of the Maskilic network in Eastern Europe.

One manifestation of this connection was the book market.[3] Maskilim who wanted to print their books beyond the reach of the Russian censor sent them to the Austrian side, where they were printed in Galicia. In Kraków and Lemberg (Lwów), large centers of Hebrew printing, numerous works by authors from various parts of Eastern Europe were published. Galicians read the works of Russian subjects, writing in Hebrew and Yiddish, and the printers of Lemberg, seeking to profit from the demand for popular literary material, often printed the most sought-after books without obtaining permission from the authors. *Dos poylishe yingl* (The Polish lad), a fiercely anti-Hasidic work by Isaac Joel Linetzky (1829–1915), a native of Ukraine, published in *Kol mevasser* in Odessa in the late 1860s, was later printed in Galicia without the author's permission, which naturally aroused his ire. Periodicals in Lemberg published the works of authors from Kiev and Warsaw. For example, a Hebrew newspaper, *Ivri anokhi,* appeared in Lemberg for twenty-five years and printed articles by writers from all parts of Eastern Europe.[4]

Insofar as all the large Jewish movements of the nineteenth century were concerned, the Jews of Galicia and their coreligionists on the Russian side continued to be part of one cultural world, its taste, languages, and diverse spiritual orientations. The Jews of Galicia in the second half of that century were also part of an ethnic-cultural entity that transcended borders, was distinct from the surrounding culture, and came into the modern era without losing any of the features of the identity it shared with other sectors of the Eastern European Jewish population.

The difference that nonetheless existed between the two Jewish societies on both sides of the Russian-Austrian border stemmed from the different political character of the governments in each of these countries. Jewish society in Galicia was still traditional and linked to premodern economic systems until nearly the end of the nineteenth century. But when this traditional society was exposed to conditions of equal political rights and a parliamentary system of government, it gained a path to politicization that was unique to Galicia. In any discussion of what happened to Jews after 1868, one must first relate to the difference in the status of the Poles, the erstwhile rulers of the area until the end of the eighteenth century. On the Russian side, the Polish aristocracy had lost its power after the failure of the Polish uprisings of 1831 and 1863. In Russia in the 1860s and 1870s, Polish nationalism was regarded as the foremost political enemy and cultural rival. In Galicia, on the other hand, after 1867, the Poles dominated the political scene and enjoyed a broad autonomy, even though the members of other ethnic groups, including the Jews and the Ukrainians, had equal rights. Since Polish peasants and Polish townsmen lived in Galicia (particularly in the western part) in numbers that bore no resemblance to the demographic situation in the various parts of the Pale of Settlement, the area was a kind of Polish national-political unit. In Austria (unlike in the neighboring Russian empire) during those years, the government did not exercise a centralized policy of identifying culture with politics, so Jews who identified with German, the state language, found themselves in constant conflict with Polish demands for cultural dominance.

The most salient difference in the reaction to emancipation existed between the Jews in the large cities and those in the towns and villages. The two large cities in Galicia were Lwów (Polish; Lemberg in German, L'viv in Ukrainian), the major city in eastern Galicia; and Kraków (Polish; Krakau in German), in western Galicia. After 1848, these two cities were the major centers of the acculturation of Jewish society in Galicia. While the Jews in the villages and towns in the areas surrounding these cities still clung to the traditional Jewish culture, in Lwów and Kraków a class of Jewish bourgeoisie sprang up that adopted Polish culture and identified with the Poles' political aspirations. One segment of this group continued to identify with the state culture, clinging to the German language and sending their children to German schools. These two alternative routes to acculturation were often intermixed. One distinct example of the complex play between the imperial culture and the Polish culture was the fact that some of the most ardent expressions of Polish patriotism in poetry and prose were written by Jews between the 1840s and the 1860s in the German language.[5]

Although the government was Austrian-German and a certain number of the higher-ranking officials in Galicia were German-speaking Austrians (at least until 1868), the Poles were the dominant element, so the local administration remained in their hands. In this Polish quasi-autonomy, large segments of the Jewish public continued to maintain traditional relations with the aristocracy, as they had from time immemorial. Again, this was in marked contrast to the situation in the Russian empire at the time, where the Polish aristocracy had lost most of its political and economic clout. The strong political ties between the Jews and the surrounding society was in part a new version of the link between the traditional Jewish elite and the Polish aristocracy that also occupied the senior administrative positions in the district. As a result, an alliance of interests existed in Galicia, one that had disappeared from the Russian part of Eastern Europe after 1863. The traditional Jewish elite—the rabbinate and the large leaseholders who had ties with members of the upper Polish aristocracy—basically supported the Poles, were loyal to them, and even identified with their political conservatism. In other words, there was a coalition between the Polish conservatives and the Jewish traditional elite. The leaseholders in the villages and towns supported the Polish aristocracy because they wanted to maintain the sources of their livelihood. Some of this support also stemmed from the fear of anti-Jewish riots, like those that took place in Kraków and Lwów in the 1830s and 1840s.

The politicization of Jewish society that began after 1868 gave rise to a unique social-political triangle. On the one hand, the alliance of interests between the traditional Jewish elite and the Polish aristocracy became political in character and was translated into election platforms and voter recruitment campaigns. On the other hand, the tendency of the Jewish bourgeoisie to become socially and culturally integrated into the Polish milieu was translated into ideological declarations that were Polish nationalist in character. In this triangle, an open, declared competition took place between two elitist strata in Jewish society. One, the conservative-traditional (Orthodox) stratum, believed it possible to be politically loyal to the Poles without adopting Polish culture. The liberal stratum (sometimes derogatively termed the assimilatory element) believed that loyalty to the Poles ought to be manifested through cultural integration and acceptance of the Polish language and culture as vital elements of the new Jewish identity that would emerge in Galicia.[6] Within the liberal camp, the affinity for the German language and culture, connected to loyalty to the Austrian empire, was also kept alive.

The relations between Jews and Poles were greatly affected by the fact that the Jews were becoming immersed in Polish culture and attending Polish institutions of higher learning. The two universities in Galicia, in Lwów and Kraków, were well-established, prestigious strongholds of Polish culture. In the first half of the nineteenth century, Jews in Galicia had been admitted to these two universities, and in the second half of the century the number of Jews attending institutions of higher learning in Galicia grew considerably. In Kraków, they formed 20 percent of the student body. In these universities, Jews primarily studied law or medicine. These graduates constituted a professional class that had received a Polish education and participated in public and political life.[7] In the 1890s, a class of Jewish scholars specializing in various branches of science emerged, some of whom would later engage in studying the history and culture of the Jewish people. Hundreds of members of the Jewish intelligentsia also emigrated from Galicia to Vienna and to other large cities in Germany. Many of the Jewish professionals in the large cities of Germany and Austria were from Galicia, graduates of its universities who had chosen the German cultural option, namely, the imperial culture, preferring it to the Polish one.

The Orthodox and the liberals competed with each other over the political connection with the Polish elite. Although there were divergent views among the Poles on this point, they tended to support the conservative side. An interesting example is the close alliance between the Orthodox, led by Rabbi Shimon Sofer of Kraków, and the Polish camp in the 1879 elections. Orthodoxy in Galicia, which evolved into a political organization in every sense of the word, did not resemble its counterpart that was taking shape in Lithuania during those years. Although the Orthodox in Galicia viewed the Maskilim and acculturating Jews as their chief enemy, its leaders, unlike their opposite numbers in the Russian empire, regarded themselves first as allies of the ruling establishment and succeeded in becoming an active part of the new political system that was created when emancipation was granted in 1867, while their rivals in the liberal camp were being relegated to the sidelines. This trend continued in Galicia from the 1830s and 1840s. Rabbi Dov Ber Meisels, whom I have mentioned, is an example of the continuity of the Polish alliance with the Orthodox in the days of the 1848 revolutions. Meisels, a member of the Jewish economic elite who combined wealth, family lineage, and rabbinical authority, supported the Polish nationalist movement prior to the 1863 Polish uprising. His family had business dealings with the Polish aristocracy. He was a conservative in his religious views but at the same time consistently came out in favor of Polish autonomy under Austrian rule and fought an uncompromising battle against the pro-Polish liberals in Kraków's Jewish society. Rabbi Meisels, who, after the revolt against the Russians in 1863, became a mythological symbol of Jewish-Polish brotherhood, also reflects the fact that conservative Jewish politics was a dependable ally of conservative Polish politics.[8]

This conservatism was based not only on considerations of profit and loss or on the fear of attacks by the Poles. It was also based on principle: each side saw in the conservatism of the other a substantive, positive value. The Polish Catholics frequently praised Jewish conservatism, and the Jewish conservatives, for obvious reasons, preferred the political conservatism of the Catholics to the demand for total assimilation of the Jews voiced by the radical camp. This is as different as night and day from any description engraved on the Jewish collective memory in the twenty-first century of the role played by the Orthodox in the political life of Eastern Europe and their attitude toward the Gentiles. In the 1880s, the internal rivalry between the two elites over the support of the

Poles clearly ended with the triumph of the conservatives, since the Poles were understandably prepared to cooperate with the Jewish side that provided them with the most votes in the elections.[9]

The participation of all the inhabitants of the state in the general elections was an unheard-of innovation in Eastern Europe. The equal rights gained by the Jews of Galicia, within the overall reform in the Austrian kingdom (which from then on became the Austro-Hungarian empire), gave them a new type of political power in the elections to the parliament. They were now the faction that tipped the scale between the Catholic Poles and the Ukrainians. The parliamentary elections were not direct, relative, and general elections. Rather, they were indirect; small electoral bodies were chosen that held the final decision in their hands. The ratio between the two large populations, each of which formed over 40 percent (the Jews constituted about 11 percent of all the inhabitants in western and eastern Galicia) of the general population, endangered the absolute hegemony of the Poles. It also greatly reduced their chances to realize their nationalist aspirations in the region. The political elements in the Polish elite that held the key positions in the local administration in Galicia found all manner of ways to neutralize the electoral power of the Ukrainian inhabitants. It was here that the Jewish population played a significant role, because of the votes it could supply to the Polish side and because of its power to influence the votes of the Ukrainian peasants. In the election campaigns, members of the Polish aristocracy (*szlachta*) operated as "contractors" for recruiting votes in all sectors of the population: the Poles (the aristocracy, the lower aristocracy, the townsmen, and the peasants in western Galicia); the Jews (the *tzaddikim* of the Hasidim, merchants, and leaseholders in the towns and villages); and the Ukrainians (an absolute majority of all the inhabitants of the villages in eastern Galicia). The Polish aristocrats would invite Ukrainian peasants to lavish dinners at which the vodka flowed freely, in order to influence their vote. This was the origin of the term "election sausage" that was coined in Galicia, referring to the sausage that was given as a bribe for voting for one or another candidate. The Jewish leaseholders and tavern owners played an important part in these election campaigns and helped the Polish *szlachta* select the candidates who were best for them.

As a result of their participation in this new political setup, all sectors of the Jewish society organized in a manner similar to that of modern political parties. Various groups, first and foremost the pro-Polish liberals and supporters of the imperial center in the big cities, organized in political societies. One such society was the Society of Brethren (Agudat Achim), whose center was in Lwów and which had a liberal pro-Polish orientation. Another, known as Shomer Israel, was pro-Austrian. The

Orthodox organized their own group, which later became known as Machzikei Hadat (Defenders of the faith). The appearance of newspapers published by various political groups was an unmistakable sign of the emergence of a new political culture, one that had left behind the traditional social ties to become what the scholar of nationalism Benedict Anderson has termed an "imagined community."[10]

In addition to the highly developed and varied Polish press, Jewish newspapers began to appear in German, Polish, and Hebrew. One of these was the newspaper of the Orthodox group Machzikei Hadat, which printed political and polemical articles disputing with their adversaries. In the struggle over the Jewish vote, agreements were reached between groups of the various nationalities. In the case of the Orthodox, the rabbis of the large cities and several Hasidic *tzaddikim* filled key roles in the election campaigns. We have noted that Hasidism exerted much influence on large sectors of the Jewish population in the towns and villages. Through political alliances and agreements, the Poles strove to preserve their autonomous control. The Orthodox sought to defend traditional Jewish frameworks against Jewish liberals. The small liberal group in the large cities was split between those who favored the central government and wanted to curb the power of the Poles on the local scene, and those who supported the Poles and wanted to achieve cultural and social integration.

Such a political alliance between Catholic circles and traditionalist Jews was of great advantage to the Poles. A Hasidic *tzaddik* in a certain city—say, the rabbi of Belz—could instruct thousands of his followers who did not know a word of Polish to vote for the Polish candidate in the elections for the Austrian parliament. In the 1873 elections, a group of the new Jewish elite, which tended to identify with the imperial center, made an audacious attempt to oppose absolute Polish dominance in political life. This was one more manifestation of the tension between the Jews' support of the empire and their identification with local (Polish) nationalism, which characterized the Jews of Eastern Europe throughout the nineteenth century. In the election campaign, the members of Shomer Israel cooperated with the Ukrainian side, which evoked the angry reaction of the Poles.

The Orthodox went to great lengths to achieve dominance in the community leadership in the large cities, where religiously nonobservant Jews were beginning to gain positions of influence. Shimon Sofer, rabbi of Kraków in the 1870s, fought a fierce, unyielding battle against the "progressive" pro-Polish group who held positions on the community council in the city. Sofer was a loyal ally of the Polish conservatives and was even elected in 1879, with their support, to the Austrian parliament. At least until the 1880s, a modus vivendi was established in Galicia in which conservatives in both the Jewish and the Polish society did their utmost to preserve the status quo within the process of politicization.

In the early 1880s, Jewish liberals became increasingly reluctant to identify with Polish interests, which explains why several members of this group adopted Jewish nationalist views. The Jewish nationalist movement began to emerge in Galicia in the absence of pogroms or any signs of hostility on the part of the imperial government. It was the rise of strident Polish nationalism and manifestations of Polish anti-Semitism at the end of the nineteenth century that led the liberals to change course. In 1884, an editorial in *Ojcizna* (Fatherland), the newspaper of the pro-Polish organization Society of Brethren, stated that the Jews of Galicia have two possible ways of solving their political problem: to convert to Christianity or to immigrate to Palestine. The Orthodox, unlike the pro-Polish liberals, had no cause for disillusionment. From the outset, they had viewed the new Jewish politics in terms of alliances based on common interests, not as a path to integration with "brothers" in language and worldview.

The political conservatism of the Orthodox, as well as the liberal camp's support of imperial culture, had little influence on the condition of the majority of Galicia's large Jewish population, which in the 1880s numbered close to three-quarters of a million. The reader will recall that the central government in Vienna discriminated economically against the region of Galicia. Modern industry was not developed there, as it was in Russian Poland. The economic activity of the Jews still went on in a pre-industrial agricultural environment. The commercial and industrial sources of income that were still in operation in the first half of the nineteenth century languished as a result of the thriving capitalist economy in the neighboring states. Galicia's economy remained on the fringes of the industrial revolution and was seriously damaged. The international trade routes that the Jews were involved with, such as commerce in cattle or the export of grain, changed direction. The trade in alcoholic beverages also underwent change. New centers of activity did spring up here and there in Galicia: for example, oil was discovered near the city of Drohobycz, so it became a focus of Jewish entrepreneurship, and a modern Jewish community was soon established there. But despite the development of a few such economic centers, the gap between the increase in the Jewish population and the decrease in their sources of livelihood was constantly growing. It is not surprising that although the government in Galicia never politically persecuted the Jews after 1848 and they had enjoyed equal political rights there since 1868, they emigrated in large numbers from the region. The majority chose to go to Vienna, the metropolitan city of the empire, or to Germany or the countries of Western Europe; many immigrated to the United States.

Later we will discuss the beginning of the mass emigration from Russia in the wake of the pogroms in the early 1880s. Galicia, where there were no pogroms and where, prior to 1881, the government did not introduce anti-Jewish measures, was, relatively speaking, as great a source of mass Jewish immigration to the industrialized areas of the West. Apparently, hatred of Jews was not the major cause for the emigration of Jews from Eastern Europe at the end of the century. Rather, the mass emigration stemmed from the enormous demographic growth of the Jews and their deplorable economic situation. The special anti-Jewish restrictions imposed by the Russian government exacerbated the economic distress of the Jewish masses, but they probably played a secondary role in affecting the dimensions of the emigration from Eastern Europe to the West.

Chapter 12

"The Jew Is Coming!" Anti-Semitism from Right and from Left

We learned in earlier chapters that prior to 1772, no Jews were allowed to enter the Russian empire. But in 1772, the empire annexed areas of Poland where Jews lived in large numbers that then became provinces under Russian rule. A hundred years passed between the first partition of Poland and the pogroms that broke out in the southern regions of the empire in 1881. During this long period of time, political, social, and economic processes affected public opinion in the various social classes in relation to Jews. The attitude toward the Jews was complex and varied from one region to another and from one ethnic group to another. The position taken by the ruling government largely determined the degree to which these new subjects were accepted into society, and we have seen that this position changed whenever a new ruler came into power. Nonetheless, the imperial officials as well as the members of the intelligentsia were of two minds: one tendency was to integrate the Jews into Russian society or, more accurately, into the Russian state; the other was to reject, alienate, or even oust this foreign, insular population from the Russian empire, or at the very least, to distance them as far as possible from the centers of economic and cultural activity in the empire.

From the standpoint of the Maskilim, the advocates of progress, there was a bleak, frightening side to the sweeping reforms introduced during the reign of Alexander II—the rise of modern anti-Semitism in the Russian empire. The growing hostility toward the Jews during the reign of the czar, who was supposedly the most liberal of all the Russian rulers in the nineteenth century, had a decisive effect on the development of movements. It deflected, as we shall later see, the advocates of integration and the supporters of Russification to paths far from the pro-government position and led them to adopt more radical solutions for the Jewish "problem." Why was it that modern Russian anti-Semitism arose during the reign of a czar who opened the gates of the empire to certain groups of Jewish society, abolished some of the restrictions connected to the Pale of Settlement, and displayed a desire to integrate Jews into the systems of Russian government, administration, and education? The answer to this question is one particular case in the history of the phenomenon known as modern anti-Semitism. After all, in the nineteenth century, in all the countries of Europe, the pace at which Jews were integrated into political frameworks through emancipation or actively participated in the economic and social systems was directly linked to the rise of manifestations of hatred toward them. The Russian case is not exceptional in the general history of the hatred of Jews in the modern era; yet certain aspects are peculiar to Russian society and culture.

The anti-Semitism that emerged in Russia in the second half of the nineteenth century incorporated motifs of the traditional hatred of Jews in Russia, which originated in the Middle Ages, particularly during periods when the Russian Orthodox Church incited a bitter controversy over Jewish influence on the Christian faith. As a result of this polemic, known as the "affair of the Judaizers," the Jews were accused of causing a schism in the Church and of attempting to convert faithful Christians to Judaism. As a result, Jews were forbidden to live in Russia for centuries. The anti-Jewish legacy of the Byzantine Empire, whose religion was Eastern Orthodoxy, was preserved for generations in the Russian Orthodox Church. But Russia was also exposed to influences from Western and Central Europe that reached it only in the modern era—in particular, ideas and attitudes that came from Germany and France. Modern Russian anti-Semitism is linked to the emergence of modern political streams in Russia that assigned a particular role to the Jews. This characteristic is not peculiar to any one political camp. It can be found in the Russian conservative (right-wing) camp as well as in the radical (left-wing) camp.

The new Russian hatred of Jews seemingly cuts across all Russian political streams of the 1860s and 1870s. On the left-radical side, the Jews were portrayed as Western urban foreigners who live at the expense of the Russian people or the Ukrainian (and other Slavic) people and are representatives of a Western invader, promoting the industrial revolution and the spread of capitalism to Eastern Europe. The Jews were also viewed as an element that assisted the Polish exploiter from the recent past, namely, the Polish aristocrat who for many generations had owned estates in extensive areas of Eastern Europe. During Alexander II's reign, the Russian radical left espoused different shades of agrarian socialism.

Revolutionary movements such as the Narodnaya Vola (The people's freedom) held that returning to the precapitalist, premodern era would redeem Russian society. The world of tomorrow, they believed, would be based on cooperative villages of free peasants, like the imaginary communes that existed in Russia before the peasants were enslaved by the

Polish *pans* (noble landowners), the Russian czars, and the Jewish lease-holders. In this Weltanschauung, endorsed by the agrarian socialists, Jews played a particularly repugnant role. They were part of the triple alliance between the czarist regime, the Polish estate owner, and the Jewish leaseholder-exploiter.

On the conservative side, the situation was not very different. Here, too, the Jew was perceived as a representative of the West, introducing modernism into Russia, which was still free of the destructive effect of the capitalism, industrialization, and urbanization that had changed the face of Western European states. The Jew was portrayed as undermining the old order, as "German," as an enemy of the Russian kingdom, as "French," as liberal, as a "Freemason," as a member of a secret international alliance that threatened to take over Russia as part of a universal Jewish plot to rule all of humankind, to exploit it for the loathsome needs of his people. These anti-Jewish ideas and the images that accompanied them had a strong impact on Russian public opinion and were given expression in the press that had already begun to flourish at the end of the 1850s with the slackening of censorship restrictions.[1]

The growth of modern Russian anti-Semitism was linked to the politicization of Russian society and to the emergence of a modern mass media. A public forum in which sharp debates were held about the place of Jews in Russian society and economy was created in the same years that Jews began to move rapidly into areas in the heart of Russia, where a Jew had not been seen for hundreds of years. This combination of the movement of Jews from the Pale of Settlement to the economic and cultural centers of the empire and the expansion of freedom of speech, two immediate results of the reforms, culminated in virulent manifestations of anti-Semitism, which intensified in the second half of the 1860s and greatly escalated in the 1870s. Jews began to settle in the interior of Russia when wealthy Jews, members of the Jewish bourgeoisie, Jews with technical professions or academic degrees, and graduates of secondary schools were permitted to cross the boundaries of the Pale of Settlement.

These Jews settled in Moscow, Saint Petersburg, and the other big cities of Russia. In the 1860s, the same complaint appeared repeatedly in the Russian press: "The Jew is on the move"—in other words, the Jew is coming from the western districts. Until then, the Jew lived far away, in the Pale of Settlement. He was a "Polish Jew," an abstract figure known only from the literature, to whom one need not relate in everyday life. And now, this overbearing foreigner was coming from the western border, bringing with him his entire repertoire of reprehensible traits. But it was not only the Jew who was making his way into the heart of the empire that troubled Russian public opinion. His coreligionists who remained in cities and towns in Lithuania, White Russia, and Ukraine were also perceived in the most negative manner. In the public debate about the political future of the various nations in the empire, the issue of the economic harm caused by the Jews to broad sectors of the population in the western districts came up repeatedly. The claim was made that the harm caused to farmers, who constituted the majority of the population, was not a thing of the past from the days of Polish rule, but that the exploitation of the peasants was still going on to that very day.

Moreover, the reforms of Alexander II were exacerbating exploitation, since the Jews had been granted economic powers of a kind they had never before possessed. The Jewish exploiting leaseholder of the old type, who had served the Polish aristocracy, was transformed into the Jewish capitalist from the city who was gaining control of the lands of the villagers and holding all of Russia in his side pocket, by means of the new network of banks and the developing stock exchange. The new Jewish capitalist, a product of the changes in Eastern Europe from the rise to power of Alexander II, was exerting a destructive influence in his old place as well as in the places to which he had recently come. In the 1870s, the anti-Semitic press wrote extensively about the multifaceted figure of the Jew, who was inflicting damage both in his old character and in his modern metamorphosis. The influence of the stock exchange on the Russian economy and the link between the exchange and the Jews were portrayed in the Russian press as part of an undercover plot, a kind of grand Jewish conspiracy to seize control of lands and assets from the hands of the authentic Russian owners and to transfer them to the hands of the Jews.[2]

An event that aroused fervid anti-Semitic sentiments in all the contexts I previously described—in the media, in society at large, and in the public's consciousness—was the 1869 publication of *The Book of the Kahal* (*Kniga kagala* in Russian), a Russian-language version of excerpts from the minute book (*pinkas*) of the *kahal* (the Jewish autonomous ruling authority prior to its abolition in 1844) of Minsk in White Russia.[3] The book was published by Jacob Brafman (1825–79), a Jew who had converted to Christianity. Brafman, who held various positions in the civil service, was, among other things, a Hebrew teacher in the government theological seminary in Minsk. For several years, he was also the censor of publications in Hebrew and Yiddish in Vilna. The fact that the book was published by an official of the civil service, at public expense, greatly offended the Jews, and in particular dampened the high regard of the Maskilim for the Russian government in the Pale of Settlement. Moreover, Brafman was known as having been the author of caustic articles in the Russian press denouncing the Hevrat Mefitzei Haskalah (Society for the spread of enlightenment), which he claimed was part of an international Jewish conspiracy supposedly linked to the worldwide activity of the French Alliance Israelite Universelle society.[4] His translation, which in the main contained correct facts, dealt in part with the laws of *hazakah* that had been in force in Jewish society before the abolition of the *kahal*, from the Middle Ages until the first half of the nineteenth century. As we learned in earlier chapters, these laws in Eastern Europe were the halakhic way in which the Jews regulated economic activity, including their intensive involvement in the leasehold economy. One Jew was barred from arrogating the right of another Jew who had previously leased a certain estate, property, or means of production. This and other economic matters in the book seemed, in the Russian translation, to be a clear indication of a secret Jewish plan to gain economic control by regulating all financial activity and conspiring to exploit non-Jews and to sap the lifeblood of their economy.

The appearance of *The Book of the Kahal* aroused a furor, which the Russian press dealt with for a long time. The book came out in an expanded second edition in 1875. Jewish writers published apologetic articles in Russian in an attempt to refute the accusations. Scholars of Jewish history in Eastern Europe, most of whom belonged to the Haskalah movement, were panic-stricken and became reluctant to publish authentic material from the minutes of the *kahal* or of other Jewish societies. In his memoirs, the historian Simon Dubnow writes that the publication of the Russian edition of the authentic records of the Jewish organization in Lithuania, *Pinkas medinat lita*, was delayed for many years because of the fears aroused by the publication of *The Book of the Kahal*. This affair had a deleterious effect on historical research, since the records of other Jewish societies and communities contained all sorts of facts whose publication in Russian, Polish, or German, at a time when the hatred of Jews was on the rise, might have provided material for anti-Semitic accusations.[5]

The Book of the Kahal became a guidebook for some Russian government officials. It seemed to be a key for understanding that strange society that existed within their area of administrative responsibility, a society about which so little was known. In the 1870s, some of the Russian intelligentsia regarded *The Book of the Kahal* as an authentic source of information, which fortunately had been placed for the first time at the disposal of the Russian reader in faithful translation. Now, at last, they believed they would know what these Jews were furtively doing and what they were writing in their secret language while cheating and deceiving the Christians in the surrounding society.

Another case, also part of the new type of media discussion that had appeared in Russia, was linked to tensions between ethnic groups in the empire, which intensified owing to the stepped-up processes of modern-ization. The rise of Ukrainian nationalism, at the time when the imperial government was attempting to blur the separate Ukrainian identity, was connected to the place of Jews in Ukraine. Those Jews who had aban-doned their traditional environment tended to identify with the impe-rial culture—in this case, the Russian. In the 1860s, *Osnova,* a newspaper that had a Ukrainian or "Ukrainophile" orientation, published a series of articles on the Jewish question. Once again, claims were made that the Jews were injurious to the Ukrainian rural population. The foreign nature of the Jew in the Ukrainian environment was perceived to have class, cultural, and national ramifications. The Jewish Russian-language newspaper, *Sion,* came out in defense of the Jews in a series of articles that argued that there was no truth to these accusations. The *Osnova-Sion* controversy was another clear case in which the pro-Ukrainian press, published in Russian, employed a series of traditional negative images of the Jew but this time linked them to economic activity in the period when the peasants were freed from the shackles of serfdom and capitalism was on the rise. An oft-repeated claim was that the Jews did not want to integrate into Russian society but at the same time were exploiting the economic and political changes to gain control of the assets of the villagers. It referred to the fact that when serfdom was abol-ished in 1861, a considerable part of the estate lands, on which peasant serfs had been living, was put up for sale on the free market. Jewish capi-talists, members of the rising Jewish bourgeoisie, took advantage of the new opportunities in the land market and began investing funds in this real estate. The question of the rural lands became exceedingly signifi-cant in the 1880s, so much so that an explicit regulation was enacted in the early 1880s barring Jews from purchasing land outside of towns.[6]

In Russia, conservatives and radicals internalized the combination of the "old" image of premodern economic activity in the leasehold econ-omy, which went hand in hand with the traditional church hostility, and Jewish economic activity in the era of rising capitalism. The appearance of the new Jewish capitalist, the experience of the modern industrial rev-olution, and the confrontation with Western influence, as well as the physical presence of the Jews all revived the old negative image of the Jew, making it a topical, concrete issue and a contemporary political problem. This negative image influenced the historical research of Ukraine (such as the writings of the historian Nikolai Kostomarov) and the political thought of the opposition in the 1870s (one of whose prom-inent expounders was Mikhail Dragomanov).

We can see how these claims directed against Jews, which at first were local in nature, took on universal significance. One extreme case of anti-Semitism that joined the specific Russian anti-Jewish image with the view

of the Jew as an international enemy can be found in the writings of
Fyodor Dostoyevsky. In the late 1870s, his regular column appeared in
installments in two Russian newspapers. Under the heading "A Writer's
Diary," from time to time he would viciously malign the Jews. He did not
restrict his vilifying criticism to Russia, not even to the boundaries of
Eastern Europe; rather, he regarded the existence of the Jews as a global
problem.[7] During the Balkan war between Russia and the Ottoman
Empire (1876–78), anti-Semites accused the Jews of collaborating with
the enemy—the Ottomans—and of evading conscription and making
easy profits while Russian soldiers were sacrificing their lives for the sake
of the homeland. The Balkan war became a focus for the awakening of
sympathy for the small Slavic nations. The idea of pan-Slavism, which
was based on the Christian Orthodox heritage and blended national
romanticism with anti-Western sentiments, was by its very nature hostile
to the Jews.

One of the most interesting essays in the series A Writer's Diary dealt
with a hero of the Balkan war, the Jew Goldstein, a soldier who was out-
standing in his heroism in battles between the Russian army and the
Turks. Dostoyevsky wrote derisively that while there is a Goldstein who
fought courageously for the Russian homeland, this exceptional case is
not typical of the behavior of other Jews during the war. Goldstein, in
his view, did not exonerate all other Jews who had caused enormous
injury, on an international scale, to Russia in particular and to the Slavic
peoples in general. Dostoyevsky, who greatly detested Jews, linked the
policy of England, whose prime minister at the time was Benjamin
Disraeli, of Jewish origin, with the struggle of the Slavic nations to gain
their freedom from Turkish enslavement:

[C]ertainly no other people in the whole world have complained so much about
their fate, complained constantly, at their very step and every word, about their
oppression, their suffering, their martyrdom. One would think that it is not they
who rule in Europe, not they who at least control the stock exchanges there and,
accordingly, the policy, the internal affairs, and the morality of the states. The
noble Goldstein may die for the Slavic idea. But still were the Jewish idea not so
powerful in the world, that same "Slavic" question (last year's question) might
well have been solved long ago in favor of the Slavs, not the Turks. I am prepared
to believe that Lord Beaconsfield [Disraeli] himself, perhaps, has forgotten
about his descent, some time ago, from Spanish Yids (however he certainly
hasn't forgotten); but that he "regulated English Conservative policy" over the
last year in part from the viewpoint of a Yid—in this, I think, there can be no
doubt.[8]

How did the Jews of Russia react to the surge of anti-Semitism that
began to take on the proportions of a massive attack in the mid-1870s?
Even earlier, an event had taken place in the south of the empire that

greatly quelled the optimistic views of Maskilim in Russia in relation to the government's attitude toward its Jewish subjects. In 1871 in Odessa, a pogrom broke out, ten years before the infamous pogroms in the days of the "Storms of the South," in 1881–82. These riots, directed mainly against Jewish-owned shops, were perpetrated by the Greek population of Odessa, which had a large Greek community hostile to the Jews. In general, relations between Jews and Greeks were tense throughout the Mediterranean basin and the southern part of Eastern Europe, and several blood libels against Jews were fomented in Greek communities in the nineteenth century. Nor was this the first Greek pogrom in Odessa. There were anti-Jewish riots there in 1821, in the early days of the Greek war of independence against the Turks. Odessa was an important center of Greek nationalism, and anti-Ottoman sentiments were coupled with hostility toward the Jewish immigrants who were streaming into the city from Lithuania in the north and Galicia over the Russian-Austrian border. In the 1871 pogrom, which broke out against the background of the sharp economic competition between Jews and Greeks, neither Russians nor Ukrainians attacked Jews; again, it was only the Greeks. The Russian government did not rush to aid the Jews, who felt that they had been deserted by the authorities, the army, and the police.

For some Maskilim, including the author Shalom Yaakov Abramovitch (Mendele Moykher Sforim), the pogrom in Odessa was a milestone in the disappointing romance between the maskilim and the Russian government. In his allegorical work *Di kliatshe* (The mare), written in Yiddish and published in 1873 (and several decades later published in a Hebrew version entitled *Susati*), he obliquely alludes to the pogrom, fearing a more explicit reference might be expunged by the censor. Abramovitch drew a bleak picture of the growing hatred of Jews, the anti-Semitic press, and violent riots. *Di kliatshe* clearly states that the Maskilic Jew cannot expect any support or aid from the government and its educational system, nor can he hope for much from the circles opposed to the government.[9] Soon after the event, the young Jewish historian Iliya Orshanski (1845–75) wrote a biting article in his newspaper *Den*, accusing the government of responsibility for the pogrom in Odessa and demanding that it compensate the victims. As a result, the paper was closed down.[10]

The pro-government position taken by Leon Pinsker, an editor of *Sion* for a short period, was also affected by the 1871 experience, only a few years before he became a leader of Hibbat Zion in Russia.

Throughout the 1870s, the Maskilim became increasingly disillusioned about the government's attitude toward the Jews and far less enthusiastic about Alexander II's reforms. They grew more and more aware that anti-Jewish tendencies were escalating among the government authorities, in particular among the local and middle-level officials. The political-ideological program, which the Maskilim had supported until then and which had gained the government's cooperation in the days after the 1863 Polish uprising, had let them down. Maskilim inside and outside of the Pale of Settlement had given their all-out support to the government's plan to Russify all non-Russian ethnic groups, namely, the Ukrainians, Poles, Lithuanians, and other peoples in the west of the empire. As a result of this alliance, which in the 1860s had important political and social implications, large numbers of Jews entered Russian secondary schools and universities. In the 1870s, conservative Russian writers began conveying a totally different message to the Jews: there are too many Jews in the secondary and higher-education system, the number of Jews in the universities is out of all proportion to their number in the imperial population, and something must be done to rectify the situation.[11]

It was obvious that the Russian press, still under control of the censor, was able to print nearly everything against the Jews that the editor wanted to, without encountering opposition on the part of the ruling officialdom. On many occasions, government officials would express anti-Jewish views on the pages of newspapers, which the Maskilim perceived as one more sign of a change in the government's attitude. Anyone perusing the Haskalah literature of Russia from the 1870s and early 1880s could not help but notice the growing coolness in the relations between the Jews and the Russian government.

In some historical literature as well as in several textbooks used in Israeli schools, 1881 is described as the year in which the Maskilim, who had cherished such optimistic hopes, were suddenly disillusioned by the Russian government's reaction to anti-Semitism. This image of a sudden change arose out of the Zionist interpretation of the link between the pogroms and the inception of the new nationalist movement. It is largely based on an uncritical reading of several lines in the diary of Maskil Moshe Leib Lilienblum, in which he describes the shift that occurred in his worldview amid the pogroms. But things were quite different. As we saw earlier, a continual process had been taking place for close to ten years before the pogroms in Russia. In this sense, the pogroms that broke out in 1881 were the culmination of a process, not a sudden, surprising event that the Maskilim could not have foreseen.

Chapter 13

"Storms in the South," 1881–1882

On March 1, 1881 (based on the old Russian calendar), Czar Alexander II was mortally wounded when a group of revolutionaries threw a bomb at the carriage in which he was riding through the streets of Saint Petersburg. This murder brought to a violent end a reign that had lasted a quarter of a century (1855–81), during which the Russian empire underwent political, social, and economic upheavals that almost abolished the old way of life and exposed this vast country on the eastern fringes of Europe to the transformative influence of the West.

A young Jewish woman, Khasia Helfman (Gelfman in Russian), was among the revolutionaries who were arrested (in the contemporary press, they were labeled "terrorists"). Helfman was not the only Jewish woman in the radical movements that were trying to overthrow the czarist regime. In the 1870s, the number of Jewish revolutionaries who wanted to radically change the regime and bring about the salvation of the masses in the Russian empire was growing. The link between young Jews, the opposition movement, and the underground revolutionary movements became stronger as disillusionment with the government's policies and the faltering momentum of reform escalated. This disillusionment had a special Jewish feature. When the early days of the reformist period drew to a close, those Jews who had hoped to integrate into Russian society were disappointed by the government and its policy. Anti-Jewish views seemed to be deeply entrenched among government circles, which were consumers of the new anti-Semitic literature. Russian officials followed the rise of revolutionary ideas with concern and often associated them with the political and literary activity of Jews. Social radicalism, which struck a responsive chord in the hearts of young Jews, was frequently linked with the early stages of Jewish national radicalism, which reflected not only their disappointment with the government's policy as a whole, but also with its attitude toward the Jews.[1] However, in the last years before Alexander II's assassination, the social orientation, aimed at saving Russia from the evils of rising capitalism, gained ascendancy among the Jewish radicals. The image of the oppressed peasant was uppermost in the minds of the revolutionary young Jews, who believed that the solution to the peasant's problem would be an overall remedy for the ills of Russian society.[2] They assumed that the special problem of the Jews, as a minority discriminated against in the Russian empire, would be resolved automatically once a great change took place in society at large.

At one stroke, the czar's assassination coupled the authorities' fear of the outbreak of a mass revolution with the strong anti-Jewish sentiments that were intensifying in the 1870s. Ironically, members of the revolutionary organizations regarded it as an opportunity to incite a large popular revolt against the authorities by fomenting hatred of Jews among the lower classes. They even printed handbills calling on perpetrators of pogroms against Jews to turn their wrath against the government and its lackeys as well.[3] Young Jewish men and women, whom government officials regarded as instigators of the revolution, were actively participating in these same organizations. Until the present day, the argument about the role that government agencies played in the outbreak of the great wave of pogroms has not been resolved. Contemporary Jewish sources reported the arrival from the capital of elegantly dressed, French-speaking emissaries who incited the population in the cities of Ukraine.[4] Be that as it may, in the minds of Jews from various ideological camps, the events were connected to the Russian government's anti-Jewish position. Hence, the belief that the outbreak of pogroms was directly linked to the Russian authorities found its way into historical research.

In April 1881, a wave of pogroms broke out in the city of Elizavetgrad in the Russian south, in the southern provinces of Ukraine. Historians regard the czar's assassination and the pogroms as the opening of a new era in the history of Russian Jewry in particular, and of Eastern Europe in general.[5] The year 1881 appears to mark the end of one period and the beginning of another. What happened in that year (April 1881–April 1882) that made it seem to be the end of over a hundred years of Eastern European Jewish history and the beginning of a new period in the history of the largest Jewish collective in the world?

Let us begin with the pogroms themselves. The 1881–82 pogroms are given several names in the contemporary sources. They are called "storms in the *negev* [south]," "tempests in the south," "the thunderstorms," and "the earthquake," and the perpetrators are called "barefoot brigades." Historically speaking, all these names were actually code names, secret words that the Jewish press in Hebrew and Russian used to describe the pogroms in the south. The word *grom* in Russian means thunder, and *negev* in Hebrew is the south. Since nearly all the pogroms took place in Ukraine, and the Russian censor did not permit any explicit mention of pogroms against Jews, Jews wrote in the press about storms in the south, tempests, thunder, and the like.

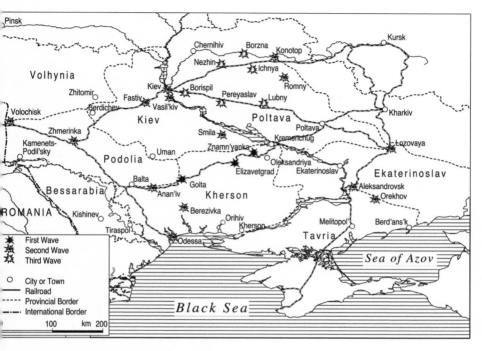

Map 2. The pogroms of spring 1881

The pogroms, which began several weeks after the czar's assassination, occurred in several waves, spread over an entire year. Some assert that the pogroms continued until 1884, but the major violent attacks against Jews took place between April 1881 and April 1882. The period of the "storms of the south" opened with three waves of pogroms in the spring of 1881, in April and early May, in the six provinces of central and south Ukraine. One of the largest pogroms took place in Odessa in the first days of May. Then there was a lull throughout late spring and summer, with the exception of instances in which Jewish property was set on fire in various parts of the Pale of Settlement. At the end of 1881, a large pogrom was carried out in Warsaw, very far from Ukraine, during the Christmas season. Again, there was a respite for several months, until in late March of 1882 during Passover, a dreadful pogrom—perhaps the largest in terms of the number of casualties—broke out in Balta in Ukraine.[6]

For an entire year, assaults were repeatedly made on the Jewish population in towns, cities, and villages. In the larger pogroms, there were several instances of murder, and in some Ukrainian cities, some Jewish women were raped. In contrast to the atrocities that occurred in the same localities in the twentieth century—for example, in the 1903–06 pogroms, the mass murders during the 1919 civil war, not to mention events in Ukraine during the Holocaust from 1941 to 1944—the 1881 pogroms were rather mild insofar as the extent of physical violence was concerned; nor were they very destructive in terms of damage to property. However, two aspects of these pogroms, not directly linked to the level of violence or the number of victims, left an ineradicable, shocking impression on the Jews. The first was their geographical magnitude—an unprecedented outbreak of violence extending over such a large area. At first, they encompassed six provinces in Ukraine, from Odessa in the distant south and areas of new Russia to the heart of historical Ukraine in the Kiev area. Then, uncontrolled, they spread outside of Ukraine to various far-off places outside the Pale of Settlement.

The second, far worse, aspect was the attitude of the Russian government toward the pogroms, which ranged, in the best case as far as the Jews were concerned, from indifference to inattention, and even in extreme cases, to cooperation by the soldiers or policemen with the perpetrators. In Odessa, for example, the police arrested Jewish students who had organized in self-defense in residential areas and commercial districts where there was a dense Jewish population.

This attitude was reflected not only in the riots themselves, but also in the trials held after them. The Jewish press was forced to face the bitter fact that the Jews and the instigators of the riots were portrayed as two sides of the same coin, namely, as participants in a violent brawl that had arisen out of economic considerations. The authorities also punished Jews who took part in organizing in self-defense or reacting with force to the attacks on them. The rioters apparently also got off with slight penalties. The Jews judged the government's response based on the fact that the police generally intervened only after three days of riots; in some cases, the military governors refused to send in the army before the pogroms when a rumor spread that an attack on Jews was imminent. All this was grievous in the eyes of the Jewish observer, but worse yet was the impression left by the official investigation of the circumstances surrounding the pogroms. The investigating commissions that were set up presumed that the Jews themselves were the direct cause of the pogroms, namely, that they were the guilty parties and that the rage of the population directed at the Jews was justified since the Jews had been economically exploiting their neighbors in the towns, villages, and cities. Not only did members of the Russian intelligentsia fail to call for support of the Jews, but many seemed to believe that the victims deserved the pogroms because of the role that they played in the economy.

In September 1881, after the wave of pogroms in the spring and the fires in the summer, inquiry commissions were established in the provinces where these incidents had occurred. In the Jewish sources of the time, these commissions were called "gubernatorial commissions." The commissions' letters of appointment stated that they were established to examine the damage that the Jews were causing to the population at large. This was exasperating to the Maskilim, who were writing in the Jewish press at the time; hence, the strongest reaction to the pogroms appeared in the Maskilic Jewish press, beginning in September 1881. This may also explain why the Jewish press began only in October 1881 to write about the desirability of encouraging Jews to emigrate from Russia.

The anxiety of the Jews was also not assuaged by the statement made to them by the Russian Minister of the Interior, Count Ignat'ev, on three occasions: "The western frontier is open to you," by which he meant that they were free to emigrate westward if they did not see fit to continue living in the Russian empire. This kind of comment reflected that the period when the Jews had entertained optimistic expectations of integrating into Russian society had come to an end. Although it was the Maskilim in Russia, a small minority in Russian Jewry, who had led this optimistic movement, the expectant mood resulting from Alexander II's reforms and the partial integration of Jews into the Russian state was shared by far broader segments of Jewish society.

But there was more to fear than hostile statements. From the early months of his reign, Alexander III, the czar who took the throne after his predecessor's assassination, introduced a clearly anti-Jewish policy. The previous government had not conducted an official anti-Jewish policy, and the new government was reversing the situation. From then on, Russian legislation on Jewish affairs would be explicitly anti-Jewish. In May 1882, a month after the pogrom in Balta, "temporary rules" were published regarding Jewish economic activity, which remained in force until the 1917 revolution. In order to restrict the Jews' ability to compete with non-Jewish merchants and to limit the economic damage that Jews were supposedly causing the village population, the law stated: "To forbid the Jews to carry on business on Sundays and Christian holidays. Hence in regard to the closing of businesses belonging to Jews on the above-mentioned days, the same arrangement will be kept as is generally determined in relation to the closing of Christian businesses."[7]

Judah Leib Gordon's call for mass emigration provides the most striking example of the change in mood among members of the Jewish intelligentsia:

We have seen evil, but we will see good once more.
We will live again in the land as we did before

If the Lord has decreed that we embark on our wanderings
Young and old, we will march as one.[8]

The "Storms in the South" mark the beginning of several new processes in Jewish history in Russia in particular and in the world in general.

Jewish Nationalism

The disillusionment with the Russian government's policy in the context
of the pogroms led the Jews to organize in a new way and to engage in
activity for the sake of the Jewish population. This activity soon took the
form of a nationalist alternative to the old ties with the government. In
April 1881, soon after the first waves of pogroms, societies to aid the victims were established in cities outside the areas that were attacked.
These aid societies provided medical help; collected facts about the incidents, which they attempted to bring to the attention of the public in
Russia and abroad; and raised funds to help Jews who had lost their
property. This spontaneous organization spread rapidly over nearly the
entire Pale of Settlement. These societies were not disbanded after the
waves of incidents died down, and their members, deeply disappointed
with the authorities and the reaction of the Russian intelligentsia to the
pogroms, continued to discuss what could be done to prevent their
recurrence. The inception of the Hibbat Zion (Love of Zion) movement
is directly linked to these aid societies, which were established around
the time of the pogroms themselves. Some of them were transformed
and within several months became the first societies of the Hibbat Zion
movement in Russia. The documents of these aid societies kept in the
Central Zionist Archives in Jerusalem indicate that between April 1881
and the end of that year, several of them became emigration societies.[9]

    The emergence of the new Jewish nationalist movement is connected,
therefore, to the chronology of the year of pogroms. In autumn 1881,
after the establishment of the gubernatorial commissions to investigate
the "damage" caused by Jews to the majority population, a public
debate was launched in the press about the solution to the Jewish "problem" through emigration from Russia. The position of the rabbinical
elite and the wealthy Jews of Saint Petersburg aroused disappointment
and criticism, since it was opposed to emigration as the solution and
failed to take more resolute steps to influence the government's policy.[10]
The question "Palestine or America" was frequently raised, and societies to help with emigration, whose members spoke explicitly about the
preservation of the national Jewish identity in the new countries, were
organizing. Within a few months, members of these societies began to
plan to purchase land in Palestine to found a colony there and even sent

emissaries to find a suitable location for settlement. In some of these societies, students, the second generation of acculturated Jews in Russia, bringing with them radical ideas in the spirit of agrarian socialism, met with Jews from more traditional circles. In general, the nationalist societies comprised Jews from diverse cultural backgrounds, from strictly observant Hasidim to Maskilim from the cities of south Ukraine to young men who spoke only Russian. This diversity left its mark on the composition of the first colonies established in Palestine some months later, in the early days of the First Aliyah.

A National Solution in the United States

Within the large wave of immigrants from Russia that inundated the countries west of the empire, there were also organized groups that sought solutions to the problem of the Jews in the Pale of Settlement that would be in the spirit of radical ideologies, from the days that preceded the pogroms. These groups coupled nationalist views with influences from Russian populism. The populist *narodnik* idea (from *narod*, meaning "people"), that human society would be redeemed through the organizing of groups of peasants and artisans living from their manual labor, was linked to the belief held by Maskilim that agricultural and productive trades had the power to repair the flaws of the Jewish people. Paradoxically, many members of the new Jewish intelligentsia agreed with the harsh criticism of the anti-Semites about the role of the Jews in the Eastern European economy, but they sought to change the Jew outside the boundaries of the empire, in agricultural colonies overseas.

In mid-1881, Jewish *gymnasium* students founded groups in several cities of the western provinces, with the aim of emigrating overseas and establishing communal colonies of farmers and artisans in their new countries. The Am Oylom society, founded in Odessa as soon as the pogroms in that city ended (May 1881), comprised students and craftsmen. It also spread to Kiev and other cities and succeeded in sending six or seven groups of settlers to the United States. Members of Am Oylom blended agrarian socialism with nationalist views. They tried to concentrate their colonies in one region in the hope of creating a Jewish entity, or even a state, in a defined territory. Some of their ideas are found in a letter that settlers sent to Peretz Smolenskin, the editor of the nationalist periodical *Hashahar*, in winter 1883: "The troubles and hardships [the pogroms] we found in the land of our fathers have stirred us to realize our ideas since that time, to abandon commerce and to engage in work on the land, and because of this we have come to America."[11]

The Jewish support institutions, among them the Alliance Israelite Universelle and Jewish organizations in the United States, were opposed to the idea of Jewish immigrants to the U.S. concentrating in one area. So against their will, members of the society dispersed throughout the large country, founding four colonies in the new continent: two in South Dakota, called Cremieux and Bethlehem, which existed until 1885; one in Louisiana, which was destroyed the same year that it was founded, when the Mississippi flooded its banks; and one in Oregon, called New Odessa, that survived until 1887. The two colonies in South Dakota were founded on a communal basis, but very soon became private farms. The daring attempt to establish colonies of Jewish farmers, from which a new type of Jew would emerge, was a continuation of a utopian vision in the spirit of Russian agrarian socialism. This attempt failed because the settlers had no vocational training, economic infrastructure, or public support for the radical ideas that the members of Am Oylam brought with them from Russia. They were unfortunate in that they did not find a generous wealthy patron, like Baron Edmond de Rothschild or Baron Maurice Hirsch. In any case, the members of this movement and their colonies were a marginal and numerically insignificant phenomenon in the mass immigration, which was provoked by the pogroms and was not motivated by any ideology.[12]

Mass Emigration

Most of the immigrants to the West flocked to the cities, crowding the poorer neighborhoods of centers of commerce and industry, such as London, New York, Philadelphia, and Boston. They were the first of the hundreds of thousands that streamed into these neighborhoods over the coming five decades. This enormous mass of poor, uneducated Jews earned their living through hard work at the most menial jobs available in the capitalist economy. Starting in 1881, a large Jewish, mostly Yiddish-speaking proletariat made its way into Western society in the modern city. The main route to integration into the modern world was not via the utopian agricultural settlement envisioned by members of Am Oylam or the Bilu movement but via the gradual rise upward in the big industrial city.

The large-scale emigration began spontaneously, with the mass flight of Jews from areas near the Russian-Austrian border, many of whom crossed the border and concentrated in large numbers on the Austrian side in the town of Brody in Galicia. The international Jewish aid to the victims of the pogroms was a continuation of the help given by Western Jewry to the needy in Eastern Europe, which had begun during the 1869 famine in Lithuania. International Jewish organizations established in the nineteenth century, such as the French Alliance Israelite Universelle and its counterparts in Austria, England, and the United States, came to the aid of the immigrants, but at the same time, they tried to stop the flood of refugees and to return those who had fled to Russia. They also wanted to prevent those who had already moved westward from remaining where their flight had ended, hoping to move them farther and disperse them in small numbers in locations as far away as possible. The attitude of Western philanthropists toward their poor brethren from the east reflected their fear that these uncultured immigrants would tarnish the positive image that the Western Jews had worked so hard to acquire. The image of the poor Eastern European immigrant, with his traditional dress and grotesque language (Yiddish) had a considerable impact on the anti-Jewish sentiments prevailing in Germany, France, England, and the United States. As a result of the pogroms, Western Jews had closer contacts with their Eastern European coreligionists, and the last thing those seeking to help the refugees wanted was to create large concentrations of members of this "uncivilized" tribe in the heart of the enlightened cultured world.[13]

In his book *The Adventure of Motel, the Cantor's Son,* the great humorist Sholem Aleichem satirically portrayed the activity of organizations set up to aid immigrants from Russia. In his book, a group of immigrants traipses from city to city, from the office of one society to that of another society, only to find that these organizations have very little to offer those in need.[14] In part, the Jewish philanthropic activities, in the wake of the "Storms of the South," stemmed from the desire to get rid of the surplus refugees, or at least to regulate their exodus, but nothing could arrest the flow of immigrants. Although in the mid-1870s, the number of Jews who emigrated from Russia to the United States because of the famine in Lithuania exceeded the number of immigrants in 1881, one can only speak of the beginning of the large wave from 1881. In the first and second decades of the twentieth century, tens of thousands of Jews immigrated each year.

From 1881 to 1914, close to a million and a half Jews emigrated from Russia to the United States. During that same period, tens of thousands immigrated to Palestine. As important as it was, the Hibbat Zion movement did not resolve the problem, except for a tiny minority of Eastern European Jews. At the time, the mass emigration overseas, in particular to the United States, offered a real solution for the masses that had been ejected from the crumbling feudal economy and subjected to real hardships in their former homeland.

New Politics

The trauma that Jewish society experienced during and after the pogroms hastened processes that had begun before 1881. A change took place in the political life of Russian Jewry, one that was clearly felt in the emergence of the new organizations and the growing influence of the press. The wealthy Jews' stronghold on the community's leadership was waning, and the leaders of the traditional sectors, including rabbis and heads of yeshivot, were losing their prestige. Maskilim and writers were taking over positions of leadership and challenging traditional Jewish politics that had failed. Organizations that represented broader sectors of society appeared, and these were also linked to radical and antigovernment streams.[15] In a sense, this process was one of the democratization of Jewish society. Young radicals had begun to challenge the existing leadership and their modes of action during the first pogroms. In his memoirs, Mordechai Ben-Ami (1854–1932), a Jewish author who wrote in Russian, tells how affluent Jews in Odessa opposed the organization of self-defense units. This is what one wealthy Odessa Jew told the angry young men who had come to ask for his help: "'Your own defense will protect you' . . . and not one word of commiseration did he have for these people who were risking their own lives to defend their brethren."[16]

Attempts to obtain protection for the Jews from the army and the police by paying them bribes, as well as the intention to conceal what was happening or to play down its importance, angered the young men. It was particularly hard to bear the reaction of the local Jewish leadership when it was obvious that the poorer Jewish quarters had been seriously damaged by the rioters, while the opulent homes of the rich were scrupulously guarded in exchange for the protection money their owners paid. In the minds of some young Jews from Russian-speaking homes, this grievous situation was connected to what they saw as a "return" to the masses of the Jewish people, that same "people" that had been abandoned by the rabbis and the wealthy Jews.

One development that may be more familiar to the Israeli reader is the emergence of the Hibbat Zion movement in the early 1880s from the spontaneous mass awakening that began with the man in the street. The idea of "auto-emancipation," namely, of self-liberation, expounded by this movement from its earliest days also reflected an aversion to the reliance on wealthy Jews and the connections that they had cultivated, which operated through the traditional system of *shtadlanut*.[17] The press called for the establishment of organizations of a new type that would draw their power from broad sectors of the population. This new political style is cogently expressed in the manifestos that some of these societies published in the Jewish press in 1881 and 1882. The manifesto of the Bilu movement, entitled *Kol b'nei haneurim* (The voice of youth), printed in May 1882 in the *Hamelitz* newspaper, is a good example of this trend. Although its authors addressed the existing elite, they do so as spokesmen of a movement that sought a new kind of activity, not as seekers of charity or help obtained through *shtadlanut*. At the same time, the members of Bilu were appealing to the masses of Jewish youth, a totally novel term in the political lexicon of contemporary Jewish society:

We, the undersigned, are all members of the young generation. Our strength is new and our world is yet before us. We have hands with which to labor and a heart with which to think and feel. And to all peoples of the world, we can say that the grand idea of rebuilding the ruins of the land of our forefathers fills all the chambers of our hearts. And the grander purpose, to which we will turn our gazes in the days to come, is to devote our physical and spiritual powers for the good of the cradle of our people, to raise it up from the rubble, to restore its honor and joy.[18]

The language of the manifesto, the ideas that inspired its writers, and the readers to whom it was addressed reflect how members of the radical nationalist society had internalized the spirit of the Russian revolutionary movement from the 1870s.[19] At the same time, it points to the shift that was taking place in Eastern European Jewish politics.

Lobbying

The extraordinary international cooperation among various circles and streams of Jewish society to help the pogrom victims was a remarkable reaction to the 1881–82 events, one that also pertained to Jewish politics. This was not a case of material or medical assistance but rather a daring attempt to arouse international public opinion. The attempt to influence the press in England, the United States, Germany, France, Italy, and other Western countries by covertly smuggling out news about the pogroms to the West was quite successful. This cooperation is fascinating because Orthodox rabbis from the Lithuanian rabbinate, who had waged a war against the Haskalah and Hibbat Zion, took part in it, working with members of these two movements and even with radical socialist Maskilim, the most prominent of whom was a socialist poet from Kiev, Judah Leib Levin (Yehalel, 1844–1925). The members of this varied group collected firsthand testimonies from the locales of the pogroms and transferred them to Kovno in Lithuania; from there, the material was smuggled over the border to the town of Memel on the German side. The Jews overseas who were participating in the endeavor made sure that the items were published in the world press. The height of success was achieved when two long articles were printed in the London *Times* on January 11 and 13, 1882. Actually, these two articles were written in part by a group of Jewish Maskilim in the towns of Ukraine. The texts in Hebrew and Yiddish were edited in Kovno by Rabbi Isaac Elchanan Spector's indefatigable anti-Zionist secretary, Jacob Halevi Lifschitz (1838–1921), and smuggled out by the rabbi's son to the rabbi in Memel, Dr. Isaac Ruelf (1831–1902), a sworn nationalist. There they were translated into German and sent to England to Lord Nathaniel Rothschild, where they were translated from German into English, and then found their way into the prestigious London newspaper.

This episode reveals a new stage in the international organization of Jewry, one in which the traditional modes of action were combined with modern tools. In times of tribulation, despite its hatred of the Maskilim and the nationalists, the Lithuanian ultraorthodox were prepared to cooperate with them to promote a common Jewish cause. They did this not out of love but because they realized that it was the Maskilim who were capable of doing what was necessary.

In the files on Hibbat Zion stored at the Central Zionist Archives in Jerusalem are dozens of letters smuggled out of Russia to the West. These letters bear the code name *heye im pifiyot* ([God,] guard the mouths [of your people's emissaries]), a name taken from a *piyyut* found in the prayer book for the High Holidays. This same slogan had been used by Jewish *shtadlanim* in previous centuries, which shows that those who initiated this endeavor had a strong consciousness of continuity. Some of the letters were written by leaders of Hibbat Zion, some by people who were socialists in their views, and some by devout rabbis. This system of communication, a kind of international Jewish network, is a fascinating case of the use of worldwide contacts to influence public opinion. What the members of this network first strove to achieve was pressure on public opinion in the West so that the governments in England or in Germany would influence the Russian government through diplomatic channels to stop or prevent the pogroms. This activity was a modern version of the traditional *shtadlanut*. At the time when Jews in Germany and England were planting material about the pogroms in the press, letters were sent to Rabbi Samson Raphael Hirsch in Germany to take advantage of contacts with a member of the German aristocracy who was related by marriage to the Russian royal house. The intent was, in addition to using the old method of *shtadlanut*, that the German side would influence its relatives to pressure Russia to stop the pogroms. Similar activity was carried out in Denmark for the purpose of exploiting connections through marriage between the Danish royal house and the czar's family.[20] Ironically, the Jewish media activity reinforced the anti-Semitic negative image of the Jew, the supposed controller of the international press.

A media event during the year of the pogroms is linked to an attempt by the British *Daily News* to deny the news items about acts of violence against Jews printed in the London *Times*. A journalist on the *Daily News* whom members of *heye im pifiyot* ironically called *dayenu* (playing on the initials of the newspaper's name) traveled to towns in southern Ukraine to try to verify the facts about the rape of Jewish women. His claim, which was backed up by Russian government officials, was that the Jews had exaggerated in their description of the events and had damaged Russia's image.

Different groups and streams in Jewish society in Russia did some soul-searching in the wake of the pogroms. Maskilim became members of Hibbat Zion, ardent socialists who changed their worldview and later became "Jewish socialists." The Jewish elite discovered the "Jewish people" just as they had the "Russian people" in the 1870s. The Jewish people, for its part, felt alienated from the Saint Petersburg elite and disappointed by the helplessness of the wealthy Jews outside the Pale of Settlement. The emigration to United States, which before the pogroms, had been modest in its proportion, now became a mass movement. Disillusionment with the government escalated. At the same time, Jewish acculturation into Russian society did not stop, but increased.

The year 1881 was a milestone in modern Jewish history. It marked the largest shift toward the emergence of the modern movements that influenced that chapter in Jewish history. As a result of the open anti-Jewish policy adopted by the government of the new czar, Alexander III, members of the Haskalah movement rarely tended to cooperate with the state any more. The social class that had acculturated and identified with the Russian urban milieu was struck a hard blow by the glaring change in the government's policy vis-à-vis the Jews.

Their disillusionment with the cold, hostile reaction of Russian intellectuals during the pogroms and the following years led many radicals among the Jewish intelligentsia to develop a national Jewish consciousness. In the new Jewish nationalist thinking, a historical model was shaped that attempted to explain the emergence of the Jewish nationalist movement. This model, which would reproduce itself many times throughout the twentieth century in every attempt by Jews to cope with hostility toward them, had three stages: it opened with the hope of integration, continued with the outright rejection by the non-Jewish side, and culminated in a renewed awakening of the old Jewish identity in a new national guise. Moses Leib Lilienblum called this process, which he experienced from the 1860s to the early 1880s, *derekh teshuvah* ("the road to repentance," also "the road back").[21] For many years, this model played a key role in Zionist historiography and directly connected the period of the pogroms in Russia to the inception of the new settlement in Palestine.

Another historical process, given great momentum by the pogroms, may have left a more significant mark on the course of Jewish history.

This was the mass emigration from Eastern Europe to the West. From 1882 to 1914, hundreds of thousands of Jews moved along a route between the impoverished towns in the Pale of Settlement to the large cities of Western Europe and the United States. Within one generation, a large segment of Eastern European Jewry was uprooted from a traditional way of life, which had just begun to change, and was confronted by the challenges of urbanization and the economic and social ills of the capitalist era. From then on, the Jewish community in the United States occupied a central place in the Jewish world, and its social and cultural character was shaped through the gradual merging of millions of Jews form Eastern Europe with the German Jews who had arrived in the new country several decades earlier. The national movement and the mass immigration, two historical phenomena that involved vast numbers of Jews in the wake of the events of 1881–82, gave birth to two new large centers of Jewish life in the twentieth century: the United States and Israel.

*   *   *

We opened the story of the history of Eastern European Jewry with a corporative society, integrated into a feudal economy in a "republic" of noblemen. The economic and political infrastructure of Poland-Lithuania was the firm basis upon which a religious society was built, a society whose spiritual world was filled by talmudic scholarship and Jewish esoterica. The partitions of Poland exposed the Jews to the disruptive forces of the centralized state and the modernist influences coming from the West. A century later, the Jews were being rudely ousted from their traditional cycles of existence and were moving in masses from the town to the city, from the Old World to the New World overseas. The attempts of Eastern European Jews to grapple with questions of their identity and to adapt to the changing reality around them gave rise to diverse ideas, streams, and movements that became the great contours of modern Jewish history. The world of Eastern European Jews more than a century ago seems very distant from contemporary Israeli reality; but if we delve more deeply into the history of this large society, we will probably find quite a few lines of continuity that link the "nation," which, in the nineteenth century, lived within three empires, to the Jewish-Israeli "nationality."

Jews as an Ethnic Minority in Eastern Europe

When Simon Dubnow, the Jewish historian and a man of the Russian empire, set out to explain how Eastern European Jewry fit into the ethnic-political tapestry of the sixteenth and seventeenth centuries, he chose to underscore the dualism that typified their social situation: "Every Jewish community was, in a sense, a small cell in the body of Jewish autonomy, and the aggregation of all these cells became a national force that created a solid organization in the great Jewish centers in Poland and Lithuania. The Jewish people, distanced from activity in general state-building, managed to build its inner structure in a manner at least no worse than the Polish nation, which was subordinate to its ruling classes."[1]

With these remarks, Dubnow, the national historian and exponent of the centers theory, noted the parallelism and resemblance that, in his opinion, existed between the Jewish corporate organization and social organizations in the non-Jewish surroundings. Concurrently, however, Dubnow stressed the dissociation between the autonomous Jewish organization and the non-Jewish political systems.[2] Like Dubnow, other Jewish historians who espoused a nationalist worldview tended to trace their modern national perceptions back to the Middle Ages. Modern Jewish nationalism in its various hues, the social radicalism that typified many writers of Jewish history in Eastern Europe, and the intensive political life of the early twentieth century, in which Eastern European intellectuals were immersed, all left a significant imprint on the way historians perceived relations between Jews and the various ethnic groups in their surroundings. National and social perceptions that painted an anachronistic picture of reality worked their way into the historiography of Eastern European Jewry. Ideas and attitudes of the modern era focused on questions that were at the forefront of the modern public debate in Russia and Poland: class conflicts prompted by economic factors; the national identity of ethnic groups; and struggles between "progressive" and "conservative" social elements. Keeping in mind Simon Dubnow's remarks, we ask: Were the Jews, a minority group that resided in Eastern Europe for several centuries, a deviant, exceptional phenomenon in terms of status and function, or was Eastern European Jewry a sector that had integrated into its surroundings and functioned as an organic part of it?

Although Dubnow applied a plenitude of anachronistic national concepts to Eastern European Jewish history, he stands apart from Zionist-oriented historians in one striking respect. Since his vision of the political future espoused an integration of the autonomous Jewish communities into the political life of the modern multinational empire, the Russian Jewish historian tended to seek the origins of the desired future integration in the sociopolitical reality of the recent past. In contrast, Ben–Zion Dinur, the most salient representative of the Zionist outlook, underscored the alienness and difference that typified the Jews vis-à-vis their Eastern European surroundings. In one instance, Dinur cited a parable by R. Solomon Eidels (the Maharsha) about the condition of the Jews in exile in order to substantiate what he considered to be the actual situation of Polish Jewry in the sixteenth and early seventeenth centuries. The Polish Jewish sage used an anecdote by the talmudic hyperbolist Raba bar bar Hanna: "Once we were traveling by ship and we saw a fish on whose back sand was rising and large reeds were growing. Thinking that he was dry land, we went up and baked and cooked on his back, and when the fish's back became hot, he flipped over. Had the ship not been close by, we would have drowned in the sea."[3] The fish that the passengers likened to dry land was the Polish diaspora, living in ostensible security until buffeted by the next spate of violence, which destabilized and destroyed a seemingly stable and eternally sustainable situation. The historians Dubnow and Dinur differed in their degree of optimism—after the fact, of course—about the likelihood of the Jews' integrating into the surrounding social and political systems. Dubnow believed that the Jews would continue to exist in the Diaspora as a national group within a multinational empire and would be, concurrently, equally privileged citizens and possessors of national rights.

Dubnow's optimism was largely grounded in his dialectical understanding of history. In an excerpt from his diary written in early 1901, he expressed his hope that the next century would be better than the previous one:

We are entering the twentieth century. What will it bring us, mankind in general and Jews in particular? Judging by the history of the last decades of the past century, one might think that mankind is entering a new Middle Ages, what with the horrors of war and national struggle, and the destruction of the highest ethical principles in politics and private life. But I do not want to believe in such over-generalizations. The current, vile wave of reaction must bring a counterreaction. The eighteenth century was the age of intellectual revolutions, the nineteenth century—the age of political revolutions and scientific and intellectual progress.

The twentieth century must bring a moral revolution. An ethical revolution in the conscience of the majority, now corrupted by the growth of materialistic culture at the expense of spiritual culture, must take place.[4]

Dinur, in contrast, foresaw irresolvable difficulties in the process of Jewish integration into the sociopolitical fabric of their surroundings. Here we deal neither with Dubnow's political optimism, which was carried forward in the historical writings of Salo Baron,[5] nor with the Zionists' pessimism, which was reinforced in a horrific manner with the destruction of Eastern European Jewry in World War II.[6] Our concern is with the integration itself, namely, with its structural aspects, the changes that occurred in forms of integration into general social and political contexts, and the acceptance of these forms in Jewish society and the societies surrounding it. Indeed, the more optimistic approach, the one enunciated by Dubnow and Baron, also assumes more openness in Jewish-Gentile relations and a strong correspondence between various phenomena in the Jewish and non-Jewish societies. However, even the more pessimistic historiography did not categorically rule out some degree of relations between Jews and their surroundings nor did it totally obscure the parallels and similarities that existed between the Jewish community and non-Jewish society.

Corporative Jewry in the Polish-Lithuanian Commonwealth

Our point of departure in examining this issue is a model of Eastern European society in which each social group had singular characteristics in a number of domains. To explain this model, which was valid at least until the middle of the nineteenth century in the areas that had been controlled by the Polish-Lithuanian Commonwealth before the partitioning of Poland (1772–95), we use the opening paragraph of the memoirs of Dov Ber of Bolechów. Dov Ber (1723–1805), a long-established eighteenth-century wine dealer whom we quoted at the beginning of this book, describes how his father amassed his wealth:

And he traded there in Hungarian wines and ordered the building of a fair cellar where the wines were laid. And sold them each year to the *pritzim* [Polish nobles] . . . at a certain profit and waxed rich. . . . [A]nd since in the mountainous property they have few fields fit for sowing, my father was obliged to enter into negotiations with the uncircumcised [Ruthenians] who were his serfs . . . and came to an agreement with the lessees of the salt trade in the town of Bolechów to supply him with timber from the forest, and in return for a wagonload of timber to be brought to the salt factory he was to give him one barrel of good-quality salt, and this they did all through the winter, and when summer came . . . all the uncircumcised from the village set out with their wagons and each took with him ten barrels of salt, and they traveled to the district of Podolia and exchanged the salt for grain. . . . [A]nd from the grain they manufactured vodka, which many people purchased and took to the land of Hungary in large quantities . . . thereby making a profit.[7]

This excerpt, in which the merchant presents a detailed account of his father's economic activity, portrays an ethnic environment in which three distinct groups are active (with the exception of the Hungarians, who live elsewhere). Each group has its own language, religion, political and legal status, occupations, and geographically distinct places of residence. The first group, cited in the text as the *pritzim* or the *srores*, is the nobility.[8] The members of this group were Poles, or Polonized members of other ethnic groups; they spoke Polish, professed the Catholic faith, had active political rights (suffrage privileges in the local and national class assemblies), and were entitled to own land and means of production. They lived in rural estates or urban residences in towns that they owned.

The second group—the "uncircumcised," the "serfs," and the "enslaved"—consisted of Ruthenian peasants. They spoke Western Ukrainian, professed (in this part of southeastern Poland) the Greek Catholic faith, had no occupation save cultivating the land of the rural estate, and had no political rights. They had extremely limited property rights, were required to cultivate the nobles' lands, and, for the most part, dwelled in villages or on the fringes of towns.

The third group, represented in the foregoing excerpt by Dov Ber's father, were the Jews. Their vernacular was Yiddish (as part of the Hebrew-Yiddish diglossia that traditional Ashkenazi society practiced until the twentieth century),[9] they practiced the Jewish faith, and they had townsmen's privileges, extensive community autonomy, and the legal right to own urban properties. They earned much of their livelihood by leasing means of production from the Polish nobility and employing the serfs, but they also engaged in import-export. The Jews dwelled in cities or legally constituted part of an urban community if they lived in villages. Although the above account of the economic activity of Dov Ber's father pertains to one town in southern Poland, it reflects the situation throughout the commonwealth of Poland-Lithuania until the late eighteenth century,[10] a situation that, in the western districts of the Russian empire[11] and in Austrian-ruled Galicia,[12] persisted until the second half of the nineteenth century.

In Eastern Europe, there was a strong correlation between ethnic origin, language, religion, legal status, political rights, occupation, and place of residence. The Polish state, until it was partitioned, had a class system in which a sizable minority of nobles controlled political life and rural and urban means of production, in contrast to a large majority of serfs of various ethnic affiliations. Different regions had ethnically and

religiously differentiated serfs. In Lithuania, the serfs were Catholic Lithuanians or Greek Orthodox Belorussians; in Eastern Ukraine, they were
Greek Orthodox Ukrainians; and in the Western Ukraine (where Dov
Ber lived), they were Greek Catholic West Ukrainians (Ruthenians).
Although the Jewish sources term all of them, collectively, 'arelim (the
uncircumcised) or meshu'abadim (the enslaved), without drawing a
precise ethnic differentiation, there is an awareness of the religious difference among the groups.[13] The Jews, whose population in Poland-
Lithuania in the late eighteenth century verged on one million and
exceeded that of the nobility,[14] were sharply and clearly differentiated
from nobles as well as serfs. Although there were non-Catholic nobles
and townsmen from several ethnic groups, the model is generally valid.
The Jews were part of the urban class, which included several ethnic sub-
groups (such as the Scots,[15] the Greeks, and the Germans). The status
of the Jews in Poland was immeasurably better than that of the peasant
serfs in every respect: they enjoyed the freedom of movement and the
right to own urban properties, and their letters of privileges gave them
total religious freedom and judicial autonomy.[16]

Thus, in the political reality of the Polish-Lithuanian Commonwealth
in the eighteenth century, Jews were clearly players in a system in which
class, religion, and economic function converged with ethnicity and language. Obviously, since the members of this corporate entity were Jews,
a religious minority in a Christian environment, everything related to
Jewish otherness in medieval society applied to the Jews in the commonwealth. The Catholic Church in Poland and the far-reaching activity of
the Jesuit order, from the Counter-Reformation era, magnified the
effect of this otherness in the seventeenth and eighteenth centuries.[17]
However, this did not have much of an impact on the daily lives of the
Jews, particularly since the Jewish community had developed efficient
defense mechanisms against excessive church meddling in its affairs.
The supra-communal organizations utilized relations that members of
the Jewish elite had established with Polish government officials. The
leasing, commercial, and financial transactions that took place between
thousands of Jews and numerous families of the nobility throughout the
commonwealth made it possible to intervene continually on the behalf
of individuals and communities.

A much more significant concern in the Jews' sociopolitical integration was the hostility and rivalry that emanated from the Christian burgher class, the class closest to them in terms of legal privileges and
economic affairs. The weakness of this class relative to the strength of
the nobility allowed the Jews to maintain their place in the system. Even
when the strength of the burgher class increased, the Jews solved the
problem of their integration by migrating to the east and taking part in

the new town-building endeavor that the upper nobility had initiated in the Polish frontier areas in the southeastern part of the commonwealth.[18]

Although corporate Jewry was exceptional in that it practiced a different religion and engaged in fierce rivalry with the non-Jewish townsmen, the Jews in the Polish-Lithuanian Commonwealth generally held their ground with the active assistance of the upper nobility. Thus, the Jews in this region not only waged a struggle based on an ethnic background and an economic rivalry, but they also developed a modus operandi for life within the existing social constellation. Until the end of the eighteenth century, corporate Jewry managed to function successfully as a group with distinctive traits as long as the Polish state remained corporate in nature. The menace to the Jews' future as an integral part of the previously defined system stemmed neither from the threat posed by the Church nor from the struggle with the Christian townsmen. It came, foremost, from the very destabilization of the feudal-corporate system in which the Jews, until the partitions, lived as a sector that had a specific role and visible, recognizable characteristics within the framework of the general system.

The Centralized State and Corporate Jewry

The feudal-corporate system in which the Jews were immersed crumbled in the nineteenth century in the wake of the partitioning of Poland, the waning political strength of the Polish nobility, and the ascendancy of capitalist economies in Eastern Europe. The centralized states that carved up the Polish-Lithuanian Commonwealth did not accept the socioeconomic model that had existed in the annexed areas with respect to the Jews. Even the Polish social reformers and statesmen changed their minds about the Jews' role in the sociopolitical reality of Eastern Europe. Sweeping reforms of the Jews' status, designed to sever the Jewish population from the rural leasing economy, had been proposed as early as the second half of the eighteenth century. This reform activity took place in the dying days of the independent Kingdom of Poland, during the the four-year *Sejm* (1788–91), the reign of Joseph II in Galicia (in the 1780s), and during the reforms carried out at the beginning of the reign of Czar Alexander I in Russia, which gave rise to the Jewish constitution of 1804.

Two aims challenged the Jews' role in the Eastern European socioeconomic constellation from the mid-eighteenth century: (1) to disincorporate Jewish society and to integrate the Jews into the general frameworks of the state administration; and (2) to identify the Jews as an inseparable part of the townsmen class (even though some in Austria and Congress

Poland believed that the Jews could be integrated into all possible social classes). The ultimate intent of these two trends—which are clearly identifiable in Russian, Austrian, and Polish (in the autonomous areas that had a separate legal status in the nineteenth century) legislation pertaining to the Jews until the second half of the nineteenth century—was to destroy the status of the Jewish sector within the old model of life. Their aims were much more radical vis-à-vis the Jews than merely to undermine the general model itself. The gradual repeal of Jewish autonomy was meant to separate the Jews' ethnic identity from their legal status and religious singularity and to integrate them into a much broader corporate entity embracing Christians and Jews, thereby abolishing the Jews' separate legal jurisdiction. The purpose of identifying the Jews as an integral part of the urban class, expressed recurrently in Russian legislation between 1785 and the era of Czar Alexander II's reforms in 1856–63, was to eliminate the exclusivity of the Jews' economic specialization and abolish the link between occupation and legal status. The ideas of the European Enlightenment movement, coupled with the activity of the centralized state, provided an ideological infrastructure for the undermining of the Jews' role in the sociopolitical system.

Many of the Jews' occupations, which until the end of the eighteenth century were regarded as desirable, were now portrayed as unproductive, injurious to the state economy, and harmful to the well-being of the majority group in the population (the peasantry). For example, a memorandum by the Russian senator Drezhavin, who had been sent by Czar Pavel I to investigate the reasons for the famine that struck the White Russian provinces annexed from Poland in the first partition in 1772, cites the Jews' lack of productivity as the main cause of economic impoverishment in the region. The Haskalah movement, although largely bereft of influence on economic processes and political changes in Eastern Europe, internalized almost unquestioningly the criticism of the Jews' place within the old model.

Thus, as exogenous processes beyond the Jews' control were seriously disrupting their place in the feudal economy, the images of the old Jewish way of life were challenged by critics from within and without. It is no wonder that the most conspicuous supporters of the old model, including the Jews' role in it, were the first exponents of Jewish Orthodoxy in Eastern Europe. They discerned—correctly, from the historical perspective—a strong connection between the old-style corporate identity and the preservation of the world of traditional values. A salient example was the chief rabbi of Kraków (subsequently the chief rabbi of Warsaw at the time of the 1863 Polish uprising against Russia), Dov Ber Meisels (1798–1870), who linked the political fate of Polish Jewry to the conservative wing of the Polish nobility. According to Meisels's logic, the traditional Jewish world could exist only if the old model, in which the political alliance between the Polish nobility and the Jews also sustained the Jews' economic role and legal autonomy, continued to exist.[19]

The policy of the absolutist governments was but one manifestation of the assault against the old model. While the governments of Austria and Russia acted consistently to redefine the Jews' position in the socio-political system, the Polish national movement from its very inception pondered the future role of the Jews in the framework of the Polish nation. Until the second half of the nineteenth century, the Polish nation, at least in the minds of many national activists, was identical to the status of the Polish aristocracy. Thus, the Jews were perceived as elements that should integrate into the Polish nation as townsmen. In various parts of partitioned Poland, considerable efforts were made to encourage urban Jews to adopt the Polish culture. The key players in this endeavor were educators and heads of the Polish universities in Russian-ruled Vilnius (Vilna), independent Kraków (under Austrian patronage), and Warsaw (in Congress Poland).[20] The imperial option and the Polish option vied with each other throughout the nineteenth century. After the 1863 uprising, the Russian influence on Jews in the eastern regions of Lithuania and Belorussia increased, and Polish influence had the upper hand in Austrian Galicia. However, the weakness of the non-Jewish urban class in these areas ruled out any possibility of Jews' integrating into the local urban element. The Jews remained ethnically and culturally separate, and their Russian or Polish acculturation did not result in assimilation.

National Movements and Nation-States

The gap between the intentions and plans—of the ruling officialdom in the absolutist state, or alternatively, of the Polish national movement—to integrate the Jews and what actually happened in nineteenth-century Eastern Europe led to the third phase in the history of the disintegration of the old corporate order. Corporate Jewry, with its religious and cultural uniqueness and diverse social and cultural functions, did not change as quickly as its external and internal critics desired. Undoubtedly, a major factor in the lack of correspondence between the political change that was occurring in the states of Eastern Europe and the pace of social and economic change among the Jews in these countries was the numerical size and wide geographical dispersion of the Jewish population.[21]

The Jews' "separatism," condemned by Russian and Austrian government officials, the Polish elite, as well as by the Maskilim, underwent a transformation in the mid-nineteenth century: what had been perceived as an interim situation worthy of change became a seemingly permanent and immutable trait. The appearance of national movements in Eastern Europe in the nineteenth century, movements that no longer accepted the exclusivity of the definition of "nation," which until then had been associated with the Polish nobility across the multinational empires, created a link between the premodern corporate situation and the "national" picture of the future.

The old model, as portrayed by Dov Ber of Bolechów, now became part of a "national" picture of the past, in which three national groups competed with one another. The first was the imperial nation, which sought to identify the dominant nation with the autochtonous nations. A salient example was the imperial Russian policy, which, instead of recognizing Ukrainian nationhood, deemed Ukrainians to be "Little Russians." The second group was that of the autochtonous nations, which sought to fortify their own distinct linguistic, cultural, or political identity. This group included the Ukrainians, the Belorussians, the Lithuanians, and other peoples of the western Russian empire and the eastern part of the Austro-Hungarian empire. The third group was the Jews. They found it difficult to integrate into the imperial nation (according to the political vision of the Haskalah movement) and were loathe to join the autochtonous nations among which they dwelled.

When the Jews were identified as a pro-imperial element, the ethnic and national tension mounted. According to the reconstruction of the Ukrainian national past, carried out as best as can be done from the writings of nineteenth-century Ukrainophiles such as Kostomarov, the peasants had been robbed of their independence by the Polish occupier, with the assistance of his Jewish agent.[22] The Ukrainian people was urged to liberate itself from the Jews' economic domination, which had lasted from the time of the Polish occupation of the Ukraine to the rule of the Russian czars. The depiction of Jewish-Ukrainian relations in broadsheets of revolutionary movements, mentioned in the previous chapter, urging the masses to participate in the pogroms of 1881 is typical:

That is not how things were in the Ukraine back then, in the days of our forefathers. The peasants owned all the land; back then there were no *pans* [nobles] or *zhids* [Jews]. The people were free Cossacks, they answered to the elected community elders only. . . . That is how things were until the Russian czars came to the Ukraine. As soon as they arrived, this cheerful country dressed itself in sorrow. They deprived the people of all the land, handed some of it to the *pans*, their close associates, and sold some of it to the Jewboys, and handed the freemen to them as slaves.[23]

This use of the past for political mobilization is a distinct indicator of the change that had occurred in the relations among ethnic groups in Eastern Europe. The Jews were perceived as aliens at both the ethnic and the economic-class levels. In contradistinction to the pre-partition period, the former serfs were portrayed as a full-fledged "people" for whom full political privileges were claimed as well as the ouster of the other elements of the old order (nobles and Jews). Exponents of the Jewish national movement, which appeared on the political map of Eastern Europe in the 1880s, when the remarks cited above were written, tended to accept the derogatory description of the Jews' role in their Eastern European surroundings. From their standpoint, it was an inevitable result of the anomaly of the Jewish situation in the Diaspora. To correct this state of affairs, the old order, a legacy of the Polish-Lithuanian Commonwealth era, should be swept aside and the Jews should spread into all fields of economic activity. In other words, the Jewish nationalists, like the Ukrainophiles, considered the Jews a "class" of the old style. Furthermore, the Jews' anomalous situation should be corrected, at least in the opinion of the Zionist (and territorialist) nationalists, by removing them from the economic and ethnic mold of Eastern Europe.

This anachronistic reading of the late nineteenth-century situation made it impossible to continue regarding the Jews as an integral component of a socioeconomic system. Furthermore, the modern national movements left no room for the continued existence in the present of the remnants of that system. The Jewish national vision presumed that the Jews who inhabited each area of the multinational empires that succeeded the Polish-Lithuanian Commonwealth would undergo a process of transition from a class to a nation. In other words, the Jewish nation would shift from a state of occupationally specialized corporate ethnicity to a state in which economic and political activity would be dispersed among the various segments of the ethnic group. On this point, there was total consensus between the Jewish nationalists and each of the national movements that emerged in Eastern Europe at the turn of the nineteenth and twentieth centuries. This consensus viewed a corporate entity with unique markers, separate political status, and economic specialization as an anomaly that should be assimilated into the local nationality or, alternatively, banished from the national territory.

Paradoxically, the Jews were inclined at this stage to rely on the imperial regime, the very regime that aspired from the outset to undermine the old, premodern model that had survived from the pre-partition era. The autonomism of several prominent Jewish national movements, including Simon Dubnow's Jewish People's Party, the Bund, and the

Avodat Hahoveh of the Zionist movement at the turn of the century, were simply manifestations of a political attempt to sustain Jewry as an "integrated sector" that, ironically, maintained its premodern uniqueness with the assistance of the imperial regime. Within the framework of the multinational empire, Eastern European Jewry could continue to function as one of several ethnic minorities, sustaining in a somewhat evolutionary fashion the corporate nature of the previous centuries. For example, the political platforms of the three aforementioned movements explicitly mentioned representative institutions that they perceived as outgrowths of the premodern autonomy. Dubnow aptly defined this type of Jewish ethnic integration into the modern state as a situation in which "Jews in each and every country who take an active part in civic and political life enjoy all rights given to the citizens, not merely as individuals, but also as members of their national groups."[24]

The demise of the multinational empire as a consequence of World War I and the ascendancy of single-nation states in the interwar period eliminated the evolution option that mainstream currents in Jewish politics had espoused. The Ashkenazi diaspora, which until 1918 dwelled within the confines of three multinational empires, disintegrated into separate units within the single-nation states that came into being on the ruins of the old imperial order. The disintegration of the empires ostensibly augured the possibility of carrying out the autonomist venture. This is because the victorious powers ordered new states that had been granted independence on a national basis (such as Poland and the Baltic countries) to recognize the rights of the minority groups under their rule. However, the new nation-states resisted these demands, regarding them as a crude intervention into their internal affairs. The Jews' singularity was defined in national terms both by spokespersons of ruling nations in the new single-nation states and by exponents of the Jewish national movements themselves.

A by-product of the ascendancy of single-nation states in Eastern Europe was the erosion of the erstwhile image of European Jewry as an integrated sector and an upturn in the strength of the Zionist narrative. This narrative, with which we began our remarks, left no further room for the Dubnow-style historical account. Only in recent years has a new generation of historians, trained in the United States, begun to reexamine the extent of the Jews' integration into the political and social tapestry of Eastern Europe.[25] Their works and those of several Israeli and Polish historians repeatedly question the degree of the Jews' integration into the premodern social and economic systems. These inquiries underscore the commonalities and similarities rather than the differences and dissimilarities between the systems.

Summary

In portraying Eastern European Jewry, the world's largest Jewish community in the modern era, in its ethnic and political milieu, historiography uses terms borrowed from the lexicon of various Jewish ideological movements prior to World War II. Modern Jewish nationalism in its various versions, social radicalism, and Russian liberalism have left a significant imprint on the profile of relations between the Jews and the various ethnic groups in their surroundings. Apologetics stemming from the immediate needs of Jewish minorities in various countries added an anachronistic shade of a different kind.

Here an attempt was made to create a model of Eastern European society in which Jewry was integrated as a cell in an organism in which each ethnic group was characterized by a string of unique markers and specific social and economic functions. This model, which corresponded to historical reality in the Polish-Lithuanian Commonwealth until the end of the eighteenth century, gradually ceased to exist in the nineteenth century. In the nineteenth and twentieth centuries, various attempts were made—by governments in states inhabited by Jews from partitioned Poland and by various groups in the Jewish population—to make the Jews adapt to other models of integration. This integration was supported by the administrative apparatus of the centralized state, which sought to integrate the Jews as subjects; but it was impeded by separatist trends of various ethnic groups in the multinational empires.

The history of the premodern Jewish community, the Haskalah movement in Eastern Europe, and the growth of the modern national movement were, according to the model portrayed here, consummate manifestations of three phases in the relations between the Jews and their surroundings: (a) the premodern corporate entity as an element of the general corporate system; (b) subjects of the centralized empire; and (c) a different and separate nation amid a multinational reality of crumbling empires.

Notes

Introduction

1. E. Orren, "Yiddish Journalism in the London East End, 1883–87: The Turning Point between Socialism and Hibbat Zion" (Hebrew), *Hatsionut* 2 (1972): 47–63.

2. Tsvi (Heinrich) Graetz, *Essays, Memoirs, Letters* (Hebrew), ed. S. Ettinger (Jerusalem, 1969), pp. 213–34.

3. G. D. Hundert, *Jews in Poland-Lithuania in the Eighteenth Century: A Genealogy of Modernity* (Berkeley, Calif., 2004), p. 4.

4. E. Zerubavel, *Time Maps: Collective Memory and the Social Shape of the Past* (Chicago, 2003), p. 96.

5. In H. H. Ben-Sasson, ed., *A History of the Jewish People* (Cambridge, Mass., 1976), p. 853.

6. On the way in which ideology, politics, and historical writing were linked by this Israeli historian, see I. Bartal and J. Frankel, "An Engaged Historian: Shmuel Ettinger on the History of the Jews in Eastern Europe" (Hebrew), in S. Ettinger, *On the History of the Jews in Poland and Russia: Collected Essays*, ed. I. Bartal and J. Frankel (Jerusalem, 1995), pp. xi–xxiii; I. Bartal, "Eastern Europe as a Focal Point for Modern Jewish History: Preliminary Reflections on the Teaching of Shmuel Ettinger" (Hebrew), in *Studies in Modern Jewish History*, ed. S. Ettinger (Jerusalem, 1992), pp. 27–30.

7. S. Ettinger, *History of the Jews from the Age of Absolutism to the State of Israel* (Hebrew) (Jerusalem, 1968), pp. 165–68, 193–98.

8. J. Frankel, *Prophecy and Politics: Socialism, Nationalism, and the Russian Jews, 1862–1917* (New York, 1981), p. 49.

9. B. Nathans, *Beyond the Pale: The Jewish Encounter with Late Imperial Russia* (Berkeley, Calif., 2002), p. 9.

10. S. E. Aschheim, *Brothers and Strangers: The East European Jew in German and German Jewish Consciousness, 1800–1923* (Madison, Wisc., 1982), pp. 3–31.

11. On the "invention" of Eastern Europe, see Larry Wolff, *Inventing Eastern Europe: The Map of Civilization on the Mind of the Enlightenment* (Stanford, Calif., 1994).

12. N. Hanover, *Yeven metsula* (Venice, 1653). In English translation, *Abyss of Despair* (New York, 1950).

13. See C. Gartner's innovative article "The Beginning of Orthodox Historiography in Eastern Europe: A Reassessment" (Hebrew), *Zion* 67 (2002): 293–336. See also A. Rapoport-Albert, "Historiography with Footnotes: Edifying Tales and the Writing of History in Hasidism," *History and Theory* 27 (1988): 119–59; I. Bartal, "True Knowledge and Wisdom: On Orthodox Historiography," *Studies in Contemporary Jewry* 10 (1994): 178–91.

14. S. Dubnow, "Nahpesah ve-nakhkorah," *Pardes* 1 (1892): 226. Here cited from S. Zipperstein, *Imagining Russian Jewry: Memory, History, Identity* (Seattle, 1999), p. 90.

15. S. Y. Fuenn, *Kiryah ne'emanah*, expanded 2d ed. (Vilna, 1914), p. 19. On the writer and on the circumstances in which this book was written, see M. Zalkin, introduction to H. N. Magid (Steinshneider), *Ir Vilna* (Hebrew) (Jerusalem, 2002), 2:20.

16. S. Buber, *Anshei shem asher shimshu bakodesh be'ir Levuv* (Kraków, 1895), p. vii.

17. I. Howe and R. Wisse, eds., *The Best of Sholem Aleichem* (New York, 1982), p. xviii.

18. I. Bartal, "Dubnov's Image of Medieval Autonomy," in *A Missionary for History: Essays in Honor of Simon Dubnov*, ed. K. Groberg and A. Greenbaum (Minneapolis, 1998), p. 15.

19. I. Bartal, "Responses to Modernity: Haskalah, Orthodoxy, and Nationalism in Eastern Europe," in *Zionism and Religion*, ed. S. Almog, J. Reinharz, and A. Shapira (Hanover, N.H., 1998), pp. 13–24.

20. Zipperstein, *Imagining Russian Jewry*, p. 20.

Chapter 1

1. Israel Halpern, *Eastern European Jewry: Historical Studies* (Hebrew) (Jerusalem, 1969), pp. 9–33.

2. Chone Shmeruk, "Young Men from Germany in the Yeshivot of Poland" (Hebrew), in *The Call for a Prophet*, ed. Israel Bartal (Jerusalem, 1999), pp. 3–17.

3. See, for example, Gershon David Hundert, "The *Kehilla* and the Municipality in Private Towns at the End of the Early Modern Period," in *The Jews in Old Poland, 1000–1795*, ed. A. Polonsky, J. Basista, and A. Link-Lenczowski (New York, 1993), pp. 174–85.

4. Simon Dubnow, *Nationalism and History: Essays on Old and New Judaism*, ed. with an introduction by K. S. Pinson (Philadelphia, 1961), p. 133.

5. Shmuel Ettinger, "The Council of the Four Lands," in *The Jews in Old Poland*, ed. Polonsky et al., pp. 93–109; Israel Bartal, "The *Pinkas* of the Council of the Four Lands," in ibid., pp. 110–18.

6. Israel Halpern, "The Structure of the Councils in Central and Eastern Europe in the Seventeenth and Eighteenth Centuries" (Hebrew), in idem, *Eastern European Jewry*, pp. 55–60.

7. Jacob Goldberg, "The Council of the Four Lands in the Social and Political Regime of the Polish-Lithuanian Kingdom" (Hebrew), in *The Jewish Society in the Polish Commonwealth* (Jerusalem, 1999), pp. 125–42. A previous version of this chapter was published in English: Jacob Goldberg, "The Jewish *Sejm*: Its Origins and Functions," in *The Jews in Old Poland*, ed. Polonsky et al., pp. 147–65.

8. Moshe Rosman, "The Authority of the Council of the Four Lands outside of Poland" (Hebrew), *Yearbook of Bar-Ilan University* 24–25 (1989): 11–30.

9. Israel Halpern, ed., *The Records of the Council of the Four Lands* (Hebrew) (Jerusalem, 1945), p. 312.

Chapter 2

1. Judith Kalik, *The Polish Nobility and the Jews in the Deitine Legislation of the Polish-Lithuanian Commonwealth* (Hebrew) (Jerusalem, 1997), pp. 25–36.

2. Israel Halpern, ed., *The Records of the Council of the Four Lands* (Hebrew) (Jerusalem, 1945), p. 312.

3. *The Memoirs of Ber of Bolechów*, trans. M. Wischnitzer (London, 1922), p. 143. See also Israel Bartal, "Dov of Bolechów: A Diarist of the Council of the Four Lands in the Eighteenth Century," *Polin* 9 (1996): 187–91.

4. *The Memoirs of Ber of Bolechów*, p. 150.

5. Halpern, *The Records of the Council of the Four Lands*, p. 440.

6. Artur Eisenbach, "The Four Years' *Sejm* and the Jews," in *The Jews in Old Poland, 1000–1795*, ed. A. Polonsky, J. Basista, and A. Link-Lenczowski (New York, 1993), pp. 73–89; Gershon D. Hundert, *Jews in Poland-Lithuania in the Eighteenth Century: A Genealogy of Modernity* (Berkeley, Calif., 2004), pp. 216–31.

7. Material relating to the status of the Jews in the four-year *Sejm* was published in the sixth volume of the debates of this parliament (ed. Artur Eisenbach et al. [Warsaw, 1969]). See Jacob Goldberg, "From Lobbying to Statesmanship: Community Representatives in the Time of the Four-Year *Sejm*, 1788–92" (Hebrew), in *The Jewish Society in the Polish Commonwealth* (Jerusalem, 1999), pp. 217–31; Adolf Haber, "Jewish Innkeepers in the Writings of Polish Publicists of the Grand *Sejm*, 1788–92" (Hebrew), *Gal-ed* 2 (1975): 1–24.

8. Frances Malino, *A Jew in the French Revolution: The Life of Zalkind Hourwitz* (Oxford, 1996), pp. 84–85; Hundert, *Jews in Poland-Lithuania*, pp. 216–20.

9. Israel Bartal, "Heroes or Cowards: Jews in the Armies of Poland, 1794–1863" (Hebrew), in *The Broken Chain: Polish Jewry through the Ages*, ed. Israel Bartal and Israel Gutman (Jerusalem, 1997), 1:358.

10. Ibid., 1:359.

11. Yehezkel Kotik, *Journey to a Nineteenth-Century Shtetl: The Memoirs of Yehezkel Kotik*, introduced by David Assaf (Detroit, 2002), p. 341.

Chapter 3

1. For an up-to-date summary on the subject, see Shaul Stampfer, "Population Growth and Immigration among Polish-Lithuanian Jewry" (Hebrew), in *The Broken Chain: Polish Jewry through the Ages*, ed. Israel Bartal and Israel Gutman (Jerusalem, 1997), 1:263–85.

2. On the Jewish community of Odessa, see Steven Zipperstein, *The Jews of Odessa: A Cultural History, 1794–1881* (Stanford, Calif., 1985).

3. Ben-Zion Dinur, "The Historical Shape of Russian Jewry and Problems of Studying It" (Hebrew), in *Generations and Records: Studies in Jewish Historiography, Historical Writings* (Jerusalem, 1978), 4:202–3.

4. Raphael Mahler, *Hasidism and the Jewish Enlightenment: Their Confrontation in Galicia and Poland in the First Half of the Nineteenth Century* (New York, 1985), pp. 105–19, 197–98.

5. Michael Hendel, *Crafts and Craftsmen among the Jewish People* (Hebrew) (Tel Aviv, 1955), p. 106.

6. Magdalena Opalski, *The Jewish Tavern Keeper and His Tavern in Nineteenth-Century Polish Literature* (Jerusalem, 1986).

7. Bina Garncarsha-Kadary, "The Jews in the Economic Development of Poland in the Nineteenth Century" (Hebrew), in *The Broken Chain*, ed. Bartal and Gutman, 1:315–36; idem, "The Jews and Factors in the Development and Location of Industry in Warsaw" (Hebrew), *Gal-ed* 2 (1975): 25–58; idem, "The Legal and Socioeconomic Situation of Kraków Jewry, 1796–1868" (Hebrew), in

Kroke-Kazimierz-Kraków: Studies in the History of Kraków Jewry, ed. Elchanan Reiner (Tel Aviv, 2001), pp. 89–118.

Chapter 4

1. Moshe Idel, *Hasidism: Between Ecstasy and Magic* (New York, 1995), p. 27.
2. Gershom Scholem, "*Devekut* or Communion with God," in *The Messanic Idea in Judaism* (New York, 1971), pp. 203–27.
3. Recently, several innovative studies on the Besht's biography, personality, and doctrine, as well as the ways that the Hasidic movement spread, have been published. Among these are Immanuel Etkes, *The Besht: Magician, Mystic and Leader* (Hanover, N.H., 2004); Moshe Rosman, *Founder of Hasidism: A Quest for the Historical Ba'al Shem Tov* (Berkeley, Calif., 1996).
4. Israel Bartal, "From an Intimate Circle to a Mass Movement: The Emergence of Hasidism," *Studia Judaica* 3 (1994): 7–16.
5. On the *kloiz*, see Elchanan Reiner, "Wealth, Social Position, and the Study of Torah: The Status of the *Kloiz* in Eastern European Jewish Society in the Early Modern Period" (Hebrew), *Zion* 57 (1993): 287–328.
6. Chone Shmeruk, "The Social Significance of Hasidic Ritual Slaughtering" (Hebrew), in *The Call for a Prophet*, ed. Israel Bartal (Jerusalem, 1999), pp. 33–63.
7. Idem, "Hasidism and Leasehold Transactions," in ibid., pp. 64–77.
8. Ibid., p. 69, based on *Sefer hitgalut hatzadikim* (Hebrew) (Warsaw, 1901), pp. 42–43.
9. Shmuel Ettinger, "Hasidism and the *Kahal* in Eastern Europe," in *Hasidism Reappraised*, ed. Ada Rapoport-Albert (London, 1996), pp. 63–75.
10. David Assaf, *The Regal Way: The Life and Times of Rabbi Israel of Ruzhin* (Stanford, Calif., 2002), pp. 181–87.
11. From *Zmir aritzim* (Warsaw, 1798), cited in M. Wilensky, *Hasidim and Mitnagdim: A Study of the Controversy between Them in the Years 1772–1815* (Hebrew) (Jerusalem, 1970), 2:192–93.
12. On the Gaon of Vilna's anti-Hasidic views, see Immanuel Etkes, *The Gaon of Vilna: The Man and His Image* (Berkeley, Calif., 2002), pp. 73–95.
13. Idem, *Rabbi Israel Salanter and the Mussar Movement: Seeking the Torah of Truth* (Philadelphia, 1993), pp. 30–56.
14. On the Volohzin yeshiva and its role in social and cultural developments in nineteenth-century Eastern Europe, see Shaul Stampfer, *The Formation of the Lithuanian Yeshiva* (Hebrew) (Jerusalem, 1995), pp. 217–25.
15. Arthur Green, *Tormented Master: A Life of Rabbi Nahman of Bratslav* (Tuscaloosa, Ala., 1979).
16. Shmuel Feiner, "*Sola Fide!* The Polemic of Rabbi Nathan of Nemirov against Atheism and Haskalah" (Hebrew), in *Studies in Hasidism*, ed. David Assaf, Joseph Dan, and Immanuel Etkes (Jerusalem, 1999), pp. 89–124. For an Orthodox version of R. Nathan, see Chaim Kramer, *Through Fire and Water: The Life of Reb Noson of Breslov* (Jerusalem, 1993).
17. Joseph Perl, *Hasidic Tales and Letters* (Hebrew), ed. Shmuel Werses and Chone Shmeruk (Jerusalem, 1969).
18. Shmuel Werses, "Hasidism in the Eyes of Haskalah Literature: From the Polemic of Galician Maskilim" (Hebrew), in *Trends and Forms in Haskalah Literature* (Jerusalem, 1990), pp. 91–109.

19. Dov Taylor, *Joseph Perl's Revealer of Secrets: The First Hebrew Novel* (Boulder, Colo., 1997).

20. *In Praise of the Baal Shem Tov* [*Shivhei ha-Besht*], trans. and ed. Dan Ben-Amos and Jerome R. Mintz (Bloomington, Ind., 1972).

Chapter 5

1. John D. Klier, *Russia Gathers Her Jews: The Origins of the "Jewish Question" in Russia, 1772–1825* (Dekalb, Ill., 1986), p. 60.

2. Shmuel Ettinger, "Major Factors in Russian Policy toward the Jews in the Time of the Partitions" (Hebrew), in *On the History of the Jews in Poland and Russia*, ed. Israel Bartal and Jonathan Frankel (Jerusalem, 1995), pp. 217–33.

3. R. Pipes, "Catherine II and the Jews: The Origins of the Pale of Settlement," *Soviet Jewish Affairs* 5, no. 2 (1975): 3–20.

4. Klier, *Russia Gathers Her Jews*, pp. 69–75.

5. Ibid., p. 75.

6. Simon Dubnow, *History of the Jews in Russia and Poland*, trans. I. Friedlaender (Philadelphia, 1946), 1:316.

7. Shmuel Ettinger, "The Statute of 1804" (Hebrew), in *On the History of the Jews in Poland and Russia*, ed. Bartal and Frankel, pp. 243–56.

8. Klier, *Russia Gathers Her Jews*, p. 141.

9. Israel Halpern, *Eastern European Jewry: Historical Studies* (Hebrew) (Jerusalem, 1969), pp. 340–47; Arthur Green, *Tormented Master: A Life of Rabbi Nahman of Bratslav* (Tuscaloosa, Ala., 1979); Eli Lederhendler, *The Road to Modern Jewish Politics: Political Tradition and Political Reconstruction in the Jewish Community of Tsarist Russia* (New York, 1989), p. 180 n. 53.

10. Israel Bartal, "Heroes or Cowards: Jews in the Polish Armies, 1794–1863" (Hebrew), in *The Broken Chain: Polish Jewry through the Ages*, ed. Israel Bartal and Israel Gutman (Jerusalem, 1997), 1:353–67.

11. Dubnow, *History of the Jews in Russia and Poland*, 2:18–19.

12. On Uvarov's views on the Jews and their "reeducation," see Michael Stanislawski, *Tsar Nicholas I and the Jews: The Transformation of Jewish Society in Russia, 1825–1855* (Philadelphia, 1983), pp. 45–47, 59–69.

13. On the arrangement of the Ministry of Education's control over all the institutions of learning and science of the Jews, June 22, 1842, *Polnoe sobranie zakonov rossiiskoi imperii*, 2nd series (Saint Petersburg, 1830–84), vol. 17, no. 15571.

14. Stanislawski, *Tsar Nicholas I and the Jews*, pp. 123–27.

15. For a detailed survey of alternative autonomous organizations, see Isaac Levitats, *The Jewish Community in Russia, 1844–1917* (Jerusalem, 1981); Azriel Shochat, "Community Leadership in Russia after the Abolition of the *Kahal*" (Hebrew), *Zion* 42 (1977): 143–233.

16. On Montefiore's journey to Russia in 1846, see L. Loewe, ed., *Diaries of Sir Moses and Lady Montefiore* (London, 1983), pp. 320–84; Chimen Abramsky, "The Visits to Russia," in *The Century of Moses Montefiore*, ed. S. Lipman and V. D. Lipman (Oxford, 1985), pp. 254–65; Israel Bartal, "Nationalist before His Time, or a Belated *Shtadlan*?" (Hebrew), in *The Age of Moses Montefiore*, ed. I. Bartal (Jerusalem, 1987), pp. 5–24.

17. Israel Bartal, "Simon the Heretic: A Chapter in Orthodox Historiography" (Hebrew), in *According to the Custom of Ashkenaz and Poland: Studies in Jewish*

Culture in Honor of Chone Shmeruk, ed. I. Bartal, E. Mendelssohn, and C. Turniansky (Jerusalem, 1993), pp. 244–46.

18. Immanuel Etkes, *Rabbi Israel Salanter and the Mussar Movement: Seeking the Torah of Truth* (Philadelphia, 1993), p. 140.

Chapter 6

1. Abraham Brawer, *Galicia and Her Jews: Studies in the History of Eighteenth-Century Galicia* (Hebrew) (Jerusalem, 1965), p. 11.

2. Ibid., pp. 147–48.

3. Rabbi Yehezkel Landau, *Noda bi-Yehudah, Mahadura Tinyana, Even Ha'ezer,* 54; quoted here from Israel Halpern, *Eastern European Jewry: Historical Studies* (Hebrew) (Jerusalem, 1969), p. 300.

4. Edward Breuer, "Naphtali Herz Wessely and the Cultural Dislocations of an Eighteenth-Century Maskil," in *New Perspectives on the Haskalah*, ed. Shmuel Feiner and David Sorkin (London, 2001), pp. 27–47.

5. N. H. Wessely, *Divrei shalom ve'emet* (Berlin, 1782–85), chap. 8. On the Italian connection of the early Jewish Enlightenment, see Lois Dubin, "Trieste and Berlin: The Italian Role in the Cultural Politics of the Haskalah," in *Toward Modernity: The European Jewish Model*, ed. Jacob Katz (New Brunswick, N.J., 1987), pp. 189–224.

6. On Homberg's textbooks for Jewish children, see Mordecai Eliav, *Jewish Education in Germany in the Period of Enlightenment and Emancipation* (Hebrew) (Jerusalem, 1960), index.

7. Herz Homberg, *Imre shefer* (Vienna, 1808), pp. 360–62.

8. Joseph Perl, *Megaleh temirin* (Vienna, 1819), p. 3.2. Here cited from Dov Taylor, *Joseph Perl's Revealer of Secrets: The First Hebrew Novel* (Boulder, Colo., 1997), p. 24.

9. "R. Israel Loebel's Tractate in German" (Hebrew), in M. Wilensky, *Hasidim and Mitnagdim: A Study of the Controversy between Them, 1772–1815* (Jerusalem, 1970), 2:336. On the Austrian government's attitude toward the Hasidim after the death of Joseph II, see I. Kuperstein, "Inquiry at Polaniec: A Case Study of Hasidic Controversy in Eighteenth-Century Galicia," *Yearbook of Bar-Ilan University* 24–25 (1989): 25–39; Raphael Mahler, *Hasidism and the Jewish Enlightenment: Their Confrontation in Galicia and Poland in the First Half of the Nineteenth Century* (New York, 1985).

10. Israel Bartal and Antony Polonsky, "Introduction: The Jews of Galicia under the Habsburgs," *Polin* 12 (1999): 3–24.

11. Rachel Manekin, "*Daitshen*, Poles, or Austrians?: The Identity Dilemma of Galician Jews, 1848–51" (Hebrew), *Zion* 68 (2003): 223–62.

12. Israel Bartal, "Heroes or Cowards: Jews in the Polish Armies, 1794–1863" (Hebrew), in *The Broken Chain: Polish Jewry through the Ages*, ed. Israel Bartal and Israel Gutman (Jerusalem, 1997), 1:363.

13. Ibid., 1:362–63.

Chapter 7

1. I. L. Peretz, *My Memoirs*, trans. Fred Goldberg (New York, 1964), pp. 98–99, emphasis in original.

2. Artur Eisenbach, "The Central Representation of the Jews in the Warsaw

Duchy 1807–15" (Hebrew), in *The Broken Chain: Polish Jewry through the Ages,* ed. Israel Bartal and Israel Gutman (Jerusalem, 1997): 287–313.

3. For a detailed study of the emancipation of the Jews in nineteenth-century Poland, see Artur Eisenbach, *The Emancipation of the Jews in Poland, 1780–1870* (Oxford, 1991).

4. See chap. 2 in this vol., pp. 30–32.

5. D. Friedländer, *Über die Verbesserung der Israeliten in Königreich Pohlen* (Berlin, 1819).

6. The most updated study on the Polish authorities and Hasidism is M. Wodzinski, *Oswiecenie żydowskie w Królestwie Polskim wobec Chasydyzmu: Dzieje pewnej idei* (Warsaw, 2004), pp. 81–120.

7. Mordechai Zalkin, *A New Dawn: The Jewish Enlightenment in the Russian Empire—Social Aspects* (Hebrew) (Jerusalem, 2000), pp. 193–203.

8. Sabina Levin, "The Rabbinical Seminary in Warsaw, 1826–63" (Hebrew), *Gal-ed* 11 (1989): 35–58.

9. Jacob Shatzki, *Geshikhte fun yidn in varshe* (New York, 1948), 2:218–19, 234–35.

10. Magdalena Opalski and Israel Bartal, *Poles and Jews: A Failed Brotherhood* (Hanover, N.H., 1992), pp. 85–86.

11. The "national government" handbill was printed in Shatzki's *Geshikhte fun yidn in varshe,* 2:291–97.

12. Yosef Salmon, "David Gordon and His Periodical *Hamaggid,* 1860–80" (Hebrew), *Zion* 47 (1982): 145–64; Israel Bartal, "Loyalty to the Crown or Polish Patriotism: The Metamorphoses of an Anti-Polish Story of the 1863 Insurrection," *Polin* 1 (1986): 81–95.

Chapter 8

1. A. B. Gottlober, "Hagezera vehabeniya," in *Zikhronot umasaot,* ed. Reuven Goldberg (Jerusalem, 1976), 2:70.

2. Shmuel Feiner, "The Invention of the Modern Age: A Chapter in the Rhetoric and Self-Consciousness of the Haskalah" (Hebrew), *Dappim lemechkar hasifrut* 11 (1998): 28–29.

3. Israel Bartal, "The Image of Germany and German Jewry in Eastern European Jewish Society during the Nineteenth Century," in *Danzig between East and West: Aspects of Modern Jewish History,* ed. I. Twersky (Cambridge, Mass., 1985), pp. 3–17; idem, " 'The Heavenly City of Germany' and Absolutism à la Mode d'Autriche: The Rise of the Haskalah in Galicia," in *Toward Modernity: The European Jewish Model,* ed. Jacob Katz (New Brunswick, N.J., 1987), pp. 33–42.

4. Immanuel Etkes, "The Question of the Forerunners of the Haskalah in Eastern Europe" (Hebrew), *Tarbiz* 57 (1987): 95–114. See also David Sorkin, "The Early Haskalah," in *New Perspectives on the Haskalah,* ed. Shmuel Feiner and David Sorkin (London, 2001), pp. 9–26.

5. Shmuel Feiner, "Isaac Euchel: Entrepreneur of the Haskalah Movement in Germany" (Hebrew), *Zion* 52 (1987): 427–69.

6. Steven M. Lowenstein, "The Readership of Mendelssohn's Bible Translation," *Hebrew Union College Annual* 52 (1982): 179–213.

7. Israel Klausner, "Joseph Pesseles: The Enlightened Relative of the Gaon of Vilna" (Hebrew), *He-avar* 2 (1954): 73–85.

8. S. Feiner, "Between the Clouds of Foolishness and the Light of Reason:

Yehudah Hurwitz, an Early-Eighteenth-Century Maskil" (Hebrew), in *Within Hasidic Circles: Studies in Hasidism in Memory of Mordecai Wilensky*, ed. Immanuel Etkes et al. (Jerusalem, 1999), pp. 111–60.

9. See a special monograph devoted to the circle in Shklov: David Fishman, *Russia's First Modern Jews* (New York, 1995).

10. The most innovative work on Mendel Lefin is N. B. Sinkoff, "Tradition and Transition: Mendel Lefin of Satanów and the Beginnings of the Jewish Enlightenment in Eastern Europe, 1749–1826" (Ph.D. diss., Columbia University, 1996).

11. Michael Stanislawski, *Tsar Nicholas I and the Jews: The Transformation of Jewish Society in Russia, 1825–1855* (Philadelphia, 1983), pp. 49–59, 109–22.

12. Israel Bartal, "True Knowledge and Wisdom: On Orthodox Historiography," *Studies in Contemporary Jewry* 10 (1994): 178–92.

13. Idem, "To Forget and Remember: The Land of Israel in the Eastern European Haskalah Movement" (Hebrew), in *The Land of Israel in Modern Jewish Thought*, ed. A. Ravitsky (Jerusalem, 1998), pp. 413–23.

14. Shmuel Werses, "Hasidism in the Eyes of Haskalah Literature: From the Polemic of Galician Maskilim" (Hebrew), in *Trends and Forms in Haskalah Literature* (Jerusalem, 1990), pp. 91–109.

15. On the singular nature of the Haskalah in the areas of the Polish autonomy, see Mordechai Zalkin, "The Jewish Enlightenment in Poland: Points for Discussion" (Hebrew), in *The Broken Chain: Polish Jewry throughout the Ages*, ed. Israel Bartal and Israel Gutman (Jerusalem, 2001), 2:391–413.

16. Israel Bartal, "From Traditional Bilingualism to National Monolingualism," in *Hebrew in Ashkenaz: A Language in Exile*, ed. Lewis Glinert (New York, 1993), pp. 141–50.

17. For an up-to-date summary of the attitudes of Eastern European Maskilim toward Yiddish, see Shmuel Werses, "The Right Hand Repels and the Left Draws It Closer: On the Attitude of the Haskalah Writers toward the Yiddish Language" (Hebrew), *Huliot* 5 (1999): 9–49.

18. For a detailed description of early Eastern European Hebrew journals and newspapers, see Menucha Gilboa, *Hebrew Periodicals in the Eighteenth and Nineteenth Centuries* (Hebrew) (Jerusalem, 1992). On book reading in foreign languages, see Iris Parush, *Reading Women: The Benefit of Marginality in Nineteenth-Century Eastern European Jewish Society* (Hebrew) (Tel Aviv, 2001).

19. David Patterson, *The Hebrew Novel in Czarist Russia* (Edinburgh, 1964), pp. 129–56.

20. Dan Miron, *From Romance to the Novel: Studies in the Emergence of the Hebrew Novel in the Nineteenth Century* (Hebrew) (Jerusalem, 1979), pp. 256–65.

21. Dan Miron, "The Headdress of Pearls, or on the Benefit of Forgery: Reality in the Novel *Das Shterentichel* by Israel Axenfeld" (Hebrew), in *From Romance to the Novel*, pp.179–216; Israel Bartal, "From a Distorted Reflection to a Historical Fact: Haskalah Literature and Research on the Hasidic Movement" (Hebrew), *Jewish Studies* 32 (1992): 7–17; idem, "The Imprint of Haskalah Literature on the Historiography of Hasidism," in *Hasidism Reappraised*, ed. Ada Rapoport-Albert (London, 1996), pp. 367–75.

Chapter 9

1. Simon Dubnow, *History of the Jews in Russia and Poland*, trans. I. Friedlander (Philadelphia, 1946), 2:166.

2. Yehuda Slutsky, *The Russian Jewish Press in the Nineteenth Century* (Hebrew) (Jerusalem, 1970), p. 27. See also Benjamin Nathans, *Beyond the Pale: The Jewish Encounter with Late Imperial Russia* (Berkeley, Calif., 2002), pp. 214–25.

3. V. O. Levanda, *Complete Chronological Collection of Laws and Statutes concerning Jews 1649–1873* (Russian) (Saint Petersburg, 1874), p. 1033.

4. Slutsky, *The Russian Jewish Press*, pp. 13–36; Nathans, *Beyond the Pale*, pp. 214–25.

5. Israel Bartal, "Non-Jews and Gentile Society in Eastern European Hebrew and Yiddish Literature, 1856–1914" (Hebrew) (Ph.D. diss., Hebrew University, 1980), pp. 15–37, 83–90.

6. In Judah Leib Gordon, *Igrot* (Warsaw, 1894), 1:90.

7. Israel Bartal, "From Traditional Bilingualism to National Monolingualism," in *Hebrew in Ashkenaz: A Language in Exile*, ed. Lewis Glinert (New York, 1993), pp. 183–94.

8. On Gordon's Yiddish poems, see Michael Stanislawski, *For Whom Do I Toil?: Judah Leib Gordon and the Crisis of Russian Jewry* (New York, 1988), pp. 70–71, 82–83.

9. Chone Shmeruk, "The Jewish Press in Warsaw" (Hebrew), in *Calling on the Prophet: Studies in History and Literature*, ed. Israel Bartal (Jerusalem, 1999), p. 167.

10. Yosef Salmon, "David Gordon and His Periodical *Hamaggid*, 1860–80" (Hebrew), *Zion* 47 (1982): 145–64; Eli Lederhendler, *Jewish Responses to Modernity: New Voices in America and Eastern Europe* (New York, 1994), pp. 31–32.

11. On the author Lev Levanda and his positions regarding Russia and Poland, see Magdalena Opalski and Israel Bartal, *Poles and Jews: A Failed Brotherhood* (Hanover, N.H., 1992), pp. 80–86, 91–93, 111–12. See also Nathans, *Beyond the Pale*, pp. 215–16; Gabriella Safran, *Rewriting the Jew: Assimilation Narratives in the Russian Empire* (Stanford, Calif., 2000), p. 63.

12. Benzion Netanyahu, in Leo Pinsker, *Road to Freedom* (New York, 1944), pp. 7–73; Shlomo Breiman, "The Change in the Public Thought of the Jews in the 1880s" (Hebrew), *Shivat Zion* 2–3 (1953): 205–27.

13. Immanuel Etkes, *Rabbi Israel Salanter and the Mussar Movement: Seeking the Torah of Truth* (Philadelphia, 1993), pp. 276–85.

Chapter 10

1. David R. Roskies, *The Jewish Search for a Usable Past* (Bloomington, Ind., 1999), p. 9; see also Israel Bartal, "No More Tradition's Chains Shall Bind Us": The Jewish Labor Movement—Revolutionary Socialism versus National Continuity" (Hebrew), in *Workers and Revolutionaries: The Jewish Labor Movement* (Tel Aviv, 1994), pp. 26–31.

2. Jacob Goldberg, "Jewish Initiatives in Polish Industry in the Eighteenth Century: A Priest and a Jew Establish a Small Metal-Products Industry in Greater Poland" (Hebrew), in *Jewish Society in the Polish-Lithuanian Kingdom* (Jerusalem, 1999), pp. 251–63. On Jewish entrepreneurs in the textile industry of western Russia, see John D. Klier, *Russia Gathers Her Jews* (Dekalb, Ill., 1986), pp. 155–61.

3. On the tobacco industry in Vilna in the 1870s, see a detailed report by A. S. Liberman, *Writings in Vpered, 1875–76* (Hebrew), ed. M. Mishkinsky (Tel Aviv, 1977), pp. 119–24.

4. Published in *Hashahar* (1875). On this satiric poem, see Michael Stanislaw-

ski, *For Whom Do I Toil?: Judah Leib Gordon and the Crisis of Russian Jewry* (New York, 1988), pp. 251–63.

5. J. L. Gordon, *Kol shirav* (Tel Aviv, 1931), 4:15–16.

6. Sholem Aleichem, *Ale Verk, Forverts,* ed. (New York, 1944), 7:43–153. For a discussion of the impact of the author's biography on his work, see Dan Miron, "Sholem Aleykhem: Person, Persona, Presence," Uriel Weinreich Memorial Lecture, YIVO Institute for Jewish Research (New York, 1972); idem, *Sholem Aleichem: Two Related Essays* (Hebrew) (Ramat Gan, 1970).

7. S. J. Zipperstein, "Russian Maskilim and the City," in *The Legacy of Jewish Migration: 1881 and Its Impact,* ed. D. Berger (New York, 1983), pp. 31–45; idem, "Haskalah, Cultural Change, and Nineteenth-Century Russian Jewry: A Reassessment," *Journal of Jewish Studies* 34 (1983): 191–207; idem, "Assimilation, Haskalah, and Odessa Jewry," in *The Great Transition: The Recovery of the Lost Centers of Modern Hebrew Literature,* ed. G. Abramson and T. Parfitt (Totowa, N.J., 1985), pp. 91–98. For a detailed study of the Odessa community, see idem, *The Jews of Odessa: A Cultural History 1794–1801* (Stanford, Calif., 1985).

8. Gordon, *Kol shirav,* p. 16.

9. For a critical study of Liberman's life and ideas, see Jonathan Frankel, *Prophecy and Politics: Socialism, Nationalism, and the Russian Jews, 1862–1917* (Cambridge, 1981), pp. 28–48. See also M. Mishkinsky, "The Historical Image of A. S. Liberman and His Writings in *Vpered,*" in Liberman, *Writings in Vpered,* pp. 9–55.

10. On A. U. Kovner, see M. Weinreich, *Fun beyde zaytn ployt: Dos shturmdike lebn fun Uri Kovnern, dem nihilist* (Buenos Aires, 1966); L. Grossman, *Confession of a Jew,* trans. R. Moab, 2nd ed. (New York, 1979); Shmuel Feiner, "Jewish Society, Literature, and Haskalah in Russia as Represented in the Radical Criticism of I. E. Kovner" (Hebrew), *Zion* 55 (1990): 427–69 (on A. U. Kovner's brother).

11. A. Kovner, "An Investigation" (Hebrew), in *Kol ketavav* (Tel Aviv, 1947), p. 45.

12. On the emergence of Orthodoxy as a modern phenomenon, see Jacob Katz, "Orthodoxy in Historical Perspective," in *Studies in Contemporary Jewry* 2 (1986): 3–17; N. Katzburg, "Orthodoxy," *Encyclopaedia Judaica* (Jerusalem, 1971), 12:1486–92; C. Liebman, "Orthodox Judaism," *The Encyclopedia of Religion* (Chicago, 1987), 2:114–15. For regional aspects of Orthodoxy, see Israel Bartal, "Responses to Modernity, Haskalah, Orthodoxy, and Nationalism in Eastern Europe," in *Zionism and Religion,* ed. S. Almog, J. Reinharz, and A. Shapira (Hanover, N.H., 1998), pp. 15–24; D. H. Ellenson, "German Jewish Orthodoxy: Tradition in the Context of Culture," in *The Uses of Tradition,* ed. J. Wertheimer (New York, 1992), pp. 5–22; A. S. Ferziger, "Hierarchical Judaism in Formation: The Development of Central European Orthodoxy's Approach toward Nonobservant Jews, 1700–1918" (Hebrew) (Ph.D. diss., Bar-Ilan University, 2001); M. Silber, "The Emergence of Ultra-Orthodoxy: The Invention of Tradition," in Wertheimer, *The Uses of Tradition,* pp. 23–85.

13. For Orthodox responses to the American threat to traditional lifestyle, see A. Hertzberg, "*Treifene Medine*: Opposition to Emigration to the United States," *Eighth World Congress of Jewish Studies* (Jerusalem, 1984), pp. 1–31; K. Caplan, *Orthodoxy in the New World: Immigrant Rabbis and Preaching in America, 1881–1924* (Hebrew) (Jerusalem, 2002).

14. Stanislawski, *For Whom Do I Toil?,* pp. 125–28, 213–14; E. Lederhendler, *The Road to Modern Jewish Politics* (New York, 1989), pp. 86–88.

15. M. L. Lilienblum, *Ways of the Talmud* (Hebrew), in *Kol ketavav* (Kraków, 1910), 1:27 (this series of articles first appeared in *Hamelitz* in 1868).

16. *Letters by M. L. Lilienblum to J. L. Gordon* (Hebrew), ed. S. Breiman (Jerusalem, 1968), 74–75.

17. M. L. Lilienblum, *Kol Ketavav*, 1:39, 41. Cf. Yosef Salmon, "Tradition, Modernization, and Nationalism: The Maskilic Rabbi as a Reformist in Russian Jewish Society" (Hebrew), in *Studies in Religious Zionism and Jewish Law Submitted in Honor of Dr. Zerach Warhaftig* (Ramat Gan, 2001), pp. 29–34; idem, "Enlightened Rabbis as Reformists in Russian Jewish Society," in *New Perspectives on the Haskalah*, ed. Shmuel Feiner and David Sorkin (London, 2001), pp. 166–83.

Chapter 11

1. For a summary of the political changes in the empire from 1849 to 1867, see Robert A. Kann, *A History of the Habsburg Empire, 1526–1918* (Berkeley, Calif., 1977), pp. 318–66.

2. On R. Israel of Ruzhin, see the detailed biography by David Assaf, *The Regal Way: The Life and Times of Rabbi Israel of Ruzhin*, trans. David Louvish (Stanford, Calif., 2002).

3. Chagit Cohen, "At the Bookseller's Shop: Jewish Bookshops in Eastern Europe during the Second Half of the Nineteenth Century" (Hebrew) (master's thesis, Bar-Ilan University, 2000), pp. 88–97, 139–47, 149–57.

4. Menucha Gilboa, *Hebrew Periodicals in the Eighteenth and Nineteenth Centuries* (Hebrew) (Jerusalem, 1992), pp. 213–20.

5. Such as the pro-Polish poem "Bajazzo," by Moritz Rappaport (Leipzig, 1863). On the multilingualism of Jewish culture in the Polish context, see Magdalena Opalski and Israel Bartal, *Poles and Jews: A Failed Brotherhood* (Hanover, N.H., 1992), p. 122.

6. Ezra Mendelsohn, "Jewish Assimilation in Lvov: The Case of Wilhelm Feldman," *The Slavic Review* 28 (1969): 577–90; idem, "From Assimilation to Zionism: The Case of Alfred Nossig," *Slavonic and East European Review* 49 (1971): 521–34.

7. Israel Bartal, "Jews in Eastern European Higher Education" (Hebrew), in *The History of the Hebrew University in Jerusalem: Origins and Beginnings*, ed. S. Katz and M. Heyd (Jerusalem, 1997), pp. 80–82.

8. Idem, "Loyalty to the Crown or Polish Patriotism: The Metamorphoses of an Anti-Polish Story of the 1863 Insurrection," *Polin* 1 (1986): 81–95.

9. Rachel Manekin, "Orthodox Jewry in Kraków at the Turn of the Twentieth Century" (Hebrew), in *Kroke-Kazimierz-Kraków: Studies on the History of Kraków Jewry*, ed. E. Reiner (Tel Aviv, 2001), pp. 155–90; idem, "Politics, Religion, and National Identity: The Galician Jewish Vote in the 1873 Parliamentary Elections," *Polin* 12 (1999): 100–119.

10. Benedict Anderson, *Imagined Communities: Reflections on the Origins and Spread of Nationalism* (New York, 1991), p. 44. On Galician Jewish protonationalism and the Yiddish press, see Joshua Shanes, "Papers for the *Folk*: Jewish Nationalism and the Birth of the Yiddish Press in Galicia," *Polin* 16 (2003): 187 n. 79.

Chapter 12

1. Shmuel Ettinger, *Modern Anti-Semitism: Studies and Essays* (Hebrew) (Tel Aviv, 1978), pp. 145–67.

2. Idem, "Jewish Exploitation in the Russian Press in the Early 1880s" (Hebrew), in *Studies in Modern Jewish History* (Jerusalem, 1992), 1:237–57.

3. Jacob A. Brafman, *Kniga kagala* (Vilna, 1869).

4. John D. Klier, *Imperial Russia's Jewish Question, 1855–1881* (Cambridge, 1995), pp. 263–83; Gabriella Safran, *Rewriting the Jew: Assimilation Narratives in the Russian Empire* (Stanford, Calif., 2000), pp. 30–31, 97–100; Benjamin Nathans, *Beyond the Pale: The Jewish Encounter with Late Imperial Russia* (Berkeley, Calif., 2002), pp. 174–75, 257–58.

5. Israel Bartal, "Dubnov's Image of Medieval Autonomy," in *A Missionary for History: Essays in Honor of Simon Dubnov*, ed. K. Groberg and A. Greenbaum (Minneapolis, 1998), pp. 12–13.

6. "Temporary Rules" (May 1882); see Simon Dubnow, *History of the Jews in Russia and Poland* (Philadelphia, 1946), 2:312.

7. On Dostoyevsky's opinions on the Jews, see David I. Goldstein, *Dostoyevsky and the Jews* (Austin, Tex., 1981); Nathans, *Beyond the Pale*, pp. 135, 258. See also Joshua Kunitz, *Russian Literature and the Jew: A Sociological Inquiry into the Nature and Origin of Literary Patterns* (New York, 1929), pp. 59–94.

8. F. Dostoyevsky, "Pro and Contra," in *A Writer's Diary*, trans. Kenneth Lantz (Evanston, Ill., 1994), 2:904–5.

9. Israel Bartal, "Between Radical Haskalah and Jewish Socialism" (Hebrew), *Proceedings of the Eighth Congress on Jewish Studies* (Jerusalem, 1984), pp. 13–20. See also E. Lederhendler, *The Road to Modern Jewish Politics: Political Tradition and Political Reconstruction in the Jewish Community of Tsarist Russia* (New York, 1989), pp. 144–46.

10. Yehuda Slutsky, *The Russian-Jewish Press in the Nineteenth Century* (Hebrew) (Jerusalem, 1970), pp. 62–64.

11. Israel Bartal, "Jews in Eastern European Higher Education" (Hebrew), in *The History of the Hebrew University of Jerusalem: Origins and Beginnings*, ed. S. Katz and M. Heyd (Jerusalem, 1997), pp. 75–89; Nathans, *Beyond the Pale*, pp. 257–60.

Chapter 13

1. Jonathan Frankel, "Jewish Socialism, 1882–90: From Jewish Populism to Cosmopolitanism" (Hebrew), *Proceedings of the Eighth World Congress of Jewish Studies* (Jerusalem, 1984), pp. 21–53; Israel Bartal, "Between Radical Haskalah and Jewish Socialism" (Hebrew), in ibid., pp. 13–20.

2. On the ideal image of the peasant in late Haskalah literature, see Israel Bartal, "Non-Jews and Gentile Society in Eastern European Hebrew and Yiddish Literature, 1856–1914" (Hebrew) (Ph.D. diss., Hebrew University of Jerusalem, 1980), pp. 68–78; idem, "The *Porets* and the *Arendar*: The Depiction of Poles in Jewish Literature, 1800–1914," *The Polish Review* 33, no. 4 (1987): 357–69.

3. Jonathan Frankel, *Prophecy and Politics: Socialism, Nationalism, and the Russian Jews, 1862–1917* (Cambridge, 1981), pp. 98–101; Y. Maor, "The Anti-Semitic Proclamation of the Narodnaya Volya" (Hebrew), *Zion* 15 (1950): 150–55; Moshe Mishkinsky, "The South Russian Workers' Union and the 1881 Kiev Pogrom" (Hebrew), *Shvut* 1 (1973): 62–73.

4. Ruelf Collection, A1/V-1/4. Central Zionist Archives, Jerusalem.

5. Frankel, *Prophecy and Politics*, p. 49; E. Lederhendler, *The Road to Modern Jewish Politics: Political Tradition and Political Reconstruction in the Jewish Community*

of Tsarist Russia (New York, 1989), pp. 4–5. For a somewhat critical view regarding the centrality of the 1881–82 pogroms in modern Jewish history, see B. Nathans, *Beyond the Pale: The Jewish Encounter with Late Imperial Russia* (Berkeley, Calif., 2002), pp. 7–13.

6. Yehuda Slutsky, "The Geography of the 1881 Pogroms" (Hebrew), *He-avar* 9 (1961): 16–25; idem, "The Pogroms in 1882–84" (Hebrew), *He-avar* 10 (1963): 144–49.

7. "Temporary Rules" (May 1882); see Simon Dubnow, *History of the Jews in Russia and Poland* (Philadelphia, 1946), 2:312.

8. Judah Leib Gordon, "Old and Young, We Will Go" (Hebrew), in *Kol shirav* (Tel Aviv, 1929), 1:50; Michael Stanislawski, *For Whom Do I Toil?: Judah Leib Gordon and the Crisis of Russian Jewry* (New York, 1988), p. 175.

9. Israel Klausner, *When a Nation Awakens* (Hebrew) (Jerusalem, 1962).

10. Ben-Zion Dinur, "The Projects of Count Ignatiev to Solve the Jewish Question" (Hebrew), *He-avar* 9 (1961): 5–82; Nathans, *Beyond the Pale*, pp. 188–98.

11. "Letter to the Editor of *Hashahar*" (Hebrew), in *Documents and Sources*, ed. Israel Bartal, pp. 314–16.

12. On Am Oylom, see Abraham Menes, "The Am Oylom Movement," *YIVO Annual* 6 (1949): 9–33; Hasia Turtle, "The Am Olam Movement" (Hebrew), *He-avar* 10 (1963): 124–43.

13. On the encounter between German Jews and the *Ostjuden*, see Jack Wertheimer, *Unwelcome Strangers: East European Jews in Imperial Germany* (New York, 1987).

14. Sholem Aleichem, *Motel peyse dem hazens*, in *Ale Verk, Forverts* ed. (New York, 1944), 1:183–244.

15. Frankel, *Prophecy and Politics*, pp. 49–107; Lederhendler, *The Road to Modern Jewish Politics*, pp. 149–53.

16. Mordechai Ben-Ami, "The 1881 Odessa Pogroms and the First Self-Defense," *Evreiski Mir* 1 (1909). Hebrew version in *Book of Heroism*, ed. I. Halpern (Tel Aviv, 1950), 2:86–87.

17. Intercession. From the Hebrew term *shtadlan*, designating Jews who represent the interests of their fellow Jews vis-à-vis the non-Jewish authorities, currying favor with officials and at times offering bribes, what in modern times would be called lobbying. On *shtadlanut*, see Lederhendler, *The Road to Modern Jewish Politics*, pp. 100–110; Scott Ury, "The *Shtadlan* of the Polish-Lithuanian Commonwealth: Noble Advocate or Unbridled Opportunist?" *Polin* 15 (2002): 267.

18. "The Voice of Youth" (Hebrew), *Hamelitz* 4 (May 16, 1882).

19. Frankel, *Prophecy and Politics*, pp. 95–97; Shulamit Laskov, *The Biluim* (Hebrew) (Tel Aviv, 1979), pp. 38–48; Yosef Salmon, "Ideology and Reality in the Bilu Movement" (Hebrew), in *Shalem: Studies in the History of the Jews in Eretz Israel* (Jerusalem, 1981), 3:149–84.

20. Israel Halpern, *Jews and Judaism in Eastern Europe* (Hebrew) (Jerusalem, 1969), pp. 357–70.

21. Moshe Leib Lilienblum, *Autobiographical Writings* (Hebrew), ed. Shlomo Breiman (Jerusalem, 1970), 2:146–201; Nathans, *Beyond the Pale*, pp. 10–12.

Conclusion

1. Simon Dubnow, *World History of the Jews* (Hebrew), 6th rev. ed. (Tel Aviv, 1958), p. 176.

2. On Dubnow's approach to premodern Jewish autonomy, see Simon Dubnow, *Nationalism and History: Essays on Old and New Judaism*, ed. with an introduction by K. S. Pinson (Philadelphia, 1961); idem, *Lettres sur le judaisme ancien et nouveau*, ed. Renée Poznanski (Paris, 1989); Israel Bartal, "Dubnov's Image of Medieval Autonomy," in *A Missionary for History: Essays in Honor of Simon Dubnov*, ed. K. Groberg and A. Greenbaum (Minneapolis, 1998), pp. 11–18.

3. Ben-Zion Dinur, *Historical Writings* (Hebrew) (Jerusalem, 1978), 4:199.

4. S. Dubnova-Erlikh, *The Life and Work of S. M. Dubnov* (Bloomington, Ind., 1991), p. 115.

5. This, despite the fact that Baron criticized Dubnow for not having sufficiently practiced in his own research what he preached, namely, the proper degree of integration between Jewish history and general history: "Simon Dubnow, who gave his book of Jewish history the bombastic title *Divrei yemei am olam*, in doing so alluded to his desire to discuss the subject from the standpoint of its nexus to world events. Nonetheless, in fact he did not do much more in this regard than his predecessors, including Graetz" (Salo W. Baron, "World Dimensions of Jewish History" [originally published in Hebrew, *Hadoar* 42, nos. 24–25 (1962): 382–84, 416–18], in idem, *The World Dimensions of Jewish History*, ed. with an introduction by Y. T. Assis and R. Liberles [Jerusalem, 1996], p. 37).

6. A particularly telling example can be found in the words of Dinur himself at the beginning of his article "Galuyot vehurbanan," published during the Holocaust (1942): "The great holocaust that has befallen us in our generation, which in its dimensions and its horrors is unparalleled in our entire two-thousand-year history—we are incapable now of grasping it in all of its authenticity and all its results. . . . Unquestionably, the enormous shocks of our generation have nearly wiped out the feeling of the distance in time between us and our forefathers in former periods. Systems of generations, worlds of 'diasporas and their destruction' have suddenly been illuminated by the blinding light of the conflagrations of the diasporas going up in flames in front of our eyes. Things that seemed obscure to us have now become clear and distinct, and shadows that reached us dimly from the remote generations now fill our souls and our whole beings with their moans." In *Historical Writings*, 4:175.

7. *The Memoirs of Ber of Bolechów, 1723–1805*, trans. M. Wischnitzer (London, 1922), p. 50. On the eighteenth-century memoirs, see A. N. Frenk, "Zikhronot R. Dov me-bolechow," *Ha-Tkufa* 20 (1923): 521–25; I. Bartal, "Dov of Bolechów: A Diarist of the Council of the Four Lands in the Eighteenth Century," *Polin* 9 (1996): 187–91.

8. On the names given in traditional Jewish society to various groups in non-Jewish society, see Israel Bartal, "Non-Jews and Gentile Society in Eastern European Hebrew and Yiddish Literature, 1856–1914" (Hebrew) (Ph.D. diss., Hebrew University, 1980).

9. On the Ashkenazi diglossia as part of the premodern corporative system, see Chone Shmeruk, *Yiddish Literature: Aspects of Its History* (Hebrew) (Tel Aviv, 1978); Israel Bartal, "From Traditional Bilingualism to National Monolingualism," in *Hebrew in Ashkenaz: A Language in Exile*, ed. Lewis Glinert (New York, 1993), pp. 141–50.

10. Gershon D. Hundert, *The Jews in a Polish Private Town: The Case of Opatów in the Eighteenth Century* (Baltimore, 1992), pp. 46–68. In the town of Opatów, most of the wine merchants were not Jews (five out of eight), but in contrast to the eight non-Jewish merchants in the city, there were sixty-one Jewish merchants.

11. See, for example, the descriptions of economic activity in White Russia in the nineteenth century in the memoirs of Hayyim Chemerinsky: *My Town Motele* (Hebrew), introduction by D. Assaf (Jerusalem, 2002); *Journey to a Nineteenth-Century Shtetl: The Memoirs of Yehezkel Kotik*, ed. D. Assaf (Detroit, 2002).

12. Abraham Brawer, *Galicia and Her Jews: Studies in the History of Eighteenth-Century Galicia* (Hebrew) (Jerusalem, 1965), pp. 104–23.

13. Bartal, "Non-Jews and Gentile Society," pp. 68–78.

14. Shaul Stampfer, "Population Growth and Immigration among Polish-Lithuanian Jewry" (Hebrew), in *The Broken Chain: Polish Jewry through the Ages*, ed. I. Bartal and I. Gutman (Jerusalem, 1997), 1:263–85.

15. Gershon D. Hundert, "On the Jewish Community in Poland during the Seventeenth Century: Some Comparative Perspectives," *Revue des Etudes Juives* 142 (1983): 349–72.

16. Jacob Goldberg, ed., *Jewish Privileges in the Polish Commonwealth* (Jerusalem, 1983).

17. Judith Kalik, "The Catholic Church and the Jews in the Polish-Lithuanian Commonwealth" (Hebrew), in *The Broken Chain*, 1:193–208.

18. Shmuel Ettinger, "Jewish Participation in the Settlement of Ukraine in the Sixteenth and Seventeenth Centuries," in *Ukrainian-Jewish Relations in Historical Perspective*, ed. P. J. Potichnyj and H. Aster (Edmonton, 1988), pp. 23–30.

19. A. Kupfer, *Ber Mayzels* (Yiddish) (Warsaw, 1952). This monograph describes Meisels's activity in a Marxist-Leninist spirit, the very opposite of what I have written about the reasons for the rabbi's support of the Polish nationalists. See Israel Bartal, "Heroes or Cowards: Jews in the Polish Armies, 1794–1863" (Hebrew), in *The Broken Chain*, 1:361–62.

20. Israel Bartal, "Jews in Eastern European Higher Education," in *The History of the Hebrew University: Origins and Beginnings*, ed. S. Katz and M. Heyd (Jerusalem, 1997), pp. 75–89; Mordechai Zalkin, *A New Dawn: The Jewish Enlightenment in the Russian Empire—Social Aspects* (Hebrew) (Jerusalem, 2000), pp. 193–98.

21. On the connection between the size and geographical dispersion of the Jewish population and the "national" character of Russian Jewry, see Ben-Zion Dinur, *Historical Writings*, 4:202–28.

22. On Kostomarov and his attitude toward the role of the Jews in Ukrainian history, see Shmuel Ettinger, *Modern Anti-Semitism: Studies and Essays* (Hebrew) (Tel Aviv, 1978), pp. 132–34.

23. Yitzhak Maor, "The Anti-Semitic Proclamation of the Narodnaya Vola" (Hebrew), *Zion* 15 (1950): 153. See also Moshe Mishkinsky, "The South Russian Workers' Union and the 1881 Kiev Pogrom" (Hebrew), *Shvut* 1 (1973): 62–73.

24. Dubnow, *Nationalism and History*, p. 137.

25. Such as studies by Hundert (*The Jews in a Polish Private Town*, pp. 216–17) and Rosman (Moshe Rosman, *The Lords' Jews: Magnate-Jewish Relations in the Polish-Lithuanian Commonwealth during the Eighteenth Century* [Cambridge, Mass., 1990]). The studies by Jacob Goldberg have been a major influence in this direction; a Hebrew collection of them has recently been published: *The Jewish Society in the Polish Commonwealth* (Jerusalem, 1999) (Hebrew). Studies by Adam Teller and Judith Kalik, written as doctoral dissertations under his guidance, also have taken this direction. See, for example, articles by Teller and Kalik in Hebrew in *The Broken Chain*, ed. Bartal and Gutman, vol. 1.

Bibliography

Abramsky, Chimen. "The Visits to Russia." In *The Century of Moses Montefiore*, ed. S. Lipman and V. D. Lipman. Oxford, 1985, pp. 254–65.

Anderson, Benedict. *Imagined Communities: Reflections on the Origins and Spread of Nationalism*. New York, 1991.

Aschheim, S. E. *Brothers and Strangers: The East European Jew in German and German Jewish Consciousness, 1800–1923*. Madison, Wisc., 1982.

Ascoly, Aaron Ze'ev. *Hasidism in Poland* (Hebrew). Introduction by David Assaf. Jerusalem, 2000.

Assaf, David, Israel Bartal, Immanuel Etkes, and Elchanan Reiner, eds. *Within Hasidic Circles: Studies in Hasidism in Memory of Mordecai Wilensky* (Hebrew). Jerusalem, 1999.

Assaf, David, ed. *The Regal Way: The Life and Times of Rabbi Israel of Ruzhin*. Stanford, Calif., 2002.

———. *Tzaddik and Devotees: Historical and Sociological Aspects of Hasidism* (Hebrew). Jerusalem, 2001.

Baron, Salo Wittmayer. *The Jews under Tsars and Soviets*. New York, 1976.

Bartal, Israel. "Between Radical Haskalah and Jewish Socialism" (Hebrew). *Proceedings of the Eighth Congress on Jewish Studies*. Jerusalem, 1984, pp. 13–20.

———. "Dov of Bolechów: A Diarist of the Council of the Four Lands in the Eighteenth Century." *Polin* 9 (1996): 187–91.

———. "Dubnov's Image of Medieval Autonomy." In *A Missionary for History: Essays in Honor of Simon Dubnov*, ed. Kristi Groberg and Avraham Greenbaum. Minneapolis, 1998, pp. 11–18.

———. "Eastern Europe as a Focal Point for Modern Jewish History: Preliminary Reflections on the Teaching of Shmuel Ettinger" (Hebrew). In Shmuel Ettinger, *Historya vehistoryonim*. Jerusalem, 1992, pp. 27–30.

———. *Exile in the Homeland: Essays* (Hebrew). Jerusalem, 1994.

———. "From a Distorted Reflection to a Historical Fact: Haskalah Literature and Research on the Hasidic Movement" (Hebrew). *Jewish Studies* 32 (1992): 7–17.

———. "From an Intimate Circle to a Mass Movement: The Emergence of Hasidism." *Studia Judaica* 3 (1994): 7–16.

———. "From Traditional Bilingualism to National Monolingualism." In *Hebrew in Ashkenaz: A Language in Exile*, ed. Lewis Glinert. New York, 1993, pp. 141–50.

———. "'The Heavenly City of Germany' and Absolutism à la Mode d'Autriche: The Rise of the Haskalah in Galicia." In *Toward Modernity: The European Jewish Model*, ed. Jacob Katz. New Brunswick, N.J., 1987, pp. 33–42.

———. "Heroes or Cowards: Jews in the Polish Armies, 1794–1863" (Hebrew). In *The Broken Chain: Polish Jewry through the Ages*, ed. Israel Bartal and Israel Gutman, 1:353–67. Jerusalem, 1997.

————. "The Image of Germany and German Jewry in East European Jewish Society during the Nineteenth Century." In *Danzig between East and West: Aspects of Modern Jewish History*, ed. I. Twersky. Cambridge, Mass., 1985, pp. 3–17.

————. "The Imprint of Haskalah Literature on the Historiography of Hasidism." In *Hasidism Reappraised*, ed. Rapoport-Albert, pp. 367–75.

————. "Jews in Eastern European Higher Education" (Hebrew). In *The History of the Hebrew University: Origins and Beginnings*, ed. Shaul Katz and Michael Heyd. Jerusalem, 1997, pp. 75–89.

————. "Loyalty to the Crown or Polish Patriotism: The Metamorphoses of an Anti-Polish Story of the 1863 Insurrection." *Polin* 1 (1986): 81–95.

————. "Nationalist before His Time, or a Belated *Shtadlan*?" (Hebrew). In *The Age of Moses Montefiore*, ed. Israel Bartal. Jerusalem, 1987, pp. 5–24.

————. "No More Tradition's Chains Shall Bind Us: The Jewish Labor Movement, Revolutionary Socialism versus National Continuity" (Hebrew). In *Workers and Revolutionaries: The Jewish Labor Movement.* Tel Aviv, 1994, pp. 26–31.

————. "Non-Jews and Gentile Society in Eastern European Hebrew and Yiddish Literature, 1856–1914" (Hebrew). Ph.D. diss., Hebrew University, 1980.

————. "The *Pinkas* of the Council of the Four Lands." In *The Jews in Old Poland, 1000–1795*, ed. Antony Polonsky, Jakub Basista, and Andrzej Link-Lenczowski. New York, 1993, pp. 110–18.

————. "The *Porets* and the *Arendar*: The Depiction of Poles in Jewish Literature, 1800–1914." *The Polish Review* 32, no. 4 (1987): 357–69.

————. "Responses to Modernity: Haskalah, Orthodoxy, and Nationalism in Eastern Europe." In *Zionism and Religion*, ed. Shmuel Almog, Jehuda Reinharz, and Anita Shapira. Hanover, N.H., 1998, pp. 13–24.

————. "Simon the Heretic: A Chapter in Orthodox Historiography" (Hebrew). In *According to the Custom of Ashkenaz and Poland: Studies in Jewish Culture in Honor of Chone Shmeruk*, ed. Israel Bartal, Ezra Mendelsohn, and Chava Turniansky. Jerusalem, 1993, pp. 243–68.

————. "To Forget and Remember: The Land of Israel in the Eastern European Haskalah Movement" (Hebrew). In *The Land of Israel in Modern Jewish Thought*, ed. Aviezer Ravitsky. Jerusalem, 1998, pp. 413–23.

————. "True Knowledge and Wisdom: On Orthodox Historiography." *Studies in Contemporary Jewry* 10 (1994): 178–92.

————, Rachel Elior, and Chone Shmeruk, eds. *Hasidism in Poland* (Hebrew). Jerusalem, 1994.

Bartal, Israel, and Jonathan Frankel. "Historya veshlikhut: Shmuel Etinger hoker yahadut mizrakh eyropa." In Shmuel Ettinger, *Beyn polin lerusya.* Jerusalem, 1994, pp. xi–xxiii.

Bartal, Israel, and Israel Gutman, eds. *The Broken Chain: Polish Jewry through the Ages* (Hebrew). Vol. 1, Jerusalem, 1997; vol. 2, Jerusalem, 2001.

Bartal, Israel, and Antony Polonsky. "Introduction: The Jews of Galicia under the Habsburgs." *Polin* 12 (1999): 3–24.

Beizer, Michael. *The Jews of Saint Petersburg: Excursions through a Noble Past.* Philadelphia, 1989.

Ben-Ami, Mordechai. "The 1881 Odessa Pogroms and the First Self-Defense" (Russian). *Evreiski Mir* 1 (1909).

Ben-Sasson, H. H., ed. *A History of the Jewish People.* Cambridge, Mass., 1976.

Ber, Dov. *The Memoirs of Ber of Bolechów, 1723–1805.* Trans. Mark Wischnitzer. London, 1922.

Brafman, Jacob A. *Kniga kagala.* Vilna, 1869.

Brawer, Abraham. *Galicia and Her Jews: Studies in the History of Eighteenth-Century Galicia* (Hebrew). Jerusalem, 1965.

Breiman, Shlomo. "The Change in the Public Thought of the Jews in the 1880s" (Hebrew). *Shivat Zion* 2–3 (1953): 83–227.

Breuer, Edward. "Naphtali Herz Wessely and the Cultural Dislocations of an Eighteenth-Century Maskil." In *New Perspectives on the Haskalah,* ed. Shmuel Feiner and David Sorkin. London, 2001, pp. 27–47.

Caplan, Kimmy. *Orthodoxy in the New World: Immigrant Rabbis and Preaching in America, 1881–1924* (Hebrew). Jerusalem, 2002.

Chemerinsky, Hayyim. *My Town Motele* (Hebrew). Introduction by David Assaf. Jerusalem, 2002.

Cohen, Chagit. "At the Bookseller's Shop: Jewish Bookshops in Eastern Europe during the Second Half of the Nineteenth Century" (Hebrew). Master's thesis, Bar-Ilan University, 2000.

Dan, Joseph. *The Hasidic Story: Its History and Development* (Hebrew). Jerusalem, 1975.

Dinur, Ben-Zion. *Historical Writings* (Hebrew). Vol. 1, Jerusalem, 1955; vol. 4, Jerusalem, 1978.

———. "The Projects of Count Ignatiev to Solve the Jewish Question" (Hebrew). *He-avar* 10 (1963): 5–82.

Dubin, Lois. "Trieste and Berlin: The Italian Role in the Cultural Politics of the Haskalah." In *Toward Modernity: The European Jewish Model,* ed. Jacob Katz. New Brunswick, N.J., 1987, pp. 189–224.

Dubnova-Erlikh, S. *The Life and Work of S. M. Dubnov.* Bloomington, Ind., 1991.

Dubnow, Simon. *History of Hasidism* (Hebrew). Tel Aviv, 1960.

———. *History of the Jews in Russia and Poland.* Trans. I. Friedlaender. Vols. 1–3, Philadelphia, 1916–20.

———. *Letters on Old and New Judaism* (Hebrew). Tel Aviv, 1937.

———. *Lettres sur le judaisme ancien et nouveau.* Ed. Renée Poznanski. Paris, 1989.

———. "Nahpesah venakhkorah." *Pardes* 1 (1892): 220–41.

———. *Nationalism and History: Essays on Old and New Judaism.* Edited with an introduction by K.S. Pinson. Philadelphia, 1961.

———. *World History of the Jews* (Hebrew). 6th rev. ed. Tel Aviv, 1958.

Dynner, G. "Men of Silk: The Hasidic Conquest of Polish Jewry, 1754–1830." Ph.D. diss., Brandeis University, 2002.

Eisenbach, Artur. "The Central Representation of the Jews in the Warsaw Duchy, 1807–15" (Hebrew). In *The Broken Chain,* ed. Bartal and Gutman. Jerusalem, 1997, 1:287–313.

———. *The Emancipation of the Jews in Poland, 1780–1870.* Oxford, 1991.

———. "The Four Years' Sejm and the Jews." In *The Jews in Old Poland, 1000–1795,* ed. Antony Polonsky, Jakub Basista, and Andrzej Link-Lenczowski. New York, 1993, pp. 73–89.

———, et al., eds. *Materials on the History of the Four-Year Sejm* (Polish). Vol. 6. Wroclaw, 1969.

Eliav, Mordecai. *Jewish Education in Germany in the Period of Enlightenment and Emancipation* (Hebrew). Jerusalem, 1960.

Ellenson, David H. "German Jewish Orthodoxy: Tradition in the Context of Culture." In *The Uses of Tradition,* ed. Jack Wertheimer. New York, 1992, pp. 5–22.

Etkes, Immanuel. *The Besht: Magician, Mystic and Leader* Hanover, N.H., 2004.

———. *The Beginning of the Hasidic Movement* (Hebrew). Tel Aviv, 1998.

————, ed. *The Eastern European Enlightenment* (Hebrew). Jerusalem, 1993.

————. *The Gaon of Vilna: The Man and His Image.* Berkeley, Calif., 2002.

————. "The Question of the Forerunners of the Haskalah in Eastern Europe" (Hebrew). *Tarbiz* 57 (1987): 95–114.

————. *Rabbi Israel Salanter and the Mussar Movement: Seeking the Torah of Truth.* Philadelphia, 1993.

————. "The Study of Hasidism: Past Trends and New Directions." In *Hasidism Reappraised*, ed. Rapoport-Albert, pp. 447–64.

Ettinger, Shmuel. "The Council of the Four Lands." In *The Jews in Old Poland, 1000–1795*, ed. Antony Polonsky, Jakub Basista, and Andrzej Link-Lenczowski. New York, 1993, pp. 93–109.

————. "Hasidism and the *Kahal* in Eastern Europe." In *Hasidism Reappraised*, ed. Rapoport-Albert, pp. 63–75.

————. *History of the Jews from the Age of Absolutism to the State of Israel* (Hebrew). Jerusalem, 1968.

————. "Jewish Participation in the Settlement of Ukraine in the Sixteenth and Seventeenth Centuries." In *Ukrainian-Jewish Relations in Historical Perspective*, ed. P. J. Potichnyj and H. Aster. Edmonton, 1988, pp. 23–30.

————. *Modern Anti-Semitism: Studies and Essays* (Hebrew). Tel Aviv, 1978.

————. *On the History of the Jews in Poland and Russia* (Hebrew). Ed. Israel Bartal and Jonathan Frankel. Jerusalem, 1995.

————. *Studies in Modern Jewish History* (Hebrew). Vol. 1, Jerusalem, 1992.

Feiner, Shmuel. "Between the Clouds of Foolishness and the Light of Reason: Yehudah Hurwitz, an Early Eighteenth-Century Maskil" (Hebrew). In *Within Hasidic Circles*, ed. Assaf et al., pp. 111–60.

————. "The Invention of the Modern Age: A Chapter in the Rhetoric and Self-Consciousness of the Haskalah" (Hebrew). *Dappim lemechkar hasifrut* 11 (1998): 9–28.

————. "Isaac Euchel: Entrepreneur of the Haskalah Movement" (Hebrew). *Zion* 52 (1987): 427–69.

————. "Jewish Society, Literature, and Haskalah in Russia as Represented in the Radical Criticism of I. E. Kovner" (Hebrew). *Zion* 55 (1990): 283–316.

————. "*Sola Fide*! The Polemic of Rabbi Nathan of Nemirov against Atheism and Haskalah" (Hebrew). In *Studies in Hasidism*, ed. David Assaf, Joseph Dan, and Immanuel Etkes. Jerusalem, 1999, pp. 89–124.

————, and David Sorkin, eds. *New Perspectives on the Haskalah.* London, 2001.

Ferziger, Adam. "Hierarchical Judaism in Formation: The Development of Central European Orthodoxy's Approach toward Nonobservant Jews, 1700–1918" (Hebrew). Ph.D. diss., Bar-Ilan University, 2001.

Fishman, D. E. *Russia's First Modern Jews: The Jews of Shklov.* New York, 1995.

Frankel, Jonathan. "Jewish Socialism, 1882–90: From Jewish Populism to Cosmopolitanism" (Hebrew). *Proceedings of the Eighth World Congress of Jewish Studies.* Jerusalem, 1984, pp. 21–53.

————. *Prophecy and Politics: Socialism, Nationalism, and the Russian Jews, 1862–1917.* Cambridge, 1981.

Friedländer, David. *Über die Verbesserung der Israeliten in Königreich Pohlen.* Berlin, 1819.

Fuenn, Shmuel Yosef. *Kiryah ne'emanah.* Expanded 2nd ed. Vilna, 1914.

Garncarska-Kadary, Bina. "The Jews and Factors in the Development and Location of Industry in Warsaw" (Hebrew). *Gal-ed* 2 (1975): 25–58.

————. "The Jews in the Economic Development of Poland in the Nineteenth

Century" (Hebrew). In *The Broken Chain*, ed. Bartal and Gutman. Jerusalem, 1997, 1:315–36.

———. "The Legal and Socioeconomic Situation of Kraków Jewry, 1796–1868" (Hebrew). In *Kroke-Kazimierz-Kraków: Studies in the History of Kraków Jewry*, ed. Elchanan Reiner. Tel Aviv, 2001, pp. 89–118.

Gertner, Haim. "The Beginning of Orthodox Historiography in Eastern Europe: A Reassessment" (Hebrew). *Zion* 67 (2002): 293–336.

———. "Gvulot hahaspa'a shel rabanut galizia ba'mea hatsha-esre." Master's thesis, Hebrew University, 1997.

———. "Rabbis and Rabbinical Judges (*Dayanim*) in Galicia in the First Half of the Nineteenth Century: A Typology of Traditional Leadership in Crisis" (Hebrew). Ph.D. diss., Hebrew University, 2004.

Gilboa, Menucha. *Hebrew Periodicals in the Eighteenth and Nineteenth Centuries* (Hebrew). Jerusalem, 1992.

Goldberg, Jacob. *Jewish Privileges in the Polish Commonwealth*. Jerusalem, 1983.

———. "The Jewish *Sejm*: Its Origins and Functions." In *The Jews in Old Poland, 1000–1795*, ed. Antony Polonsky, Jakub Basista, and Andrzej Link-Lenczowski. New York, 1993, pp. 147–65.

———. *Jewish Society in the Polish Commonwealth* (Hebrew). Jerusalem, 1999.

Goldstein, David I. *Dostoyevsky and the Jews*. Austin, Tex., 1981.

Gordon, Judah Leib. *Igrot*. Vol. 1, Warsaw, 1894.

———. *Kol shirav*. Vols. 1–4, Tel Aviv, 1929–31.

Gottlober, Abraham Baer. *Zikhronot umasaot*. Ed. Reuven Goldberg. Vol. 2, Jerusalem, 1976.

Graetz, Tsvi (Heinrich). *Essays, Memoirs, Letters* (Hebrew). Ed. Shmuel Ettinger. Jerusalem, 1969.

Green, Arthur. *Tormented Master: A Life of Rabbi Nahman of Bratslav*. Tuscaloosa, Ala., 1979.

Greenbaum, Abraham. *Jewish Scholarship in Soviet Russia: 1918–1941*. Boston, 1959.

Greenberg, L. *The Jews in Russia: The Struggle for Emancipation, 1772–1880*. Vol. 1, New York, 1976.

Gries, Zeev. *Conduct Literature (Regimen Vitae): Its History and Place in the Life of Beshtian Hasidism* (Hebrew). Jerusalem, 1989.

Grossman, Leonid. *Confession of a Jew*. Trans. Ranne Moab. 2nd ed. New York, 1979.

Haber, Adolf. "Jewish Innkeepers in the Writings of Polish Publicists of the Grand *Sejm*, 1788–92" (Hebrew). *Gal-ed* 2 (1975): 1–24.

Halpern, Israel, ed. *Book of Heroism* (Hebrew). Vol. 2, Tel Aviv, 1950.

———. *Eastern European Jewry: Historical Studies* (Hebrew). Jerusalem, 1969.

———, ed. *The Records of the Council of the Four Lands* (Hebrew). Jerusalem, 1945.

Hannover, Nathan Note. *Yeven metsula*. Venice, 1653. In English translation: Abraham J. Mesch, *Abyss of Despair*. New York, 1950.

———. *Yeven metsula*. Ed. Israel Halpern. Tel Aviv, 1945.

Hendel, Michael. *Crafts and Craftsmen among the Jewish People* (Hebrew). Tel Aviv, 1955.

Hertzberg, Arthur. "*Treifene Medine*: Opposition to Emigration to the United States." *Eighth World Congress of Jewish Studies*. Jerusalem, 1984, pp. 1–31.

Homberg, Herz. *Imre shefer*. Vienna, 1808.

Howe, Irving, and Ruth R. Wisse, eds. *The Best of Sholem Aleichem*. New York, 1982.

Hundert, Gershon David. *Jews in Poland-Lithuania in the Eighteenth Century: A Genealogy of Modernity*. Berkeley, Calif., 2004.

————. *The Jews in a Polish Private Town: The Case of Opatów in the Eighteenth Century*. Baltimore, 1992.

————. "The *Kehilla* and the Municipality in Private Towns at the End of the Early Modern Period." In *The Jews in Old Poland 1000–1795*, ed. Antony Polonsky, Jakub Basista, and Andrzej Link-Lenczowski. New York, 1993, pp. 174–85.

————. "On the Jewish Community in Poland during the Seventeenth Century: Some Comparative Perspectives." *Revue des Etudes Juives* 142 (1983): 349–72.

————, and Gershon Bacon. *The Jews in Poland and Russia: Bibliographical Essays*. Bloomington, Ind., 1984.

Idel, Moshe. *Hasidism: Between Ecstasy and Magic*. Albany, N.Y., 1995.

In Praise of the Baal Shem Tov. Trans. and ed. Dan Ben-Amos and Jerome R. Mintz. Bloomington, Ind., 1972.

Kalik, Judith. "The Catholic Church and the Jews in the Polish-Lithuanian Commonwealth" (Hebrew). In *The Broken Chain*, ed. Bartal, 1:193–208. Jerusalem, 1997.

————. *The Polish Nobility and the Jews in the Deitine Legislation of the Polish-Lithuanian Commonwealth* (Hebrew). Jerusalem, 1997.

Kann, Robert A. *A History of the Habsburg Empire, 1526–1918*. Berkeley, Calif., 1977.

Karlinski, Nahum. *Counter History, The Hasidic Epistles from Eretz-Israel: Text and Context* (Hebrew). Jerusalem, 1998.

Katz, Jacob. "Orthodoxy in Historical Perspective." *Studies in Contemporary Jewry* 2 (1986): 3–17.

————. *Tradition and Crisis: Jewish Society at the End of the Middle Ages* (Hebrew). Jerusalem, 1958; New York, 1993 (English).

Katzburg, Nathaniel. "Orthodoxy." *Encyclopaedia Judaica*, 12:1486–92. Jerusalem, 1971.

Klausner, Israel. "Joseph Pesseles: The Enlightened Relative of the Gaon of Vilna" (Hebrew). *He-avar* 2 (1954): 73–85.

————. *Vilna: Jerusalem of Lithuania, 1495–1881* (Hebrew). Tel Aviv, 1988.

————. *When a Nation Awakens* (Hebrew). Jerusalem, 1962.

Klier, John D. *Imperial Russia's Jewish Question, 1855–1881*. Cambridge, 1995.

————. *Russia Gathers Her Jews: The Origins of the "Jewish Question" in Russia, 1772–1825*. Dekalb, Ill., 1986.

————, and Shlomo Lambrosa, eds. *Pogroms: Anti-Jewish Violence in Modern Russian History*. Cambridge, 1992.

Kotik, Yehezkel. *Journey to a Nineteenth-Century Shtetl: The Memoirs of Yehezkel Kotik*. Ed. David Assaf. Detroit, 2002.

Kovner, Abraham Ury. "An Investigation" (Hebrew). In *Kol ketavav*. Tel Aviv, 1947, pp. 5–45.

Kramer, Chaim. *Through Fire and Water: The Life of Reb Noson of Breslov*. Jerusalem, 1993.

Kunitz, Joshua. *Russian Literature and the Jew: A Sociological Inquiry into the Nature and Origin of Literary Patterns*. New York, 1929.

Kuperstein, I. "Inquiry at Polaniec: A Case Study of Hasidic Controversy in Eighteenth-Century Galicia." *Yearbook of Bar-Ilan University* 24–25 (1989): 25–39.

Kupfer, A. *Ber Mayzels* (Yiddish). Warsaw, 1952.

Laskov, Shulamit. *The Biluim* (Hebrew). Tel Aviv, 1979.

Lederhendler, Eli. *Jewish Responses to Modernity: New Voices in America and Eastern Europe*. New York, 1994.

————. *The Road to Modern Jewish Politics: Political Tradition and Political Reconstruction in the Jewish Community of Tsarist Russia*. New York, 1989.

Levanda, V. O. *Polny Khronologicheskii Sbornik Zakonov i Polozhenii Kasaiushchikhsia Evreev Opublikovany 1649–1873* [Complete chronological collection of laws and statutes concerning Jews]. Saint Petersburg, 1874.

Levin, Sabina. "The Rabbinical Seminary in Warsaw, 1826–63" (Hebrew). *Gal-ed* 11 (1989): 35–58.

Levitats, Isaac. "Critique of the Book of the *Kahal*" (Hebrew). *Zion* 3 (1938): 170–78.

————. *The Jewish Community in Russia, 1772–1844*. New York, 1943.

————. *The Jewish Community in Russia, 1844–1917*. Jerusalem, 1987.

Liberman, Aharon Shmuel. *Writings in Vpered, 1875–76* (Hebrew). Ed. Moshe Mishkinsky. Tel Aviv, 1977.

Liebman, Charles. "Orthodox Judaism," *The Encyclopedia of Religion*, 2:114–15. Chicago, 1981.

Lilienblum, Moshe Leib. *Autobiographical Writings* (Hebrew). Ed. Shlomo Breiman. Jerusalem, 1970.

————. *Kol ketavav*. Vol. 1, Kraków, 1910.

————. *Letters to Judah Leib Gordon* (Hebrew). Ed. Shlomo Breiman. Jerusalem, 1968.

Loewe, Louis, ed. *Diaries of Sir Moses and Lady Montefiore*, London, 1983.

Lowenstein, Steven M. "The Readership of Mendelssohn's Bible Translation." *Hebrew Union College Annual* 52 (1982): 179–213.

Luz, Ehud. *Parallels Meet: Religion and Nationalism in the Early Zionist Movement*. Philadelphia, 1988.

Mahler, Raphael. *Hasidism and the Jewish Enlightenment: Their Confrontation in Galicia and Poland in the First Half of the Nineteenth Century*. New York, 1985.

Malino, F. *A Jew in the French Revolution: The Life of Zalkind Hourwitz*. Oxford, 1996.

Manekin, Rachel. "*Daitshen*, Poles, or Austrians?: The Identity Dilemma of Galician Jews, 1848–51" (Hebrew). *Zion* 68 (2003): 223–62.

————. "Orthodox Jewry in Kraków at the Turn of the Twentieth Century." In *Kroke-Kazimierz-Kraków: Studies on the History of Kraków Jewry* (Hebrew), ed. E. Reiner. Tel Aviv, 2001, pp. 155–90.

————. "Politics, Religion, and National Identity: The Galician Jewish Vote in the 1873 Parliamentary Elections." *Polin* 12 (1999): 100–119.

Maor, Yitzhak. "The Anti-Semitic Proclamation of the Narodnaya Vola" (Hebrew). *Zion* 15 (1950): 150–55.

Mendelssohn, Ezra. "From Assimilation to Zionism: The Case of Alfred Nossig." *Slavonic and East European Review* 49 (1971): 521–34.

————. "Jewish Assimilation in Lvov: The Case of Wilhelm Feldman." *The Slavic Review* 28 (1969): 577–90.

Menes, Abraham. "The Am Oylom Movement." *YIVO Annual* 6 (1949): 9–33.

Miron, Dan. *From Romance to the Novel: Studies in the Emergence of the Hebrew and Yiddish Novel in the Nineteenth Century* (Hebrew). Jerusalem, 1979.

————. *Sholem Aleichem: Two Related Essays* (Hebrew). Ramat Gan, 1970.

————. "Sholem Aleykhem: Person, Persona, Presence." Uriel Weinreich Memorial Lecture, YIVO Institute for Jewish Research, New York, 1972.

Mishkinsky, M. "The South Russian Workers' Union and the 1881 Kiev Pogrom" (Hebrew). *Shvut* 1 (1973): 62–73.

Nathans, Benjamin. *Beyond the Pale: The Jewish Encounter with Late Imperial Russia*. Berkeley, Calif., 2002.

——. "On Russian-Jewish Historiography." In *Historiography of Imperial Russia: The Profession and Writing of History in a Multinational State*, ed. T. Sanders. London, 1999, pp. 397–432.

Opalski, Magdalena. *The Jewish Tavern Keeper and His Tavern in Nineteenth-Century Polish Literature.* Jerusalem, 1986.

——, and Israel Bartal. *Poles and Jews: A Failed Brotherhood.* Hanover, N.H., 1992.

Orbach, Alexander. *New Voices of Russian Jewry.* Leiden, 1980.

Orren, Elchanan. "Yiddish Journalism in the London East End, 1883–87: The Turning Point between Socialism and Hibbat Zion" (Hebrew). *Hatsionut* 2 (1972): 47–63.

Parush, Iris. *Reading Women: The Benefit of Marginality in Nineteenth-Century Eastern European Jewish Society* (Hebrew). Tel Aviv, 2001.

Patterson, David. *The Hebrew Novel in Czarist Russia.* Edinburgh, 1964.

Peretz, Isaac Leib. *My Memoirs.* Trans. from Yiddish by Fred Goldberg. New York, 1964.

Perl, Joseph. *Hasidic Tales and Letters* (Hebrew). Ed. Shmuel Werses and Chone Shmeruk. Jerusalem, 1969.

——. *Megaleh temirin.* Vienna, 1819.

Piekarz, Mendel. *Studies in Braslav Hasidism* (Hebrew). Jerusalem, 1972.

Pinsker, Leo. *Road to Freedom.* New York, 1944.

Pipes, Richard. "Catherine II and the Jews: The Origins of the Pale of Settlement." *Soviet Jewish Affairs* 5, no. 2 (1975): 3–20.

Polnoe sobranie zakonov rossiiskoi imperii [Complete collection of the laws of the Russian empire]. 2nd series. Saint Petersburg, 1830–84.

Rabinowitsch, Wolf Z. *Lithuanian Hasidism.* London, 1970.

Raisin, Jacob S. *The Haskalah Movement in Russia.* Philadelphia, 1913.

Rapoport-Albert, Ada, ed.. *Hasidism Reappraised.* London, 1996.

——. "Historiography with Footnotes: Edifying Tales and the Writing of History in Hasidism." *History and Theory* 27 (1988): 119–59.

Rappaport, Moritz. "Bajazzo." Leipzig, 1863.

Reiner, Elchanan. "Wealth, Social Position, and the Study of Torah: The Status of the *Kloiz* in Eastern European Jewish Society in the Early Modern Period" (Hebrew). *Zion* 57 (1993): 287–328.

Roskies, David R. *The Jewish Search for a Usable Past.* Bloomington, Ind., 1999.

Rosman, Moshe. "The Authority of the Council of the Four Lands outside of Poland" (Hebrew). *Yearbook of Bar-Ilan University* 24–25 (1989): 11–30.

——. *Founder of Hasidism: A Quest for the Historical Ba'al Shem Tov.* Berkeley, Calif., 1996.

——. *The Lords' Jews: Magnate-Jewish Relations in the Polish-Lithuanian Commonwealth during the Eighteenth Century.* Cambridge, Mass., 1990.

Safran, Gabriella. *Rewriting the Jew: Assimilation Narratives in the Russian Empire.* Stanford, Calif., 2000.

Salmon, Yosef. "David Gordon and His Periodical *Hamaggid*, 1860–80" (Hebrew). *Zion* 47 (1982): 145–64.

——. "Enlightened Rabbis as Reformists in Russian Jewish Society." In *New Perspectives on the Haskalah*, ed. Shmuel Feiner and David Sorkin. London, 2001, pp. 166–83.

——. "Ideology and Reality in the Bilu Movement" (Hebrew). In *Shalem: Studies in the History of the Jews in Eretz Israel*, 3 (1981):149–84.

——. *Religion and Zionism: First Encounters* (Hebrew). Jerusalem, 1990; in English translation, Jerusalem, 2002.

———. "Tradition, Modernization, and Nationalism: The Maskilic Rabbi as a Reformist in Russian Jewish Society" (Hebrew). In *Studies in Religious Zionism and Jewish Law, Submitted in Honor of Dr. Zerach Warhaftig*. Ramat Gan, 2001, pp. 29–34.

Scholem, Gershom. *The Messianic Idea in Judaism*. New York, 1971.

Sefer hitgalut hatzaddikim. Warsaw, 1901.

Shanes, Joshua. "Papers for the *Folk*: Jewish Nationalism and the Birth of the Yiddish Press in Galicia." *Polin* 16 (2003): 167–87.

Shatzki, Jacob. *Geshikhte fun yidn in varshe*. Vol. 2, New York, 1948.

Shimoni, Gideon. *The Zionist Ideology*. Hanover, N.H., 1995.

Shmeruk, Chone. *The Call for a Prophet* (Hebrew). Ed. Israel Bartal. Jerusalem, 1999.

———. "Hasidism and the *Kehilla*." In *The Jews in Old Poland, 1000–1795*, ed. Antony Polonsky, Jakub Basista, and Andrzej Link-Lenczowski. New York, 1993, pp. 186–95.

———. *Yiddish Literature: Aspects of Its History* (Hebrew). Tel Aviv, 1978.

———. *Yiddish Literature in Poland: Historical Studies and Perspectives* (Hebrew). Jerusalem, 1981.

Shochat, Azriel. "Community Leadership in Russia after the Abolition of the *Kahal*" (Hebrew). *Zion* 42 (1977): 143–233.

Sholem Aleichem [Shalom Rabinowitz]. *Menahem Mendel: Ale Verk. Forverts* ed., 7:43–153. New York, 1944.

———. *Motel peyse dem hazens*. In *Ale Verk. Forverts* ed. Vol. 1, New York, 1944.

Silber, Michael. "The Emergence of Ultra-Orthodoxy: The Invention of Tradition." In *The Uses of Tradition*, ed. Jack Wertheimer. New York, 1992, pp. 23–85.

Sinkoff, Nancy B. "Tradition and Transition: Mendel Lefin of Satanów and the Beginnings of the Jewish Enlightenment in Eastern Europe, 1749–1826." Ph.D. diss., Columbia University, 1996.

Slutsky, Yehuda. "The Geography of the 1881 Pogroms" (Hebrew). *He-avar* 9 (1961): 16–25.

———. "The Pogroms in 1882–84" (Hebrew). *He-avar* 10 (1963): 144–49.

———. *The Russian-Jewish Press in the Nineteenth Century* (Hebrew). Jerusalem, 1970.

Sorkin, David. "The Early Haskalah." In *New Perspectives on the Haskalah*, ed. Shmuel Feiner and David Sorkin. London, 2001, pp. 9–26.

Stampfer, Shaul. *The Formation of the Lithuanian Yeshiva* (Hebrew). Jerusalem, 1995.

———. "Population Growth and Immigration among Polish-Lithuanian Jewry" (Hebrew). In *The Broken Chain*, ed. Bartal and Gutman, 1:263–85. Jerusalem, 1997.

Stanislawski, Michael. *For Whom Do I Toil?: Judah Leib Gordon and the Crisis of Russian Jewry*. New York, 1988.

———. *Tsar Nicholas I and the Jews: The Transformation of Jewish Society in Russia, 1825–1855*. Philadelphia, 1983.

Taylor, Dov. *Joseph Perl's Revealer of Secrets: The First Hebrew Novel*. Boulder, Colo., 1997.

Turtle, Hasia. "The Am Olam Movement" (Hebrew). *He-avar* 10 (1963: 124–43.

Ury, Scott. "The *Shtadlan* of the Polish-Lithuanian Commonwealth: Noble Advocate or Unbridled Opportunist?" *Polin* 15 (2002): 267–99.

Vital, David. *Zionism: The Formative Years*. Oxford, 1982.

Weeks, Theodore R. *Nation and State in Late Imperial Russia*. Dekalb, Ill., 1996.

Weinreich, Max. *Fun beyde zaytn ployt: Dos shturmdike lebn fun Uri Kovnern, dem nihilist*. Buenos Aires, 1966.

Weinryb, Bernard D. *The Jews of Poland: A Social and Economic History of the Jewish Community in Poland from 1100 to 1800*. Philadelphia, 1973.

Werses, Shmuel. *"Awake, My People": Hebrew Literature in the Age of Modernization* (Hebrew). Jerusalem, 2001.

―――. *Haskalah and Sabbatianism: The Story of a Controversy* (Hebrew). Jerusalem, 1988.

―――. "The Right Hand Repels and the Left Draws It Closer: On the Attitude of the Haskalah Writers toward the Yiddish Language" (Hebrew). *Huliot* 5 (1999): 9–49.

―――. *Trends and Forms in Haskalah Literature* (Hebrew). Jerusalem, 1990.

Wertheimer, Jack. *Unwelcome Strangers: East European Jews in Imperial Germany*. New York, 1987.

Wilensky, Mordecai. *Hasidim and Mitnagdim: A Study of the Controversy between Them in the Years 1772–1815* (Hebrew). Vols. 1–2, Jerusalem, 1970.

Wisse, Ruth R. *I. L. Peretz and the Making of Modern Culture*. Seattle, 1991.

Wodzinski, Marcin. *Oswiecenie żydowskie w Królestwie Polskim wobec Chasydyzmu: Dzieje pewnej idei*. Warsaw, 2004.

Wolff, Larry. *Inventing Eastern Europe: The Map of Civilization on the Mind of the Enlightenment*. Stanford, Calif., 1999.

Zalkin, Mordechai. "Introduction" (Hebrew). In H. N. Magid [Steinshneider], *Ir Vilna*, 2:1–20. Jerusalem, 2002.

―――. "The Jewish Enlightenment in Poland: Points for Discussion" (Hebrew). In *The Broken Chain*, ed. Bartal and Gutman, 2:391–413. Jerusalem, 2001.

―――. *A New Dawn: The Jewish Enlightenment in the Russian Empire—Social Aspects* (Hebrew). Jerusalem, 2000.

Zerubavel, Eviatar. *Time Maps, Collective Memory, and the Social Shape of the Past*. Chicago, 2003.

Zinberg, Israel. *A History of Jewish Literature*. New York, 1976.

Zipperstein, Steven J. "Assimilation, Haskalah, and Odessa Jewry." In *The Great Transition: The Recovery of the Lost Centers of Modern Hebrew Literature*, ed. Glenda Abramson and Tudor Parfitt. Totowa, N.J., 1985.

―――. "Haskalah, Cultural Change, and Nineteenth-Century Russian Jewry: A Reassessment." *Journal of Jewish Studies* 34 (1983): 191–207.

―――. *Imagining Russian Jewry: Memory, History, Identity*. Seattle, 1999.

―――. *The Jews of Odessa: A Cultural History, 1794–1881*. Stanford, Calif., 1985.

―――. "Russian Maskilim and the City." In *The Legacy of Jewish Migration: 1881 and Its Impact*, ed. D. Berger. New York, 1983, pp. 31–45.

Index

Orthodox Church, 135; Russian, 135, 140
Orthodoxy, Jewish, 120–23, 128–29, 131, 153, 163
Osnova, 139
Ostjuden, 91
Ottoman Empire, 15, 21, 24, 41, 61, 140. *See also* Turkey

Pale of Settlement. *See* Russia
Palestine and Land of Israel, 112, 149, 151, 155; British Mandate in, 3, 11
Pavel I, 163
Pennsylvania, 114
Peretz, I. L., 11, 83
Peretz family, 43, 45
Perl, Joseph, 56–57, 76, 95, 96, 97, 98
Pesseles, Eliahu Ben Zvi, 94
Pesseles, Joseph, 94
Petersburg, 35, 68, 108, 136, 143, 148, 155
Peter the Great, 26
Philadelphia, 113, 150
Pinkas medinat lita, 138
Pinsker, Leon, 110, 141
Podolia, 47–48, 95, 98, 125
Pogroms, 3–5, 123, 133, 148, 153, 154, 155. *See also* Odessa; Storms in the South
Poland, 10, 17, 25, 39, 80, 81, 82–89, 95, 99, 125, 157; Congress (Kongresówka), 41, 42, 44, 84, 86, 89, 164; Little, 70; nationalism, 83, 129–30, 132; partitions of, 1, 19, 23–37, 54, 58, 124; uprising against Russian rule, 85–87, 88, 103, 113, 129, 163
Polish-Lithuanian kingdom, 1, 2, 6, 15–17, 23–37, 39, 82, 159, 161
Polotzk, 58
Poniatowski, Stanisław August, 27–29, 72
Posen, 19, 81
Potocki, Seweryn, 62
Potocki family, 84
Poznań. *See* Posen
Praga, 33
Press. *See* Jewish press
Prussia, 1, 23, 24, 27, 32, 34, 36, 72, 79, 81, 89, 92, 95

Raba bar bar Hanna, 158
Rabbinate and rabbis, 73
Rabinowitz, Shalom. *See* Aleichem, Sholem
Ribal. *See* Levinsohn, Isaac Baer
Roskies, David, 112
Rothschild, Edmond de, 150

Rothschild, Lord Nathaniel, 154
Ruelf, Isaac, 154
Russia, 6, 23, 27, 32, 34, 58–69, 79, 92, 133, 139, 140, 157, 162; church in, 60; empire, 1, 5, 7, 12, 26, 35–36, 44, 73, 85, 89, 102–4, 114, 115, 117–18, 122, 124, 127, 134, 144, 160, 165; Little, 62. *See also* Ukraine; new, 39, 41, 62, 63, 146; Pale of Settlement, 3, 14, 40, 41, 42, 61, 64, 65, 103–6, 113, 120, 122, 124–25, 127, 134, 142, 145, 156; Red, 70; White, 1, 2, 3, 6, 34, 40, 48, 59, 61, 64, 89, 95, 113, 125, 137. *See also* Soviet empire

Sabbatian Movement, 48, 49
Sadagora, 125
Saint Petersburg. *See* Petersburg
Salanter, Israel, 111
Salonika, 39
Satanów, 95
Secularization, 112
Sejm, 21, 25, 26, 29–31; four-year, 30, 32, 62, 85, 95, 162
Sepharadim, 15
Shabbetai Tsevi, 21
Shklov, 43, 94
Shmeruk, Chone, 50
Shneersohn, Menahem Mendel, 65
Shomer Israel, 130, 131
Shtadlanim, 25, 152–53, 154
Shtetls, 39, 103
Sion, 111, 139
Smolensk, 61
Smolenskin, Peretz, 88, 118, 149
Socialism, 112, 117–19, 155. *See also* Jewish proletariat
Society of Israelite Christians, 63
Society for Promoting Christianity among the Jews, London, 63
Sofer, Shimon, 129, 131
Soviet empire, 10
Spector, Isaac Elchanan, 153–54
Spring of the Nations, 80, 87, 124
Stern, Bezalel, 65
Sternharz, Nathan, 56
Storms in the South, 141, 143–48, 151. *See also* Pogroms
Sulamith, 107
Syracuse, New York, 120

Talmud, opposition to, 65
Tarnopol, 41, 56, 97

Acknowledgments

This book sums up over thirty years of teaching and research on the history of Eastern European Jewry. It is an outcome of classes I taught from the early 1970s at the Hebrew University of Jerusalem and was enriched by my teaching on the western side of the Atlantic at Harvard University, the University of Pennsylvania, and McGill and Rutgers Universities. The book took on its final form in 1999, when I gave a series of lectures, "The Jews in Eastern Europe, 1772–1881," on the Broadcast University of Israel Defense Forces Radio. Tirzah Yuval, editor of the academic lecture series before her untimely death, and Yishai Kordova, editor of the printed series of the Ministry of Defence Publishing House, which published the Hebrew version of the book, brought this multiyear process to a close.

When I entered the Hebrew University in the late 1960s, the founding fathers of the "Jerusalem School" were teaching and conducting research there on the history of Eastern European Jewry. They were ardent Zionists and radical world reformers for whom research, ideology, and politics were intertwined, just as they had been in their native towns in Poland and Russia. In the United States, too, the leading scholars in the field were immigrants from Eastern Europe whose spiritual world and style of academic work in no way differed from that in Israel. In the dozens of years that have passed since I began teaching and conducting research, new generations of scholars have come up to the podium for whom Eastern Europe, its way of life, and the diversity of its culture were an abstract memory. New questions have been asked, and old ideas have been rejected and forgotten. Eastern Europe has taken on a different, sometimes surprising, image in the new research.

Although I was counted as a member of the new generations, I was privileged to have studied and worked with the last of the earlier generations. Three professors from the Hebrew University—Israel Halpern, Shmuel Ettinger, and Chone Shmeruk—opened the gates to the vanished world of Eastern Europe for me. Professor Jacob Katz, although not one of the former Eastern Europeans on the Jerusalem campus, taught me much about the nature of the Ashkenazi diaspora, the emergence of Orthodoxy, and the roots of the Jewish national movement.

Shmuel Werses, dean of research on the literature of the Haskalah, was an inexhaustible source of knowledge and inspiration in the search for roots of modernity in the Jewish people.

Over the years, the members of my academic generation, who began their scholarly work during the 1970s on both sides of the Atlantic, created a network of research, information, and exchange of views whose traces are clearly evident in this book. History, literature, philosophy, mysticism, and folklore are interconnected in this network. Among these, for their influence, advice, and criticism, I am particularly grateful to my colleagues in Israel—Richard I. Cohen, Jacob Goldberg, Immanuel Etkes, Eli Lederhendler, Elchanan Reiner, Moshe Rosman, Yosef Salmon, Michael Silber, Shaul Stampfer, Chava Turniansky—and to my colleagues abroad: Gershon Hundert, Benjamin Nathans, Magdalena Opalski, Ada Rapoport-Albert, Michael Stanislawski, Ruth Wisse, and Steven Zipperstein. In conversations held in the space between New York, Ottawa, Vilna, and Jerusalem, and even more so in their writings that I read before and after their publication, they revealed new aspects to me and stimulated my thoughts and reactions. Jonathan Frankel, a true friend and wonderful colleague, with whom I taught in seminars at the Hebrew University, enriched my historical thinking. The colossal spectrum of the historical areas of his interest sharpened insights for me and connected what at first glance had seemed to be unconnected.

I have had the privilege of seeing the generation of scholars that came after me grow and break new ground in research. Some of these scholars were my students in the 1970s and 1980s, and not too many years later, I found myself garnering knowledge from their original studies and internalizing their innovative ideas. I learned about the Haskalah movement from the monumental works of Shmuel Feiner and Mordechai Zalkin, and about the Hasidic movement from David Assaf's innovative studies. Research on the emergence of Orthodoxy in Eastern Europe in the nineteenth century took a new turn with the publication of studies by Haim Gertner, Rachel Manekin, and Nahum Karlinski. And I made use of all these in my book.

This book would never have been published were it not for the help of librarians and archivists in Israel and abroad. A considerable part of my work was conducted in the National University Library in Jerusalem and in the library of the Center for Advanced Judaic Studies at the University of Pennsylvania, and I thank the dedicated staffs of these institutions for their amiability and skilled professional assistance. My special thanks go to the employees of the Institute for Advanced Studies at the Hebrew University and the staff of the Bildner Center for the Study of Jewish Life at Rutgers University, who provided me with suitable conditions for writing the book and assisted me with my scholarly work. I owe a special debt of gratitude to David Ruderman, the dynamic director of the Center for Advanced Judaic Studies at the University of Pennsylvania, whose idea it was to publish an English version of the Hebrew book. At the University of Pennsylvania Press, I want to thank Jerome Singerman for his enthusiastic support of this project; Erica Ginsburg and Theodore Mann for guiding me through the production process; and Janice Meyerson for her careful copyediting.

I am indebted to Scott Ury, who advised me on how best to adapt the Hebrew-Israeli spirit of the book into a version appropriate for the American audience, and to Jonathan Meir, who contributed his broad bibliographical knowledge and assisted with the preparation of the notes. A special thanks goes to the translator of the book, Chaya Naor, for her precise and inspired work.

The book is dedicated to the memory of my mother, Bela Bartal (1920–2003), a native of the town of Delatyn, in eastern Galicia. This town, in which several thousand Jews lived in 1939, was a microcosm that contained the grand story of Eastern European Jewry in the modern era. My father, who was born in Vienna when his parents were refugees during World War I, also grew up in Delatyn. My maternal grandmother was born and raised in the Austro-Hungarian empire. My mother was born in independent Poland and immigrated to Palestine with her mother, brothers, and sisters in 1935. In September 1939, Delatyn came under Soviet rule and in June 1941, it was occupied by the German army. Most of the town's Jews were shot to death in a nearby forest in September 1941, including all the members of my mother's family who had not emigrated, as well as my paternal grandparents along with their children, except for my father. The story of this town, one of thousands of Jewish communities destroyed in the Holocaust, has been part of me since my childhood. The political and cultural turmoil and the outburst of talent and entrepreneurship in one town on the southern fringes of Galicia were an enigma to me. The ostensibly incomprehensible combination of religious fanaticism and a naive belief in the possibility of rebelling against the social reality and totally reforming the world—which I knew from my parents' stories of their youthful experiences—called for an explanation. It is my hope that some of the things written in this book may explain the cultural and social uniqueness of Eastern European Jewry in the modern age.